Eternal Life Principles & Beyond

© 1980 by Madeline Massi Vance. All rights reserved TXu 000674301
© 1995 by Madeline Massi Vance. All rights reserved TXu 000674301
© 2001 by Madeline Massi Vance. All rights reserved TXu 000994767
© 2008 by Madeline Massi Vance. All rights reserved TX 0007049130

First Printing – December 2001
Second Printing – January 2002
Third Printing – March 2002
Fourth Printing – April 2002
Fifth Printing – October 2007
Sixth Printing – August 2008
Seventh Printing - June 2010
Eighth Printing – July 2012
Ninth Printing – January 2015

As such, the ultimate design, content, editorial accuracy, and views expressed or implied in this work are those of the author.

No part of this publication may be reproduced, stored in a retrieval system or transmitted in any form or by any means—electronic, mechanical, photocopy, recording or otherwise —without the prior permission of the copyright holder, except as provided by USA copyright law. Any unauthorized reproduction is a violation of the law and of Christian ethics.

Unless otherwise noted, all Scriptures are taken from the New American Standard Bible, © 1960, 1963, 1968, 1971, 1972, 1973, 1975, 1977 by The Lockman Foundation. American Bible Society. Used by permission.

Scripture references marked NKJV are taken from the New King James Version, © 1979, 1980, 1982 by Thomas Nelson, Inc., Publishers. Used by permission.

Supporting Scripture quotations are taken from the New Testament 26 Translations, Zondervan Bible Publishers.

Cover Design: David Hewitt, Remarkable Solutions, www.remweb.com

Rights for publishing this book in other languages may be contracted through Madeline M. Vance.

WHAT PASTORS ARE SAYING:

Eternal Life Principles & Beyond is truly a masterpiece of sound doctrine written under the admonition and anointing of the Holy Spirit. These doctrines will take your Christian experience to a much higher level. Madeline Vance ministered as our Christian Training Administrator at Beacon of Light Ministries. She is a yielded vessel that God uses to send His word to the present day believer.

Dr. Nelson Noble, Sr., Pastor
Beacon of Light Ministries

Eternal Life Principles & Beyond is a book long overdue in our Christian Education Department. This book explains the different components of the Christian life as one goes from conversion to leadership (maturity). Anyone wanting to do a work for Jesus will greatly enrich his/her Bible knowledge from this series of studies.

Pastor Dr. James W. Hendershot B.Ph.B.,D.D.
House of Prayer

Many, if not most, Christians have a weak understanding of basic doctrines and theology, mainly because no one ever taught them. They were given the "milk" but never moved on to the "meat". This lack of understanding can cause a great many problems in a believer's walk. This book, *"Eternal Life Principles & Beyond"* will help believers, both new and more experienced, move on to the "meat". It is a resource that should be on every Believer's shelf

Pastor Michael Pici, B.A. English Journalism; M.A. Biblical Studies
Agape Tower Fellowship

It's not often that textual and scriptural honesty along with simplicity show up as partners in one work....but here it is. Madeline Vance has truly come through with a dogmatic approach to the necessary *"Eternal Life Principles & Beyond"* and found a way to make these truths come alive and enjoyable. Learning, I believe, must be fun so it doesn't feel like work....this text qualifies. I encourage Church schools or places of higher learning to use this course and to apply it's principles as taught.

Pastor Ken Boaz M.Div., D.Min.
International Church of Clearwater
VISION International University

Madeline introduced her book "*Eternal Life Principles & Beyond*" to me this past summer. I find Madeline to be a person of integrity committed to excellence throughout the many years she has served in ministry. I am pleased and honored to recommend this work of the truth of the Word of God that is so detailed, researched and thorough in content. I believe that the book is destined to go to the nations, printed in many different languages to reach the world with the truth of sound doctrine.

Senior Pastor M. Joyce Frohlich, MA in Biblical Counseling
Lion of Judah Foursquare Church

Eternal Life Principles & Beyond is a thorough, well-thought out and excellent material for our university. It has a place in our curriculum.

Dr. Douglas Wingate, Founder and President
Life Christian University, FL

These four words - "Repentance from Dead Works" - have illuminated into my spirit. It has been an eye opener! I'm realizing that there are so many myths, traditions and untruths in the body of Christ. Many people say, "If I sin, God understands". When you tell a person God understands why we sin, it's a lie! It's a lot of error! I'm not bothering with a debt that has been paid! This lesson has met my needs and this book should be part of every church's program. For me, it's a cultural shock! I appreciate knowing you don't have to sin, because if you sin, in any area, there are consequences to pay.

Your Answer Classes are phenomenal and your insights are incredible. You are mature in the Word and I want to live here forever, basking in these moments. The lesson on not going back to dead works has exposed a truth that has revolutionized and revitalized me in the Lord. I cannot and will not go back to dead works! I'm having so much joy, peace and contentment that I find myself very happy and I don't believe I've ever been so consistent with the Lord. I'm excited about what I have learned in your Answer Classes. Thank you.

Elementary Principles is greatly needed in such times as these. Your teachings are alive and full of truth. So many preachers are trying to go "DEEP" and Christians don't know the basics about being a born-again believer. Madeline, I believe this is why the enemy has fought you so hard day in and day out, especially when trying to get *Elementary Principles* on the market, but in God's timing, there is His release. Just know this Madeline, this book the Lord gave you will help me help others in my congregation and others in the Body of Christ receive more rewards and suffer less at the Judgment Seat of Christ. Again, thank you.

L. Don Middleton, Pastor
New Pleasant Grove Baptist Church, FL

This book is Biblically based upon sound doctrine. We believe that it will enlighten many to the deep truths in God's word. Every lesson is also clearly explained and highly documented with Scripture.

Pastors Noel & Marylou Melendez
Winds of Praise Ministries, Inc.

This presentation of written information along with the built in study guide was well planned and executed. All of the topics from Hebrews 6:1-2 were thoroughly covered. I would like to close by extending hearty congratulations on reaching this monumental milestone in your ministry education pursuits. May God reward you richly for all of your endeavors for the King of Kings and Lord of Lords.

Dr. Douglas J. Wingate
President and Founder
Life Christian University

Comments

What Students Are Saying About This Fabulous Workbook:

These teachings are most essential in the life of every true believer. The doctrine of laying on of hands is one that many do not consider a practice for our times. They are sadly mistaken. *Eternal Life Principles & Beyond* is a most excellent piece of work. I love it. The church will love it.
Ralph Quinones, FL

I am being blessed by these teachings. My theology is being corrected and I am gaining confidence in knowing His Word. It's refreshing to know the Truth.
Pedro Ruiz, FL

I have been sitting under Madeline's teachings since 1994. With her instruction, help and much encouragement, I have grown stronger in my faith and walk with God. I thank God for her.
Sue Robe, FL

I have a better understanding of a child's baptism now. I also like your explanation of the rite of circumcision as a "permanent sermon" declaring God's people His peculiar and holy people. Praise God that "water baptism can close the door to our past." Eternal Judgment – Wow, Whoa, this is heavy stuff….but truth. *Eternal Life Principles & Beyond* is excellent reading, revelation after revelation and learning more of the Word of God. Thank you Madeline.
Paula Graham, AK

You are a prophet among us and how you manifest His Presence is found in very few believers. For in His presence is fullness of Joy! It is hard for most people to fathom who you are and where you have been. Your Bible Study teachings and your teachings in *Eternal Life Principles & Beyond* are very in-depth and Spiritual. The pathway you take is extremely narrow and your walk is the path that few are able to take. Therefore, it is difficult for others to identify with you. People must be willing to take the necessary time to learn to know "who" you really are.

God looks for those who worship, and follow, Him in Spirit and in Truth. You are such a follower. The closer you walk with Christ, and do the Will of our Father, the less, even believers, will understand you! You have to master an openness to allow them to learn how to minister to the Father, introducing them to a spiritual relationship with His Son. That's where you are…that is "where" you stand.

I know "where" you are and it is a Joy to my heart to know you and Fellowship in Truth with you. I respect your great hunger to teach, all the while learning His greater Spiritual insights. Those who come under your mantle are real seekers! They long in their hearts for this! To fully appreciate this, one must get the world out of one's mind for Satan is constantly nipping at their heels trying to draw away devoted ones from profiting from your wealth of Godly knowledge.
Sally Marlowe, N.P., Executive Director
Southeast Regional Arthritis Center, FL

Madeline, I do appreciate you and your insights of the Bible. You make me think and want to move deeper in the Word!

John Fischer, FL

I mentioned to Hospice that your class came just at the right time for me and was helpful for keeping my fundamental beliefs written on my heart during this difficult period in my life.

My initial concern with your book/class was that I thought it could be taught with more emphasis on "application." I'm glad I approached your class with that opinion as I really HAD to apply quite a bit of the truths in your work and it was helpful for me to have your book for reference at times.

Peter Vasusky
Safety Harbor, FL

What Others Are Saying:

"....by the way, regarding the lesson on the Judgment Seat of Christ, I was blessed reading through your presentation on this serious of all subjects. You were very thorough and a good writer."

Evangelist Mike Shreve
Cleveland, TN

You are God's child. He created you. He loves you. Madeline Vance has studiously and eloquently enlarged upon this message explaining biblical doctrines and how one can walk with God to find a fulfilling spiritual life

Jean Swengel Beardsley Allen, MI
Author

You have done a load of thorough work. Your research and method of compilation are remarkable.

Michael D. Evans, CFP
Vice President, South Trust Bank, FL

I'm proud of you for reaching your goal and having it in a form that can help folks. Good going! I suggest a much stronger title with more appeal. Most people arrogantly consider themselves to be beyond elementary principles.... whether or not they are!

Jeani McKeever-King, President
The Cutting Edge Ministries, OR

Madeline has brought into focus the basic fundamental truths of New Testament Doctrine as revealed in Hebrews 6:1-2. This course is a must for all new and seasoned believers alike.

Marjorie DeJohn, FL
Friend & Neighbor

Madeline, I'm overwhelmed by this all inclusive and exhaustive study. How exciting the way each lesson picks up momentum toward the end. It's amazing how you pulled each doctrine together to show its full impact and power in an easy to understand technique. Our Answer Classes certainly have been stimulating and informative. Thank you.

Ruth Smith, Coordinator
Harvest Temple Senior Adult Ministries, FL

When you've grown up in the faith, you wonder what more you can learn. Our Answer Classes certainly have been very intense and put quite a new demand on my faith.

Jacqueline Edenfield
Harvest Temple, FL

Details that Madeline has brought forth in her book on these six New Testament Doctrines are clearly stated and easy to read. In the past, a source of confusion for me had been the question on whether water baptism should be administered in the name of Jesus or in the names of the Father, Son and the Holy Spirit. I learned there should not be any debate for both beliefs are correct according to Colossians 2:9 "For the fullness of the Deity dwells in Him." During our class times, she has shared her experiences and more insights bringing a richer meaning to the Scriptures. I recommend having this book in your personal library.

Frances Rentovich
Emanuel Chapel, FL

I enjoyed your lesson on Hell, especially the distinction between a fiery place of torment and simply the place of the dead. It is the most extensive discussion on "Hell" that I have seen.

Samuel W. Townsend, Jr., Chairman
Townsend Advisory Group, FL

Madeline your book takes me to places where I have never been. It will do the same for others.

Bettie Ann Hayes, Deaconess
St. Petersburg, FL

Your teachings are alive and full of truthfulness. You are mature in the Word and have incredible insights. I'm excited for you and about what I learned in your Answer Classes.

Lori Wilson
Largo, FL

**Therefore, leaving the
elementary principles
about the Christ,
let us press on to maturity,
not laying again a foundation of
repentance from dead works,
and of faith toward God,
of instruction about washings,
and laying on of hands,
and the resurrection of the dead,
and eternal judgment.**

Hebrews 6:1-2 NAS

Table of Contents

Acknowledgments..xiii
Foreword..xiv
Preface..xv
Introduction..xvi
About the Author...xx
A Word From the Author...xxii

	Index..25
	Foundation – Historical Study...27
	Lesson Study Review 1..33
	Addendum - Lesson Study Review 2..36

Doctrine 1   **Index**..39
Repentance From Dead Works...41
Lesson Study Review 3..52
Addendum - Lesson Study Review 4..56
Index..57
Conversion – Historical Study..59
Lesson Study Review 5..67

Doctrine 2   **Index**..69
Faith Toward God...71
Lesson Study Review 6..84

Doctrine 3   **Index**..89
The Doctrine of Baptisms I...91
Lesson Study Review 7..102
Instruction About Washings II..105
Lesson Study Review 8..115
Instruction About Washings III...117
Lesson Study Review 9..126
Baptism IV..127
Additional Notes – Infant Baptism..130
Lesson Study Review 10..133

Mid-Summary Review..135

Doctrine 4   **Index**..137
Laying On Of Hands I...139
Lesson Study Review 11..146
Laying On Of Hands II..149
Lesson Study Review 12..157

Doctrine 5	**Index**..159	
	Resurrection Of The Dead I..161	
	Lesson Study Review 13...169	
	Resurrection Of The Dead II...171	
	Lesson Study Review 14...178	
	Resurrection Of The Dead III..179	
	Lesson Study Review 15...187	
Doctrine 6	**Index**..191	
	Eternal Judgment I..193	
	Lesson Study Review 16...210	
	Pivotal Judgments...213	
	Eternal Judgment II...215	
	Lesson Study Review 17...230	
	Eternal Judgment III..233	
	Lesson Study Review 18...247	
	Final Summary Review...248	
	Index..253	
	Hell – Historical Study..255	
	Index..267	
	Sin – Historical Study...269	
	Lesson Study Review 19...279	
	Answer Section..281	
	Letter of Encouragement...340	
	Congratulations..341	
	My Comments...342	
	Bibliography..345	

Dedication

....first and foremost to the glory of God and His Son, Jesus the Christ....

....to all new Believers in Christ who thirst after truth and are earnestly pressing toward a closer walk with God....

....to all maturing Believers who while running the race have never been instructed how to lay their foundation on Christ....

....to all teachers and students in the Body of Christ who desire to see that the foundations are not destroyed, but laid properly....

Acknowledgments

To Jesus for dying for me and giving me new life and to the Holy Spirit for His fullness and inspiration, desire, direction and joy for the overwhelming task of developing this study.

To my firstborn child, JudyMarie, who was fatally injured in 1977. Among the many original sayings and inspirational drawings found in the margin of her college notebooks, I chose to use one as a watermark on each doctrine index page of this book.

To Jean Swengel Allen, BA, MA, Human Ecology for her tedious scrutiny of my grammar and her challenge after critiquing the first manuscript. For her encouragement, frequent hospitality, and for providing me privacy in her lovely condo on the beautiful coastline of Sarasota to continue this work.

To Pastor Mike Pici, BA English with Journalism emphasis; MA Biblical Studies. I am exceedingly fortunate for our six year association that gave seemingly instantaneous assistance whenever I needed it. Always ready with his red pen, for input, suggestions and the many challenges of what I write, I am indebted.

To Ralph Quinones, correspondence course student, who took this course as a dry run before the first printing, throwing the manuscript into a third major revision. I am indebted to his long letters of speaking life into this work, his prayers and encouragement.

To Sue Robe, constant in season and out of season. My true friend.

To Sam Townsend and Rev. Glenn Pav, for our extensive emails and marathon theological phone conversations line by line, precept by precept. I'm forever grateful. We actually held hours of discussions without intimidation, anger or dissension. I praise God for holy men.

To David Hewitt, for his many hours of stick-to-it-tive-ness in preparing this work for the publisher.

Foreword

I first met Madeline Vance in 1993. Since I've known her, she has been involved in discipling and "special encouragement" of many ministries and applies a disciplined principle to the teaching of God's Word.

The basic principles she shares are experience-oriented and are presented to gradually change lives for the better. There is positive proof of this in the lives of those with whom she shares.

"*First [Elementary] Principles*" provides simple yet well-organized diagramming of deeper principles with delineation of experiential life teachings. The student is shown the fullness of the doctrines and how to walk by faith in a practical way. This book has need and value in this age.

Dr. Dwight D. Martin
President
Florida Beacon Bible College & Seminary

Preface

As far back as childhood, I can remember searching for truth in many matters including the Truth about God, but never found the latter until age 37, when the Lord left the ninety-nine behind, found me and called me into His Kingdom to follow Him. Since then His truth, the Bible, has become my constant companion. In my daily life, I remember almost always telling the truth or telling of an incident without manipulation or shading of the circumstances. Many times this worked to my detriment and many times I was punished or rejected, but something inside me would not allow me to skirt the truth of the matter. Today, if you ask me a question, it remains impossible for me to be any different. White-washing and politically correct is repulsive to me.

Eventually, I became frustrated as a "pew-warmer" with the infiltration of worldly elements into the church services through messages, songs, performances and religious entertainment. And are not the five Callings as spoken of in Ephesians 4:7-13 for the equipping of the saints for work of service? In 1994-95, I produced and directed a TV teaching program called *"Back To Bible Basics"* and tried to stick as close to basics as possible. This study guide also reflects Bible basics. If His word is absolute Truth why are we adulterating the purpose of assembling together by deviating from the power of God, His love for us and His desire on how to run His government?

When Dr. Martin (see About the Author) asked me to recall 18 hours of lectures into writings to be included in this study guide for the Correspondence Course Department of the college, he requested I add a Bibliography page. Although it is only recently that I have discovered books on various aspects of New Testament doctrine that include parts of Hebrews 6:1-2. I understand there are many commentaries on all the books of the Bible, but I'm not aware that a book exists which teaches exclusively these six "elementary principles" as a whole in one bound labor such as this book. I don't want to sound arrogant and there may be a book or two out there, but it hasn't crossed my path. In this labor of love, I have endeavored to interpret these verses and it is my hope that all denominations will recognize the importance of these necessary teachings. These six doctrines were not only essential to the First Century Hebrew believers, but its also essential to us 21st Century believers as well.

Since Hebrews 6:1-2 is basic to our faith in God, in all honesty, I must confess, it amazes me that "elementary principles," because they are elementary, are not part of the new Believer's handbook in all churches of all denominations.

Introduction

The Beginnings Of Our New Life In Christ

Foundations and beginnings are important to our walk with God. The ancient writer inquired:

> **"If the foundations are destroyed,**
> **What can the righteous do?"**
> **—Psalm 11:3**

Jesus taught the need for having sound foundations upon which to build our personal lives. He illustrated this truth by a parable of two houses, one built with a proper foundation and one built without a proper foundation. Under storm conditions the house with the foundation upon a rock stood, while the house built upon the earth without a solid foundation was destroyed and the "ruin of that house was great." The man who built his house upon the rock foundation was according to Jesus, wise. This parable shows: the man *came* to Christ, *heard* His words and *acted* upon them. Truly wise people do the same.

The purpose of Christ's illustration regarding the two houses was to establish the truth that the life built without Him as the foundation, is a life inevitably bound for destruction. Many professing Believers begin with every intention of raising a fine, grandiose edifice of Christianity in their lives, but before long the storms of life cause their structure to sink, lean and get-out-of-plumb. In time, their vows, prayers and good intentions are left by the wayside. Jesus said, "they would be like a foolish man, who built his house upon the sand and when the rain descended, and the floods came the house not only fell, but its fall was great."

Father God, who is the creator and maker of all things, spoke everything into being on the integrity of a solid foundation; through Jesus, the carpenter's son, "All things came into being and apart from Him nothing came into being that has come into being" (John 1:3) and through the power of the Holy Spirit. Are we to do any less than build our lives on a solid foundation? On the following pages we read of Matthew's and Luke's account of the words Jesus spoke of building a house on a foundation of rock. The Word of Jesus is the foundation and our soul is the spiritual house with which we must build upon the Word of God, strengthened in our inner man by the power of the Holy Spirit.

Therefore, the goal of this study is not just to acquire head knowledge, but also to build a strong personal foundation of faith and love toward God and become a true and steadfast Believer with heart knowledge. As Paul wrote to the church in Corinth "Knowledge makes one arrogant, but love edifies." (1 Corinthians 8:1). Acquiring head knowledge can make one conceited, but heart (core of man) knowledge will present information with humility.

In his same letter to the Corinthians, in the thirteenth chapter, Paul explains how to deliver knowledge in love. Read specifically verses 1-13.

Eternal Life Principles & Beyond

The foundation stones must, by definition, be of equal value; therefore, each doctrine has equal holding power and one doctrine does not carry more weight than another or there will be an imbalance in our lives. Although some would argue that faith in God is most important and that may be legally true, as a foundation stone their posture is positionally out-of-plumb.

Once the Believer's heart has fully grasped the foundation of what the kingdom of God is all about, he is then secure in his *Faith Toward God* to move on to maturity. Spiritual maturity carries with it solid character (James 1:4), a spirit (heart) of integrity (Proverbs 11:3; 19:1; 20:7) and walking in the fruit of the Holy Spirit (Galatians 5:22-23) regarding all circumstances keeping in mind the ultimate goal of a perfected life. James admonishes us "....If anyone does not stumble in what he says, he is a perfect man, able to bridle the whole body as well" (3:2). Since no one knows when a storm will come, the following lessons, based on the Sacred Writings, will prove to be the solid foundation from which you will draw your stability.

Therefore, this work begins with background material of Historical Study entitled *Foundations*. Throughout this course on New Testament doctrines there are three additional Historical Study sections which confirm, support and enhance certain specific doctrines. Each section is clearly identified as a Historical Study for clarity to the reader.

Over and over again it is beautiful to see the Word of God unfold within our hearts and confirm itself as the Holy Spirit teaches those with a teachable spirit. For with the help of the precious Holy Spirit, God leaves no room for doubt of His Word. If we have faith and the intent of our heart is toward His Truth, His Holy Spirit will teach us. We have no need to worry for the Apostle John scribed Jesus' spoken promise in the sixteenth chapter verse 13, "But when He, the Spirit of truth, comes, He will guide you into all truth;" and again in chapter 14 verse 26, "But the Helper, the Holy Spirit, whom the Father will send in My name, He will teach you all things...."

It is so important to God we understand His Word that He does not leave us to speculate on doctrines.

One other mention worthy of noting is what may appear as grammatical error or poor sentence construction is simply a direct quote of the Scriptures as written, which do not always follow grammatical patterns.

The following is a disclaimer regarding gender neutral. With current cultural standards being defined and challenged, please allow me to clarify the use of men or man in the context of this Bible study. It demonstrates that no person is demeaned or excluded. There are four principal Hebrew words translated "man" in the Old Testament which represent him in four inconsistent aspects: Adam, he is of the earth, earthy, Genesis 2:7; *Ish*, he is endued with immaterial and personal existence, springing from him as a contrast, i.e. husband/wife, Genesis 2:23; as *Enosh*, he is weak or incurable, or a person or in the case of angelic beings, Genesis 18:2, 16, 22; and as *Gever*, he is mighty and

Introduction

noble which are capable of being exhibited in his life and character, Genesis 6:4. Most Bible students are cognizant of the fact Adam also means firstman/man/ruddy/red/earth/mankind/person/mortal/population/someone/anyone/being and in the beginning (before Eve was created), did not represent either male or female. The personal pronoun "he" does not designate gender or sexual orientation, race or ethnicity. It simply indicates personhood. Also, according to New Testament theology there is neither male nor female in Christ Jesus - Galatians 3:28. We are spirit, soul and body and the precious Holy Spirit speaks to us through our spirit.

Also, I have avoided using the title Christian/Christians wherever possible as it is not a name ordained by God for His chosen. The word "saint" is among 1,000 other names in the Bible as God's designation of a Believer. In quoting Kenneth S. Wuest's *Word Studies from the Greek New Testament* for the English reader, he explains on page 19 of Paul's letter to the Jews in Rome the following:

> The name "Christian" was coined by the world as a term of derision. The city of Antioch in Syria had a reputation for coining nicknames. Luke says, "The disciples were called Christian first at Antioch" (Acts 11:26). The word is used three times in the New Testament, and each time as a term of reproach or derision. Agrippa also used the term when Paul was defending himself and his message before the king. Peter in his first letter (4:16), by the Holy Spirit, appropriates the title as a proper designation of a believer when he says, "If any man suffer as a Christianos."

The expressions, "the first principles of the oracles of God" in Hebrews chapter 5 verse 12, and "the principles of the doctrine of Christ" in chapter 6 verse 1, are quite different in the Greek. The word "principles" in these verses comes from two different Greek words. The expression in 5:12 *"stoicheion"* (meaning one in a row, i.e. the alphabet) refers to the elementary teachings in New Testament truth, and the expression in 6:1, *"logos"* (meaning an instruction, statement, speech or exhortation) refers to the teaching in the Gospel of Matthew whose theme is Jesus, as Messiah, was first mentioned.

Hebrews 6:1-3 – We now come to a careful study of the two Greek words translated "leaving" and "let us go on." A correct understanding of these is absolutely essential to the proper exegesis (a serious study of the Word) of the passage we are treating.

The Greek word *"aphiemi"* translated *"leaving"* is a verb meaning "to put or place," with a preposition prefixed which means "off" or "away". The preposition implies separation and is used with a case in Greek which also implies separation. The basic idea in the verb is that of an action which causes a separation. The various meanings of the word are as follows: to send away, to bid go away or depart, to let go, to send from one's self, to let alone, to let be, to disregard.

Eternal Life Principles & Beyond

In Matthew 13:36 and Mark 4:36, this word is used of the sending away of the multitudes. We could translate it thus, "Therefore, having abandoned once for all the principles of the doctrine of Christ, let us go on to perfection." The act of abandoning is the pre-requisite to that of going on. One cannot go on without first separating one's self from that to which one is attached. The word translated "let us go on" means "to carry or bear," which means the subject is passive or inactive itself and is being acted upon by some outside agent. Thus we could translate, "abandoning once for all....let us be carried along."

Since my born-again experience in 1975, I can testify how our Lord has a cunning way of carrying me along from one circumstance to another to bring about my progression toward perfection and I am guaranteed He will continue until the day of our Lord's appearing in the sky (Philippians 1:6). There has been one incident after another that caught me by surprise and usually not appreciated until after I "laid the axe to the root" or "Unless the grain of wheat falls into the earth and dies, it remains by itself alone; but if it dies, it bears much fruit."

This book is not intended to be a theological discourse for the third and fourth year seminary student, although such a one may desire to peruse New Testament doctrine as an integral part of their faith. The volume of this book is based on two Scriptures and is simply a teaching purposing to instill into the core of your very being the basics of our faith. Again, not to be redundant about searching for written material on Hebrews 6:1-2 exclusively, it was important because these six doctrines are so foundational to our faith and the key not only to this study but its importance to the hearts of the believer, which needs to be solidified.

Major portions of the above articles on "principles," "leaving" and "let us go on" were taken from Wuest's *Word Studies From the Greek New Testament*, volume two, pages 107-111, Wm. B. Eerdmans Publishing Company, Grand Rapids, MI 49502

About The Author

Madeline Massi Vance was born and raised in Camden, New Jersey of Italian and Sicilian immigrant parents. Like most during the aftermath of the depression and WWII, she began her life with difficulties and hardships which strangely continue on till today. Madeline wrote *"Eternal Life Principles & Beyond"* to prepare the way for you, the Believer, in your life's journey with Jesus, the Christ. Her heart is very much in her work which reflects her love for Jesus.

During the late winter months of 1973, Madeline experienced a life-changing encounter with Christ Jesus. She discovered Jesus is alive and that the Word of God is absolute Truth. The Holy Spirit became a dynamic part of her daily fellowship with Abba Father and witnessing and teaching became her priority in life.

As a new Believer her thirst for reading and understanding God's letters to the Body of Christ was insatiable. She was so on fire with this new knowledge that many came to "drink from her cup" as the Holy Spirit moved in power and glory. Almost immediately after her salvation experience, she was asked to give Bible studies in three different parts of the county. About three years later she began compiling Scriptures on 3x5 cards and noted that patterns of doctrine emerged. The first writing of *Eternal Life Principles & Beyond* was simply a collection of organized Scriptures referencing each doctrine using only *Strong's Exhaustive Concordance*. At this time a teacher's manual and student syllabus was developed. Titled *Elementary Principles* was comprised of 12 lessons and 12 exams and completed in 1981.

In 1982 she sold her home in New Jersey and by 1983 moved to Pinellas County, Florida. In the spring of 1992 she met Dr. Dwight Martin, President of Florida Beacon Bible College & Seminary. He hired her part-time to answer the phone. Within three months she was appointed his Administrative Assistant and working full-time. In 1994 she graduated from the college with an AA Degree in Theology.

After graduation, Madeline presented a copy of the teacher's manual and student workbook of eight lessons, with eight exams, a mid-term exam and final exam to Dr. Martin to ask about teaching *Eternal Life Principles & Beyond* to first year students. He agreed it was necessary doctrine to be added to the college curriculum. At that time, four lessons of background material were also added to complete the course work. There were now twelve one-hour lectures with twelve exams respectively, in addition to a mid-term and final exams all updated from a typewriter to a word processor. She taught *Eternal Life Principles & Beyond* for three semesters.

From 1993-2001, Madeline was the Correspondence Course Coordinator and later, Correspondence Course Director for Florida Beacon Bible College and Seminary. In 1997, Dr. Martin asked her to assemble her lectures in textbook form, and to add a bibliography page, to be used in the Correspondence Course Department. Madeline spent two full weeks diligently searching for books in particular, and not commentaries, on "first principles" or "elementary principles" and found none. Then she prayed, "Lord is this possible? Please send me something." Eventually, three booklets crossed her path with sparse information containing portions of these doctrines from which she has drawn. They are included as references on the Bibliography page. What you hold in your hands today is the revised exhaustive edition of her original work. In 2004, she earned a Master of Arts in Theology, Summa Cum Laude. On Saturday, June 6, 2015, Madeline Massi Vance walked the graduation podium one more time, and for the last time, to receive her Doctorate Degree in Theology, Magna Cum Laude. She started her Biblical education in 1979 and finished in 2015. Yes, it took her 36 years to finish her theological education.

May Eternal Life Principles & Beyond, bless your heart and help your walk with our mighty Savior Jesus, the Christ.

.

A Word From The Author

Welcome Dear Reader!

I hope that your study of the *Eternal Life Principles & Beyond — Foundation of Our Faith* will be educationally profitable for *you*. This Bible-based study has been designed primarily for Believers desiring to understand our basic New Testament beliefs. However, it can be used for group study in Home Cell Prayer Groups, Sunday School Classes, New Believers Class or Bible School Classes, Prison Ministry Outreach, Missionary Outreach, High School Home Schooling and Church Training Center.

These *Elementary Principles* are not intended as an evangelistic tool, but can be used as such. However, pastors and Bible teachers can also use it as a suggested outline for sermon preparation and reference. Missionaries can, with permission, use it as a foundational course from which they can present this valuable revelation in other languages.

As *you* study these six New Testament doctrines, it is necessary to recognize that God has established basic foundations and specifically indicated what they are in order that we may understand and do them. We don't just want to be informed of these foundational principles; simply put, they must become functional in our lives. They are essential to the development of new and mature Believers if they are to become established on a sound foundation upon which to construct an indestructible spiritual life. We should not leave the elementary teachings about the Christ and press on to becoming mature Believers until we have studied these basic New Testament Doctrines. Before we leave the Elementary Principles, which is what this book is all about and continue to become growing believers, let's make sure we have applied these principles to our lives, which are the foundation of our faith, and by doing so we can press on to maturity in Christ with a deeper application of the Word of God.

It's very important to take the time to answer all the questions in the Lesson Study Review and then check your answers in the Answer Section in the back of the book. To read *Eternal Life Principles & Beyond* as a novel will not have the significance and the full impact of the specific doctrine if you skip the Lesson Study Reviews. You will understand after checking your answers.

Read the Lesson Study Review questions carefully. Most Lesson Study Review answers are contained within that specific lesson, but not all. Take note of the maximum line space for your answer. It indicates short and on-target answers.

Some guidelines in answering the questions:

- If the question contains false information, then the answer must be false.

- Where there are essay questions in a particular quiz it is important the answer be fully obtained from that text. Do not go outside the lesson plan of that doctrine. If *you* do, it will reduce the doctrine to mediocrity.

- It is also important the answers not be evangelistic in nature or on love or the natural or spiritual gifts. Again, to do so would reduce the doctrine to mediocrity. Please stay focused on the title of the lesson.

- Essay questions in the Mid-Summary Review and Final Summary Review must be fully explained. I have listed the pertinent points in the Answer Section that must be addressed in your answer.

- My goal is for the Believer to receive heart knowledge over head knowledge; therefore, please refer back to the text for the needed answer.

I also encourage you to work from your own Bible when necessary.

May God Bless Your Growth in the Christ,

Madeline

My Inspirations, Challenges & Revelations:

INDEX

FOUNDATION – HISTORICAL STUDY

    Parable Of The Two Houses..27

    What Did The Lord Jesus Teach About Our Personal Foundation
        In The Parable Of The Two Houses?...29

    What Did The Apostles Teach About Our Personal Foundation
        Described In First Principles?..31

My Inspirations, Challenges & Revelations:

Foundation -
Historical Study

The Parable Of The Two Houses

Matthew 7:24-29	Luke 6:47-49
24 "Therefore everyone who hears these words of Mine, and acts upon them, may be compared to a wise man, who built his house upon the rock.	47 "Everyone who comes to Me and Hears My words, and acts upon them, I will show you whom he is like:
25 And the rain descended and the floods came, and the winds blew, and burst against that house; and yet it did not fall, for it had been founded upon the rock.	48 he is like a man building a house, who dug deep and laid a foundation upon the rock; and when a flood rose, the torrent burst against that house and could not shake it, because it had been well built.
26 And everyone who hears these words of mine, and does not act upon them, will be like a foolish man, who built his house upon the sand.	49 But the one who has heard, and has not acted accordingly, is like a man who built a house upon the ground without any foundation; and the torrent burst against it and immediately it collapsed, and the ruin of that house was great."
27 And the rain descended, and the floods came, and the winds blew, and burst against that house; and it fell, and great was its fall.	
28 The result was that when Jesus had finished these words, the multitudes were amazed at His teaching;	
29 for He was teaching them as one having authority, and not as their scribes."	

The importance of a sound foundation cannot be overestimated. If a building is to be useful, sturdy, and permanent, it must have a solid base. A good illustration is Bonanno Pisano's leaning tower built between 1173 and 1350 on shifting subsoil in Tuscan, Italy.

The most important feature of any solid and permanent building is the foundation. It supports a building and sets a limit to the weight, width and height of the structure to be erected upon it. A foundation set on sand is inadequate. Since this is commonly understood, God used the parable of the two houses to teach us a Divine Truth.

Foundation - Historical Study

The Bible also speaks of our lives as buildings and tells us the kind of foundation upon which they must be built. Additionally, the Bible speaks of Christ's Church as a building and tells us the kind of foundation upon which it must be built. What, then, is God's appointed foundation for the Believer's life? Here are a few Scriptures written by a variety of men starting with Paul:

> "For no man can lay a *foundation* other than the one which is laid, which is Jesus Christ."
>
> —1 Corinthians 3:11

> "Therefore, thus says the Lord God, "Behold, I am laying in Zion a stone, a tested stone, a costly cornerstone for the *foundation*, firm placed (well-laid). He who believes in it will not be disturbed."
>
> —Isaiah 28:16

Peter speaking about Jesus, also confirmed Isaiah's words in his first epistle in chapter two, verse six. Thus the Old Will and the New Will (Hebrews 8:13 & 10:9) alike agree in this vital fact: the true foundation of the Believer's life is Jesus Christ Himself. He is not a creed, not a church, not a denomination, not an ordinance or a ceremony, but the only Begotten Son of the living God, Yahweh.

In various places where the Bible compares the life of a Believer to the construction of a building, or an edifice, we read:

> "But you, beloved, *building* yourselves up on your most holy faith;...."
>
> —Jude 20

> "For we are God's fellow workers; you are God's field, God's building. According to the grace of God which was given to me, as a wise master builder, I laid the *foundation*, and another is building upon it. But let each man be careful how he builds upon it. For no man can lay a *foundation* other than the one which is laid, which is Jesus Christ."
>
> —1 Corinthians 3:9-11

> "You also are *builded* together for an habitation of God through the Spirit."
>
> —Ephesians 2:22 KJV

> "... and I consider it right, as long as I am in this earthly dwelling, to stir you up, by way of reminder, knowing that the laying aside of my earthly dwelling is imminent, as our Lord Jesus Christ has made clear to me."
>
> —2 Peter 1:13-14

> "Rooted and *built up* in Christ and established in the faith."
>
> —Colossians 2:7 KJV

> "The word of God's grace is able to *build* you up."
>
> —Acts 20:32 KJV

Eternal Life Principles & Beyond

In all these passages, the Believer's life is compared to the construction of a building. Therefore, in this series, we are going to study the personal foundation of character building, which each of us must have if we are to construct lives that are sound.

What Did The Lord Jesus Teach About Our Personal Foundation In The Parable Of The Two Houses?
Matthew 7:24-29, Luke 6:47-49

    A. What constitutes a sound life? —Luke 6:47

        1. "Everyone who comes to Me
        2. hears my words and
        3. acts upon them...."

    B. Can one hear and not do? —Luke 6:46

        1. "Why do you call Me, "Lord, Lord"
        2. and do not do what I say?"

Jesus is saying here that "this is *knowing* the Word and not doing it!" This is a very grievous situation as you will see when studying the lessons on *Eternal Judgment*.

    C. What is a man like who hears and does the Word? —Luke 6:48a

        1. "he is like a man building a house
        2. who dug deep
        3. and laid a foundation upon the rock...."

This describes the wise builder as he "dug deep", and as he dug and dug and dug he removed all the dirt between himself and the Rock. He was anticipating the magnificence of the structure he was going to build on it. The dirt not only represents our traditions, religiosity, legalisms, false indoctrinations, opinions, and unresolved conflicts, but in some cases our sins. James 3:2-6 refers to the unbridled tongue "as a fire, the very world of iniquity" (vs 6) ".... which defiles the entire body, ...and is set on fire by hell." Sin continues to be dealt with in the Believer's maturing/building process as the Believer submits to the conviction of the Holy Spirit. The wise builder makes sure that he is on solid footing. The only man who is secure in his placement is the man who is standing in God.

    D. Why must the house be erected "on a rock"? —Luke 6:48b

        "When a flood rose, the torrent burst against that house and could not
        shake it because it had been well *built*."

Foundation - Historical Study

It is the nature of life to be stormy! Read Hebrews 12:25-29. Nobody escapes the storms. The peace of God is not freedom from the storm; it is security in the midst of the storm. (Mark 4:37-40). So, how does a person begin to build upon this Rock, which is Christ?

Maturity develops as we steadfastly apply our faith toward God during the hard times and continue to draw closer to Him. One storm at a time, one trial at a time, one hardship at a time, one challenge at a time, we develop our faith for eternity with a security and confidence which no thing, or no one, can ever persuade, mislead or destroy. It is through faith and not a thought process. The mature believer seeks the promises of God and responds in faith.

    E. What happened to the house founded "on a rock"? —Luke 6:48b

        1. The torrent "could not shake it"
        2. .....it "had been well built!"

There will be storms in your walk with Christ, but if you are hearing and doing the Word of God, the storm cannot shake you. The *only* Rock, upon which true and stable faith can be based on, is in Christ Himself, therefore, your house must be built before the storm comes!!

Recorded in the Old Will are many of David's prophetically-inspired Psalms confirming the Lord as Our Rock. "The Lord is my rock.... in whom I will trust" Ps 18:2. Please read Psalm 62:1-2; 5-7. Notice the emphatic repetition of the word "only", especially in verse six. Throughout this particular Psalm, the words "rock" and "salvation" intimately relate to and reveal the person as the Lord Himself. If Believers build upon this foundation we, like David, can say: "He only is my rock and my salvation; He is my defense; I shall *not be moved.*"

    F. Who's life is in danger? —Luke 6:49a

        1. "The one who has heard and has not acted accordingly"
        2. "a man *without any foundation!*"
        3. "A life built upon the ground (sand)"

    G. What happens to the house without a proper foundation? —Luke 6:49b

        1. "The torrent burst against it" (same storm)
        2. "Immediately it collapsed"
        3. "The ruin of that house was great"

Eternal Life Principles & Beyond

What Did The Apostles Teach About Our Personal Foundation Described In First Principles?
Hebrews 6:1-2

1. "Repentance from dead works"
2. "Faith toward God"
3. "Instruction about washings"
4. "Laying on of hands"
5. "Resurrection of the dead"
6. "Eternal judgment"

Summary:

The Believer must have a good foundation if he is going to build a good house in the Lord. The foundation must be laid according to the Architect's plan. We have this plan in the Bible. We want these principles to become functional in our lives. It is important to be informed about God's truths, and apply them to our daily living till the storms that come our way dissipate. We are going to deal with six New Testament doctrines that are foundational truths. Each doctrine is an integral part of the foundation. If the building is to be useful for God's plan and purpose for your life, it must be sturdy, permanent, unshakable and uncollapsible. It must have a solid base.

Having embraced these foundational truths by the end of this study, we will then leave these "first principles" and go on toward perfection/maturity and completion (James 1:4). We don't stand around and admire a foundation. We must start building on our foundation. Spiritual growth is a continual building process of the soul. It is a process that never ceases.

Please read Paul's words to the church at Philippi in chapter three, verses eight to sixteen. These verses include the following:

> "Not that I have already obtained it, or have already become perfect, but I press on in order that I may lay hold of that for which also I was laid hold of by Christ Jesus...."

> "I press on toward the goal for the prize of the upward call of God in Christ Jesus. Let us therefore, as many as are perfect, have this attitude;...."

Additional Notes:

Foundational building, in the natural or in the spiritual, is not usually an exciting time, it is tedious, slow and hard labor to dig deep and remove stones of character weakness and which involves much perseverance. We cannot "go on unto perfection" unless these foundation stones are rightly laid. This is why so many Believers do not grow and

Foundation - Historical Study

mature in their faith. A foundation that is sound brings peace, hope and joy to the soul, but a person who does not have a solid foundation will find their house swept away by flooding rains.

Zerubbabel had the capacity to make foundation building exciting and to make it a time of celebration (See Ezra 3:10-13). And *you* can, also, if *you* keep your mind on the things for which a great foundation can prepare *you* (See Philippians 1:6). Ahead of *you* lies the road to becoming the Lord's disciple, becoming all *you* can be as a husband and father, wife and mother, student, employee, employer and, etc. Character building and becoming a person of integrity, holiness and power means the breaking of bad habits and laying the "axe to the root" of self-abasement, worry, anxiety and anger.

Foundation

Lesson Study Review 1

1. What did the Lord indicate constitutes a sound life for His Called Ones?

   Luke 6:47 _____

   _____

2. How important is a foundation to a building?

   _____

   _____

3. Is it possible to erect a building without a proper foundation? _____

   Explain Your Answer: _____

   _____

   _____

   A. List the four storms found in Colossians 2:8.

   _____   _____

   _____   _____

   B. List six storms that face families today that are not mentioned in the lesson.

   _____   _____

   _____   _____

   _____   _____

4. In the Lord's parable, what is inevitable in the lives of all human beings?

   _____

   _____

   _____

Lesson Study Review 1

5. According to the parable of the two houses what does the Lord consider to be the process to lay a good foundation?

Luke 6:48 _____

_____

   A. What is some of the dirt that many have to face in their primary relationships that can negatively impact their relationship with Jesus? (Draw from your personal experience.)

   _____   _____
   _____   _____
   _____   _____
   _____   _____

(Flesh is the inclination of our nature to self-satisfying or gratifying behavior.)

6. Describe the steps to secure a good foundation for this life.

_____
_____
_____

7. God expects us to build a good foundation when we have received information on how to do it. _____ (True or False)

Justify your answer: _____

_____
_____

8. According to Hebrews 6:1-2, what constitutes the foundation of a Believer's life?

   1 _____
   2 _____
   3 _____
   4 _____
   5 _____
   6 _____

Eternal Life Principles & Beyond

9. List some New Testament principles that enable us to progress on to spiritual maturity.

A. _____

B. _____

C. _____

D. _____

E. _____

F. _____

G. _____

H. _____

Foundation

Addendum:

Lesson Study Review 2

Read 2 Timothy 2:1-7. In Paul's second letter to Timothy, he draws three illustrations. Write out the key words that exemplify the believers' character that are to be part of the foundation of their house.

vs 1 _____

vs 2 _____

vs 3 _____

vs 4 _____

vs 5 _____

vs 6 _____

In vs 2 did Paul mention eloquent men? Did he speak of good looking men? Did he declare educated men?

_____

Name two attributes noted in vss 1-6 that Paul listed for Believers:

_____ and _____

Our heavenly Father is a God of love; therefore, He has given us the power of choice. In making decisions, we can choose the direction, but we cannot choose the results. In the following verses what virtues were Paul and Jesus exalting?

1 Timothy 1:12 _____

1 Corinthians 4:1 _____

1 Corinthians 4:2 _____

1 Corinthians 4:17 _____

Luke 16:10-12 _____

Foundation: Lesson Study Review 2

Read the following Scriptures for additional character building virtues and circle the ones that can be added to the above list.

1 Corinthians 10:13   2 Corinthians 1:18   2 Thessalonians 3:3

   Hebrews 3:5;   10:23;   11:6   1 Thessalonians 5:24   1 Peter 4:19

Two final illustrations:

Read Matthew 24:45-51 and write down what vs 48 reveals as the opposite of faithful.

_____   Notice it is not unfaithful.

In Matthew 25:14-21 Jesus spoke on the parable of the talents.

In vs 21 He calls this slave _____

In vs 23 He calls this slave _____

But in vs 26 Jesus calls this slave _____ and _____

Is this the opposite of faithful?   _____

Note: A neglected virtue among some is not "showing appreciation" when warranted.

My Inspirations, Challenges & Revelations:

DOCTRINE 1

REPENTANCE FROM DEAD WORKS

What Is The Meaning Of The Word Repentance?...42

Definitions Of The Word Repentance..42

So, What Are Dead Works Anyway?..43

How Important Is Repentance?...44

Is Repentance Required?...45

What Causes Mankind To Repent?...45

What Is Associated With Repentance?...47

Do Saints Repent?...48

How Important Is Repentance When Evangelizing..50

My Inspirations, Challenges & Revelations:

Repentance From Dead Works

1 Now in those days John the Baptist came, preaching in the wilderness of Judea, saying

2 "Repent, for the kingdom of heaven is at hand."

3 For this is the one referred to by Isaiah the prophet, saying
> "THE VOICE OF ONE CRYING IN THE WILDERNESS 'MAKE READY THE WAY OF THE LORD, MAKE HIS PATHS STRAIGHT'"

4 Now John himself had a garment of camel's hair and a leather belt about his waist; and his food was locusts and wild honey.

5 Then Jerusalem was going out to him, and all Judea, and all the district around the Jordan;

6 and they were being baptized by him in the Jordan River, as they confessed their sins.

7 But when he saw many of the Pharisees and Sadducees coming for baptism, he said to them, "You brood of vipers, who warned you to flee from the wrath to come?

8 "Therefore bring forth fruit in keeping with repentance;

9 and do not suppose that you can say to yourselves, 'We have Abraham for our father': for I say to you, that God is able from these stones to raise up children to Abraham.

10 "And the axe is already laid at the root of the trees; every tree therefore that does not bear good fruit is cut down and thrown into the fire.

11 "As for me, I baptize you with water for repentance, but He who is coming after me is mightier than I, and I am not fit to remove His sandals; He will baptize you with the Holy Spirit and fire.

12 "And His winnowing fork is in His hand, and He will thoroughly clear His threshing floor; and He will gather His wheat into the barn, but He will burn up the chaff with unquenchable fire.'"

—Matthew 3

Repentance From Dead Works

What Is The Meaning Of The Word Repentance?

Teshuvah (repentance) is one of the basic 613 commandments in traditional Judaism and is directed toward the believers.

In the Old Testament, there are two words which when translated signify repent. The one, *"nacham"* means to "lament," "to grieve", or "to be sorry" and refers to the aroused emotions of God or man when undertaking a different course of action. It is most generally employed to express the Scriptural idea of genuine repentance. It is used extensively by the prophets and indicates *A RADICAL CHANGE IN ONE'S ATTITUDE TOWARD SIN AND GOD.*

The other word *"shuwb,"* means "to withdraw," "to turn back," "to consider, convert," "fetch home again" and implies a conscious moral separation, and a personal decision to forsake sin and enter into fellowship with God.

In the New Testament, there are also two words which when translated mean repent. One of these, *"metamellomai"* is like the first Old Testament word *"nacham"* and conveys "to have a feeling or care, concern or regret".

The other word, *"metanoeo"* means "to have another mind" or "to think differently toward" and occurs in the noun and verb forms 57 times. It is also associated with the word, *"turn"* and "describes that deep and radical change whereby a sinner turns from the idols of sin and self unto God." It involves the stirring and directing of the emotions to urge the required change. It is the action of the yielded will in turning the whole man away from sin to God. It is not a suggestion. It is a command with the implications as in the military giving the order "about face!" (A 180° turn!)

Note: Teshuvah (repentance) is one of the basic 613 commandments in traditional Judaism and is directed toward the Messianics (Believers in Christ).

Definitions Of The Word Repentance

A. "Repentance expresses that mighty change in the mind, heart, and life wrought by the Spirit." —Trench

B. "Repentance may be defined as the voluntary change in the mind of the sinner whereby he turns from sin. It involves a change of view, a change of feeling, and a change of purpose." —Paddington

C. "Repentance describes that deep and radical change whereby a sinner turns from the idols of self and sin unto God, and devotes every movement of the inner and outer man to the captivity of His obedience." —Chalmers

D. "Repentance implies an intellectual and a hearty giving up of all controversy with God upon all and every point. It implies a conviction that God is wholly right, and the sinner wholly wrong, and a thorough and hearty abandonment of all excuses and apologies for sin." —Finney

E. "I stand ready to admit God is holy right and I am wholly wrong. I will change my weak attitude toward sin and fear God's sovereignty and righteousness. I will give up all wrangling and squabbling with God upon each and every point and will make a thorough and vigorous abandonment of all temptations for sin." —Author Madeline Vance

Summary statement of the above definitions:

Repentance involves reforming and changing of the mind as well as the stirring and directing of the emotions to urge the required change. The action of the yielded will then turn the whole man away from sin and to God. Heed this statement as it will be a theme through-out most of these lessons.

So What Are Dead Works Anyway?

The question now arises, "What are dead works?"

Although there is no Scripture that defines exactly what dead works are, the Bible says that after salvation, as we grow in the Lord, the Holy Spirit bears witness in our conscience mind and convicts us of sin, righteousness and judgment. Everything we do as a Believer is either done of the prompting of the Holy Spirit or prompting of the flesh. If our works are done in obedience to the Lord, it is a good work. If we do a work in the flesh (i.e. selfishly), it is a dead work. Our Father looks to and fro over the earth for those who would seek Him to do His will in Spirit and in truth.

So now the next question is, "What are living works?" Below, are references to spiritual fruit all of which are "living works." These are in contrast to "dead works."

The Bible speaks of four kinds of spiritual fruit. John the Immerser referred to one kind in the opening Scripture reading in Matthew 3:8 & 10 of this lesson. The following is but a brief overview of good fruit.

In verses 8 and 10 this fruit refers to righteous deeds, which are also called "fruit unto holiness," "fruits worthy of repentance" and being "fruitful in every good work." For further study of this fruit read James 3:18, Romans 6:22 and Colossians 1:10. Repentance is seated in the heart and a true penitent brings forth good fruit. Those who say they are sorry for their sins, but persist in them, have not "laid the axe to the root" (in their heart).

Read Matthew 7:16-20. Jesus takes no thought to repeat what his cousin John preached and concludes with this message, "So then, you will know them by their fruits." Jesus means you will know them by their persons, their words, deeds and actions and the course of their conversation. Observe how they live; their words and their works will testify for them or against them.

The second kind of "fruit" is of the divine nature of God manifesting in us as explained by Paul in his letter to the Galatians in chapter 5 verses 14-26. Read these verses and take special note of verses 22-23. Believers who daily walk in this fruit have an intense desire to please God and to do good to mankind regardless of others' attitude toward us. It is the fulfilling of the commandment to love our neighbor as we love ourselves. Also read Ephesians 5:9.

The third kind of "fruit" is of souls being added to the kingdom of God. The Apostle John describes it as gathering "fruit for life eternal". Read John 4:36.

The fourth kind of "fruit" is found in Hebrews 13:15 "Through Him then, let us continually offer up a sacrifice of praise to God, that is, the fruit of lips that give thanks to His name."

How Important Is Repentance?

A. Repentance is one reason for Christ's coming into the World

"I have not come to call the righteous, but sinners to *repentance*."
—Luke 5:32

B. Repentance is necessary to eternal life

"And when they heard this, they quieted down, and glorified God, saying, 'Well then, God has granted to the Gentiles also the *repentance* that leads to life'"
—Acts 11:18

C. Repentance is necessary for forgiveness

"And Peter said to them, 'Repent and let each of you be baptized in the name of Jesus Christ for the *forgiveness* of your sins; and you shall receive the gift of the Holy Spirit.'"
—Acts 2:38

D. Repentance is God's desire for all

"The Lord is not slow about His promise, as some count slowness, but is patient toward you, not wishing for any to perish but for all to come to repentance."
—2 Peter 3:9

E. Repentance is necessary for entrance into the Kingdom of God

> From that time Jesus began to preach and say, "Repent, for the kingdom of heaven is at hand."
>
> —Matthew 4:17

The message of repentance was one of the reasons Christ came into the world. It was His first message (Matthew 4:17). The apostles preached it. Pastors and evangelists must preach it or deny the other Scriptures as well. These are apostolic principles and we must return to them because they embrace the need for accountability. Accountability is not a favorite subject with most people as the carnal side of man fights taking responsibility for his/her sins.

Is Repentance Required?

A. Repentance is part of our Lord's commission to us

> "And that repentance for forgiveness of sins should be proclaimed in His name to all the nations, beginning from Jerusalem."
>
> —Luke 24:47

A humble heart before God admits sin at the time we sin. We must do a 180° turn. If all men repented, there would be a change in universal behavior. The answer to societal reform is not more government programs, more laws, more philosophy and psychology, but more people repenting and obeying God's Word, the Bible.

People seek either—

"Human philosophy" or "human counsel" where man is the highest court of appeal or they will seek "divine counsel" where the living God is the highest court of appeal. Those seeking God's highest court of appeal will diligently search the Word of God for His truths and law. Our beliefs and actions stem from one of these sources. When in despair and disagreement with God's Word, please don't argue—just repent!

What Causes Mankind To Repent?

A. The goodness of God causes man to repent

> "Or do you think lightly of the riches of His kindness and forbearance and patience, not knowing that the *kindness* of God leads you to repentance?"
>
> —Romans 2:4

B. Christ's call causes the unbeliever to repent

> "But *go* and learn what this means, 'I desire compassion, and no sacrifice,' for I did not come to call the righteous, but sinners."
>
> —Matthew 9:13

Repentance From Dead Works

    C. Good preaching causes man to repent

       "The men of Nineveh shall stand up with this generation at the judgment, and shall condemn it because they repented at the *preaching* of Jonah."

                                                    —Matthew 12:41

    D. A rebuke causes man to repent

       "....if your brother sins, *rebuke* him; and if he repents, forgive him."

                                                    —Luke 17:3

    E. Godly sorrow causes man to repent

       "....you were made *sorrowful*, to the point of repentance; for you were made sorrowful according to the will of God in order that you might not suffer loss in anything through us. For the *sorrow* that is according to the will of God produces a repentance without regret, leading to salvation."

                                                  —2 Corinthians 7:9-10

    F. The divine gift of repentance causes man to repent.

Repentance is a divine gift from God that causes man to seek reconciliation with God. This is illustrated by the following Scriptures:

       "Well then, God has granted to the Gentiles also the repentance that leads to life."

                                                  —Acts 11:18

       "He is the one whom God exalted to His right hand as a Prince and a Savior, to grant repentance to Israel, and forgiveness of sins."

                                                —Acts 5:31

       "....with gentleness correcting those who are in opposition, if perhaps God may grant them repentance leading to the knowledge of the truth."

                                                —2 Timothy 2:25

    G. The Holy Spirit causes men to repent.

      7 "But I tell you the truth, it is to your advantage that I go away; for if I do not go away, the *Helper* shall not come to you; but if I go, I will send Him to you

      8 And He, when He comes, will convict the world concerning sin, and righteousness and judgment;

      9 concerning sin because they do not believe in Me;

      10 and concerning righteousness, because I go to the Father, and you no longer behold Me;

      11 and concerning judgment, because the ruler of this world has been judged."

                                                —John 16

What Is Associated With Repentance?

A. Faith is associated with repentance

"....repent and *believe* in the gospel."
—Mark 1:15

"....repentance toward God and *faith* in our Lord Jesus Christ."
—Acts 20:21

B. The gift of the Holy Spirit is an accompaniment of repentance.

And Peter said to them, "Repent," and let each of you be *baptized* in the name of Jesus Christ for the forgiveness of your sins; and you shall receive the gift of the Holy Spirit."
—Acts 2:38

C. Conversion is associated with repentance

"Repent therefore and return (be converted), in order that times of refreshing may come."
—Acts 3:19

Note: There is no such thing as a repentance that does not result in a turning around. You must make a radical change in your attitude to stop walking in sin and, by the grace of God, walk in righteousness. This involves a conscious moral separation and personal decision to forsake sin and enter into fellowship with God. There are fifty-seven descriptions in the New Testament of individuals making a radical change from sin (which includes worship of idols) and then reconciling to God.

D. Good works are associated with repentance

"....and even to the Gentiles, that they should repent and turn to God, performing *deeds* appropriate to repentance."
—Acts 26:20

The works of a man will testify as to whether or not there has been true repentance.

E. Good Fruits are associated with repentance

"Therefore bring forth *fruit* in keeping with repentance."
—Matthew 3:8

John the Baptizer came preaching with the message that the "fruit" of righteous deeds should follow after a Believer repents.

Repentance From Dead Works

Do Saints Repent?

Here's another simple question in response: Do Saints, sin? First, the name saint is one of over a thousand names in the Bible that is a God ordained name for His Believers. Throughout the Holy Scriptures, we see this name mentioned because the Holy One, Jesus Christ the Righteous, indwells within us. So, yes, Believers not only sin by action but also because all people are born with a sin nature. Wherever there is sin, there must be repentance. The following Scriptures illustrate the different issues that were taking place in the early churches (the called out ones):

A. The body of Saints assembling in Corinth had to repent toward their salvation:

"I now rejoice, not that you were made sorrowful, but that you were made sorrowful to the point of *repentance*."
—2 Corinthians 7:9

"For I am afraid that perhaps when I come I may find you to be not what I wish and may be found by you to be not what you wish; that perhaps there may be strife, jealousy, angry tempers, disputes, slanders, gossip, arrogance, disturbances;"
—2 Corinthians 12:20-21

B. The body of Saints assembling in Ephesus had to repent from falling away from their first love:

"Remember therefore from where you have fallen, and *repent* and do the deeds you did at first."
—Revelation 2:4-5

C. The body of Saints assembling in Pergamum had to repent from many issues:

"Repent therefore; or else I am coming to you quickly, and I will make war against them with the sword of My mouth."
—Revelation 2:15-16

D. The body of Saints assembling in Sardis had to repent from dead works:

"Remember therefore what you have received and heard; and keep it, and *repent*."
—Revelation 3:2-3

E. The body of Saints assembling in Laodicea had to repent from being satisfied with riches:

"Those whom I love, I reprove and discipline; be zealous therefore, and repent."
—Revelation 3:19

Eternal Life Principles & Beyond

Summary:

Repentance from dead works is the first mentioned doctrine of the Elementary Principles in the Believer's foundation and is of paramount importance. We must emphasize repentance today more than ever. Dead works are discussed under Additional Notes at the end of this lesson.

> "....a foundation of repentance from dead works."
>
> —Hebrews 6:1

Repentance was preached in the New Testament by:

1. Jesus

    > "*Repent*, for the kingdom of heaven is at hand."
    >
    > —Matthew 4:17

2. The Apostles

    > And they went out and preached that men should *repent*.
    >
    > —Mark 6:12

3. Paul

    > "....solemnly testifying to both Jews and Greeks of *repentance* toward God and faith in our Lord Jesus Christ."
    >
    > —Acts 20:21

Repentance is one apostolic principle to which we must return. For a pastor or evangelist to preach only one segment of the Scriptures is to deny the others. They are not preaching a full gospel.

We are the temple of the Holy Spirit and the Lord would have us build a permanent, useful and strong house. Therefore, God will not permit us to go on to maturity if our foundation is not strong. God has provided the following as foundation stones for a solid foundation:

- Repentance from dead works
- Faith toward God
- Baptism/Washings
- Laying on of hands
- A resurrected life
- Moral government

If these are the foundations to be practiced in the life of The Called, is this what is meant by "receiving Christ"?

Repentance From Dead Works

Additional Notes:

This book, *Eternal Life Principles & Beyond*, has been written for the Believer, therefore, it does not address evangelistic modalities. On the other hand, repentance is also a requirement by the unbeliever as entrance into the Kingdom of God and for placement in their Eternal Life. Repentance is a double edged sword and is applicable to the Believer and the unbeliever. For the Believer, it will affect their rewards at the Bema Seat and for the unbeliever it's applicable initially to their salvation.

Listed here are those Scriptures needed for evangelist purposes and for the salvation of those who do not know Christ as Savior and are reading this study book and to encourage the evangelists to begin their message with the doctrine of repentance, thereby following the lead of Our Great Shepherd, the twelve apostles and Paul.

How Important Is Repentance When Evangelizing?

A. Repentance is one reason for Christ's coming into the World

"I have not come to call the righteous, but sinners to *repentance*."
—Luke 5:32

B. Repentance is necessary to avoid destruction

"I tell you, no, but, unless you *repent*, you will all likewise perish."
—Luke 13:3

C. Repentance is necessary to eternal life

"And when they heard this, they quieted down, and glorified God, saying, 'Well then, God has granted to the Gentiles also the *repentance* that leads to life'
—Acts 11:18

D. Repentance is necessary for forgiveness

"And Peter said to them, 'Repent and let each of you be baptized in the name of Jesus Christ for the *forgiveness* of your sins; and you shall receive the gift of the Holy Spirit.'"
—Acts 2:38

E. The gift of the Holy Spirit is an accompaniment of repentance

And Peter said to them, "Repent," and let each of you be *baptized* in the name of Jesus Christ for the forgiveness of your sins; and you shall receive the gift of the Holy Spirit."
—Acts 2:38

F. Repentance is necessary for entrance into the Kingdom of God

> From that time Jesus began to preach and say, "Repent, for the kingdom of heaven is at hand."
>
> —Matthew 4:17

The message of repentance was John the baptizer's first message, it was Christ's first message (Matthew 4:17) it was the apostles' first message and it was also Paul's first message. So what should our first message be?

G. God commands it immediately and universally

> "Therefore having overlooked the times of ignorance, God is now declaring to men that all everywhere should repent."
>
> —Acts 17:30

If God commands repentance immediately and unconditionally, would you not say, it must be very important?

In the next doctrine, *Faith Toward God*, we will read some verses that contain examples of good works.

Repentance From Dead Works
Lesson Study Review 3

1. Define the word REPENTANCE:

   (OT) Nacham _____

   A. _____

   B. _____

   C. _____

   (OT) Shuwb _____

   (NT) Metamellomai _____

   (NT) Metanoeo _____

2. Give Charles G. Finney's definition of "repentance"

   _____

   _____

   _____

3. What is the summary definition of "repentance"?

   A. _____

   B. _____

   C. _____

4. Describe the difference between dead works and fruitful (living) works

_____

_____

_____

5. Is repentance to be preached in all the world?

    Luke 24: 47 _____

_____

    Why? _____

_____

6. Why is repentance necessary?

    A. Luke 5:32 _____

_____

    B. Luke 13:3 _____

    C. Acts 11:18 _____

    D. Acts 2:38 _____

    E. 2 Peter 3:9 _____

    F. Matthew 4:17 _____

John the Baptist – Matthew 3:2 _____

_____

Jesus – Luke 24:47 _____

_____

_____

Lesson Study Review 3

Apostles - Mark 6:12 _____

Paul – Acts 20:21 _____

Note: Jesus preached Repentance throughout His three-year ministry as indicated in all four Gospels.

7. Is repentance required of all? _____ Give Scriptural support for your answer:

   Acts 17:30 _____

8. What brings man to repentance?

   A. Romans 2:4 _____

   B. Matthew 9:13 _____

   C. Matthew 12:4 _____

   D. Luke 17:13 _____

   E. 2 Corinthians 7:9 _____

       vs 10 _____

   F. Acts 11:15 _____

       Vs 18 _____

       Acts 5:31 _____

   2 Timothy 2:25 _____

9. What are some evidences that one has truly repented?

   A. Mark 1:15 & Acts 20:21 _____

   B. Acts 2:38 _____

   C. Acts 3:19 _____

   Explain in your own words: _____

Eternal Life Principles & Beyond

_____
_____
_____
_____
_____
_____

    D. Acts 26:20 _____

    E. Matt 3:8 _____

    F. Rev. 2:21 _____

10. Give five Biblical instances of whole local assemblies needing to repent.

    2 Corinthians 7:9 _____

    2 Corinthians 12:20-21 _____

    Revelation 2:16 _____

    Revelation 3:2-3 _____

    Revelation 3:19 _____

Repentance From Dead Works
Lesson Study Review 4

Addendum:

Now that we want to move on to good works, we need to establish what good works are.

A person who walks in the fruit of self-control is in possession of good works by righteous decisions. Works do not save us, but after salvation, that coin flips 180° and works indicate the attitude of our heart and faith toward God. Our Lord's (half) brother speaks of the profit in possessing faith in doing good works. Read from your Bible James 2:14-26 and list the four good works mentioned.

1. vss _____

2 a. vs _____

   b. therefore, vs _____

3. vs _____

Write out the key verse:

  vs 26 _____

_____

_____

4. Based on the above Scripture verses revealing what good works truly are, write a fifty word essay about three or more other disciples mentioned in the New Testament that performed good works, and tell exactly what function they carried out.

_____

_____

_____

_____

_____

_____

_____

Having completed this first doctrine, let us now do a historical study of what conversion is since it is the result of repentance from dead works.

INDEX

CONVERSION – Historical Study

    What Is The Meaning Of The Word Conversion?...60

    How Important Is Conversion?..60

    What Are The Rewards Of Conversion?..61

    What Does Conversion Involve?..62

    Can Followers Of Christ Be Converted?..63

    What Is Repentance And Conversion According To Jesus?......................................64

My Inspirations, Challenges & Revelations:

Conversion -
Historical Study

> 1 Paul and Silvanus and Timothy to the church of the Thessalonians in God the Father and the Lord Jesus Christ; Grace to you and peace.
>
> 2 We give thanks to God always for all of you, making mention of you in our prayers;
>
> 3 constantly bearing in mind your work of faith and labor of love and steadfastness of hope in our Lord Jesus Christ in the presence of our God and Father,
>
> 4 knowing, brethren beloved by God, His choice of you;
>
> 5 for our gospel did not come to you in word only, but also in power and in the Holy Spirit and with full conviction; just as you know what kind of men we proved to be among you for your sake.
>
> 6 You also became imitators of us and of the Lord, having received the word in much tribulation with the joy of the Holy Spirit.
>
> 7 so that you became an example to all the believers in Macedonia and Achaia.
>
> 8 For the word of the Lord has sounded forth from you, not only in Macedonia and Achaia, but also in every place your faith toward God has gone forth, so that we have no need to say anything.
>
> 9 For they themselves report about us what kind of a reception we had with you, and how you <u>turned</u> to God from idols to serve a living and true God,
>
> 10 and to wait for His Son from heaven, whom He raised from the dead, that is Jesus, who delivers us from the wrath to come.
>
> —1 Thessalonians 1

Since "Conversion" is so closely related to "Repentance," attention should be given to what the Scriptures teach about it.

Conversion - Historical Study

What Is The Meaning Of The Word Conversion?

The Greek word translated "convert" is "*epistrepho*". It is also translated "turn," and when used in connection with repentance and faith, means "to turn from the wrong way to the right way".

How Important Is Conversion?

A. It is necessary for blotting out sin

> "Repent therefore and *return* (turn, convert), that your sins may be wiped away, in order that times of refreshing may come from the presence of the Lord."
>
> —Acts 3:19

Peter spoke the above words in his second sermon. On the day of Pentecost and immediately after "tongues as of fire rested on each person in the upper room," Peter preached his first sermon, and the people listening were pierced to the heart and asked, "What shall we do?" "And Peter said to them, 'Repent, and let each of you be baptized in the name of Jesus Christ for the forgiveness of your sins; and you shall receive the gift of the Holy Spirit.'" (See Acts 2:38).

Jesus said:

> "....to open their eyes so that they may *turn* from darkness to light and from the dominion of Satan to God, in order that they may receive forgiveness of sins and an inheritance among those who have been sanctified by faith in Me."
>
> —Acts 26:18

Please notice there are five beneficial results to conversion in Jesus' comment.

B. It saves from spiritual death

> "....let him know that he who *turns* (converts) a sinner from the error of his way will save his soul from death, and will cover a multitude of sins."
>
> —James 5:20

This verse is of utmost importance as it is part of James' letter of exhortation addressed to the 12 tribes dispersed abroad (Chapter 1:1). The "12 tribes" indicate he had written to the entire Christian Jewish nation, no matter how widely they may have been scattered. James was a reputed leader in the first century church. James, the Lord's brother, was also chairman of the council in Jerusalem and regarded as the first bishop of the church in Jerusalem. His messages were highly practical, positive and delivered with a wealth of authority.

C. Is it necessary to enter into the kingdom?

> "....Truly I say to you, unless you are converted and become like children, You shall not enter the kingdom of heaven."
>
> —Matthew 18:3

These words of Jesus were in answer to His disciples when they asked "Who then is the greatest in the Kingdom of Heaven?"

D. The burden of apostolic preaching

> 18 (Jesus speaking) "....to open their eyes so that they may turn from darkness to light and from the dominion of Satan to God, in order that they may receive forgiveness of sins and an inheritance among those who have been sanctified by faith in Me."
> 19 (Paul speaking) "Consequently, King Agrippa, I did not prove disobedient to the heavenly vision,
> 20 but kept declaring both to those of Damascus first, and also at Jerusalem and then throughout all the region of Judea, and even to the Gentiles, that they should repent and turn to God, performing deeds appropriate to repentance.
>
> —Acts 26

Rewards Of Conversion

A. "....for the kingdom of God is not eating and drinking, but righteousness and peace and joy in the Holy Spirit."

—Romans 14:17

B. "For the kingdom of God does not consist in words, but in power."

—1 Corinthians 4:20

Righteousness, peace, joy and power belong to the people of God whom God has prepared through salvation in Jesus Christ. For those who enter His holy kingdom, these rewards become the gifts by which we are known. These gifts are the instruments of establishing a counterpart of the Kingdom of glory among men. Righteousness, the pardon of sin, is producing holiness of heart and life. Peace from above regulating, ruling and harmonizing the soul of man is a sense of God's mercy. Joy in the Holy Spirit is solid spiritual happiness from a clear sense of God's mercy and the love of God being shed abroad in the heart. Power is not in human eloquence, excellence of speech or even in doctrines, but in the mighty energy of the Holy Spirit, enlightening, quickening, converting and sanctifying Believers. This is a genuine counterpart of heaven: righteousness without sin, peace without inward disturbance, joy without any kind of mental agony of distressing fear and the dynamic energy of the Holy Spirit.

Conversion - Historical Study

What Does Conversion Involve?

A. Acknowledging the Divine Lordship

"And he [John] will turn back many of the sons of Israel to the Lord their God."

—Luke 1:16

These words were spoken by an angel of the Lord to Zacharias the high priest while he was performing his priestly service before God in the temple. He and his wife, Elizabeth, were elderly and (up to this point in their marriage) Elizabeth was barren. The Scriptures report "they were both righteous in the sight of God, walking blamelessly in all the commandments and requirements of the Lord." (See Luke 1:6). To have a child beyond childbearing years was something to be noticed. So, from the very beginning of Elizabeth's pregnancy, all eyes were on this baby. At John's birth Zacharias told the people of the visit from the angel and the words spoken about his future son, John. The angel also said his son would usher in the Messiah and make straight His path with the message of repentance and conversion.

"And all who lived at Lydda and Sharon saw him [Aeneas, who had been bed-ridden for eight years], and they *turned* to the Lord."

—Acts 9:35

"And the hand of the Lord was with them [Apostles], and a large number who believed *turned* to the Lord."

—Acts 11:21

"Therefore, it is my judgment that we do not trouble those who are *turning* to God from among the Gentiles,"

—Acts 15:19

The Apostle James, the Lord's brother, spoke the above words of wisdom during the council at Jerusalem.

B. Turning "From Darkness to Light"

"I am sending you to open their [Gentiles] eyes so that they may *turn* from darkness to light and from the dominion of Satan to God, in order that they may receive forgiveness of sins and an inheritance among those who have been sanctified by faith in Me."

—Acts 26:18 ABUV

Paul in speaking his defense before Agrippa is describing his experience of meeting Jesus on the road to Damascus and the Lord's instructions to him.

Eternal Life Principles & Beyond

C. Turning "From the Power of Satan Unto God"

> "to *turn* them....from the power of Satan unto God."
> —Acts 26:18 NKJV

D. Turning From the "Vanities of Idolatry"

> "Men, why are you doing these things? We also men of the same nature as you, and preach the gospel to you in order that you should *turn* from these vain things to a living God, Who made the heaven and the earth and the sea, and all that is in them."
> —Acts 14:15

Paul and Barnabas had fled to the city of Lycaonia and continued to preach the gospel. There a man who had never walked, lame from his mother's womb, was listening and believing. Paul, seeing that he had faith to be made well, said in a loud voice, "Stand upright on your feet." When the crowds saw what Paul had done, they raised their voices saying, "The gods have become like men and have come down to us." But when the apostles, Paul and Barnabas, heard of it they tore their robes and rushed out into the crowd ordering them not to speak such things.

> "For they themselves report about us what kind of a reception we had with you, And how you *turned* to God from idols to serve a living and true God,"
> —1 Thessalonians 1:9

Can Followers Of Christ Be Converted?

A. The Apostle Peter

Jesus speaking to Peter said,

> "Simon, Simon, behold, Satan has demanded permission to sift you like wheat; But I have prayed for you, that your faith may not fail; and you, when once you have *turned* again, strengthen your brothers."
> —Luke 22:31-32

The word "converted" translated *"turned"* in the above Scripture means to change from our ways of sin to faith toward God. How it is used here does not mean from one religion to another.

Most people have their own ideas as to what certain words mean and in this particular verse we need to consider if we really understand what this statement means as conveyed by Jesus.

Two things need to be kept in mind concerning this verse. One is, most foreign languages are difficult to translate into English word-for-word. And two, this statement by Jesus was long before the upper room experience. Peter was truly converted after the Holy Spirit rested upon him and the others on day of Pentecost. Since it is a cardinal sin to reject the Lord after being converted, my choice as author was to either omit addressing Jesus' statement altogether to avoid any confusion or include it and, hopefully, unfold its essence.

We must also consider today's social environment. Most people dislike the idea of taking personal responsibility for their actions. Today, it is also out of fashion to require personal responsibility of another person. Equally true is that teaching truth and repentance are very much to the point and may give people some difficulty, whereas conversion tickles the ears and is easier to accept. Our society has done serious damage to our thinking since the politically-correct theory. There was a time when people understood personal and corporate responsibility and adhered to it. Unfortunately, those who reject these Scriptural principles will find themselves disciplined by God until they do understand that they still exist in the spiritual realm and, by the same token, God judges countries as well as people.

Jesus knew Peter would deny Him three times. After the cock crowed a second time, Peter remembered the remark Jesus made to him and he began to weep. Although Peter was filled with remorse, Scripture does not say whether he repented or not. It would also be three more days before he would see Jesus again. Moreover, it would also be another 50 days before the day of Pentecost when the Holy Spirit would manifest as wind and fire and rest upon those in the upper room filling them with strength and power.

Now that Jesus sits on the Throne at the right hand of God, He can also send His Holy Spirit to fill us with strength and power and to stop sinning. Once we experience the infilling of the Holy Spirit, He can work His attributes through us. Peter had gotten as far as he could go till Pentecost because the Holy Spirit had not come in fire and power. Peter had his moments. However, He did not turn from Jesus; he turned from the demand of the faith. Jesus' words that Peter would deny Him three times had been a prophetic statement.

Repentance And Conversion According To Jesus

> 11 And He said, "A certain man had two sons;
> 12 and the younger of them said to his father, 'Father, give me the share of the estate that falls to me.' And he divided his wealth between them.
> 13 And not many days later, the younger son gathered everything together and went on a journey into a distant country, and there he squandered his estate with loose living."
> 14 Now when he had spent everything, a severe famine occurred in that country, and he began to be in need.

15 "And he went and attached himself to one of the citizens of that country, and he sent him into his fields to feed swine.

16 "And he was longing to fill his stomach with the pods that the swine were eating, and no one was giving anything to him.

17 But when he came to his senses, he said, 'How many of my father's hired men have more than enough bread, but I am dying here with hunger!

18 'I will get up and go to my father, and will say to him, "Father, I have sinned against heaven, and in your sight;

19 "I am no longer worthy to be called your son; make me as one of your hired men."'

20 And he got up and came to his father. But while he was still a long way off, his father saw him, and felt compassion for him, and ran and embraced him, and kissed him.

21 "And the son said to him, 'Father, I have sinned against heaven and in your sight; I am no longer worthy to be called your son.'

22 "But the father said to his slaves, 'Quickly bring out the best robe and put it on him, and put a ring on his hand and sandals on his feet;

23 and bring the fattened calf, kill it, and let us eat and be merry;

24 for this son of mine was dead, and has come to life again; he was lost, and has been found.' And they began to be merry."'

—Luke 15

In this parable of the prodigal son we see the principles of wise reasoning, repentance and conversion. He changed (*informed*) his mind, he *stirred* his emotions, and he *commanded* his will. And then he took action on that decision. His conscience brought about repentance and he asked forgiveness.

There was a process that occurred in the prodigal's mind. These are the steps that lead to his conversion:

    A. The change of mind by *informing* the mind (vs 17)

        1. When he came to his senses
        2. He is thinking "I am dying" (perishing)

    B. The decision of the will is by *stirring* the emotions (vs 18-19)

        1. I will get up and go to my father
        2. I will say to him, "Father, I have sinned against heaven, and in *your* sight."

    C. The performance of the will is by *commanding* the Will: Conversion (vs 20)

        1. And he got up (He left the old life)
        2. Came to his father (He started the new life)

Conversion - Historical Study

Conversion is the actual "doing" of the repenting immediately after commanding the will. This wise action causes one to become spiritually alive unto Yahweh and His precious Holy Spirit.

Additional Notes:

Pastor Mike Pici explains conversion is used to denote an initial turning from dead works and our sins to good works and faith toward God. Repentance can be initial or repetitive. A person is converted only once, but may repent many times.

Evangelist Mike Shreve writes "Conversion is a word with a triune meaning; to turn from, to turn toward and to return. Those who are converted turn away from this world and its carnality, turn toward God and return to that place of submission and of intimacy with Him that Adam had in the beginning. Conversion is something effected both by God's efforts and man's. It is not only an initial experience. It is an ongoing process that should be constantly evidenced by an increase of Christlikeness. This should always result in an increase of kingdom-living as well." (See Psalm 51:13; Luke 22:32 KJV; Acts 3:19; James 5:19-20 KJV.)

Conversion

Lesson Study Review 5

1. What is the meaning of the word "conversion"?

   _____

   _____

2. Is conversion essential to salvation? _____ Why? (Acts 3:19)

   A. _____
   B. _____
   C. _____

3. Can one be in the Kingdom of God without being converted? _____ (Yes or No)

   Explain why or why not? Romans 14:17 and 1 Corinthians 4:20

   _____

   _____

   _____

4. According to Paul, what happens when one is converted?

   _____

   _____

   _____

5. Describe the conversion of the Apostle Peter according to Luke 22:32.

   _____

   _____

   _____

Conversion: Lesson Study Review 5

6. Describe repentance and conversion using the story of the prodigal son. Explain the necessary conclusions.

   A. Steps Toward Repentance:

___

___

___

___

   B. Steps Toward Conversion:

      1. ___

      2. ___

      3. ___

What is the conclusion of the story?

___

___

___

___

___

___

___

___

DOCTRINE 2

FAITH TOWARD GOD

Are Faith And Repentance Inseparable?..71

How Did Paul Describe The Relationship Of Faith And Repentance......................72

What Is The Meaning Of The Word "Faith"?..72

What Are Some Definitions By Others?..73

How Does The Bible Describe Faith?...73

How Important Is Faith?..74

What Is The Extent Of Our Involvement In Believing God's Word?......................75

Who Are The Bible Examples Of Faith?...77

Does Good Works Have Anything To Do With Faith?...78

Where Are Several Places You Can Misplace Your Faith?.....................................80

My Inspirations, Challenges & Revelations:

Faith Toward God

And without faith it is impossible to please Him, for he who comes to God must believe that He is, and that He is a rewarder of those who seek Him.

—Hebrews 11:6

Unless faith/trust in God is firmly established in Believers' hearts, many will fall by the wayside. Although Christianity claims the power of God, it is not for the fainthearted. Christianity has never offered anyone a storm-free passage to heaven. Any religious person who avoids and bypasses the doctrines of trials and tribulation is in deception affecting their eternal life. God's purpose is that we become Overcomers with faith toward Him as He guides us toward our promised destination. Overcoming adversity through Christ also develops spiritual maturity. There will be adversity and everyone will be tested at one time or another!

Like a good father, God disciplines those whom He loves. Discipline is not punishment, it is training, and with encouragement from the Holy Spirit to overcome the adversity, it will help you reach your highest potential. Maturity cannot be achieved without trials and discipline (Philippians 1:6); each of us has character flaws originating from our old nature, which Father must correct and each of us have emotional, mental, and spiritual wounds that He is willing to heal. When God sets us apart to mature us by correcting character flaws, we experience a struggle of dying to self and to the pursuit of worldly gratification. (See Hebrews 12:4-11).

On the other hand, be assured that, because of God's love for us and His desire we be whole, He is always ready to heal a wounded spirit. Yes, at times there is agonizing pain while we struggle through the process of forgiving our perpetrators and at the same time, putting the wound at the foot of the cross (healing) and laying the axe to the root of the problem (deliverance). This is a three-step process (See Hebrews 12:14-15).

"Christ loved the church and gave Himself up for her that He might sanctify her, having cleansed her by the washing of water with the word that He might present to Himself the church in all her glory, having no spot or wrinkle or any such thing, but that she should be holy and blameless." (Ephesians 6:27). Believers suffer in different ways and some more than others, but God's purpose remains constant—to develop us as mature fruit, with a spirit of excellence, with integrity and holiness.

Are Faith And Repentance Inseparable?

Faith and repentance toward God are inseparable in effecting genuine conversion. As Chaplain Glenn Pav so adequately puts it: "Not that they go hand in hand and not that Faith is one hand and Repentance is the other. Rather, Repentance is the back of the hand and Faith is the front of the hand. You cannot separate the back from the front of the one hand."

Faith Toward God

Paul sums up his ministry to the lost as:

> "Testifying to both Jews and Greeks of repentance toward God and faith in our Lord Jesus Christ."
>
> —Acts 20:21

How Did Paul Describe The Relationship Of Faith And Repentance?

> "For they themselves report about us what kind of a reception we had with you, and how you turned to God from idols to serve a living and true God."
>
> —1 Thessalonians 1:9

This scripture reveals that the expected result of Paul's preaching the balanced message is two-fold. To profess to turn to God without forsaking sin through repentance is hypocrisy, purposeless and useless. To attempt to forsake sin without turning to God in faith brings failure and despair. Without a true understanding of Biblical faith, we find it impossible to come into spiritual maturity. God takes pleasure in His children as they become rich in trust toward Him.

What Is The Meaning Of The Word "Faith"?

The root words from which we get "faith" (noun) and "believe" (verb) and their derivatives are found in the New Testament 619 times. "Faith" and "believe" are used interchangeably. I encourage you to desire and embrace them in full measure since they can determine defeat or victory in Christ.

    A. Faith (pistis)

> "The conviction of the truthfulness of God, especially reliance upon Christ for salvation."
>
> —Strong's #4102

> "Trust, belief, firm persuasion, assurance, firm conviction, honesty, integrity, faithfulness, and truthfulness."

    B. Believe (pisteuo)

> "To trust in, put faith in, confide in, rely on a person or thing; have a mental persuasion; to entrust, and commit to the charge or power of."
>
> —Strong's #4100

What Are Some Definitions By Others?

A. W.A. Whitehouse—

"It is the act by which a person lays hold on God's preferred resources, becomes obedient to what God prescribes, and abandoning all self-interest and self-reliance, trusts God completely."

B. Finney's definition—

"It is receiving of Christ for just what He is represented to be in His gospel, and an unqualified surrender of the will, and of the whole being to Him."

C. JB Phillips' definition—

Now faith means putting our full confidence in the things we hope for; it means being certain of things we cannot see."

D. Derek Prince's definition—

"Now faith is the ground, or confidence, of things hoped for, a sure persuasion or conviction concerning things not seen.

How Does The Bible Describe Faith?

Faith originates directly in God's Word and is always directly related to our relationship to Him; therefore, we believe in our heart what God has said according to His Word is true. We accept this in faith and trust. Both the Old and the New Testaments emphasize and give great significance to acquiring faith toward God.

> "Now faith is the assurance of things hoped for, the conviction of things not seen."
>
> —Hebrews 11:1 NASB

> "Now faith is the assurance, the confirmation, the title deed of the things we hope for, being the proof of things we do not see, and the conviction of their reality. Faith is perceiving as real what is not revealed to the senses."
>
> —Hebrews 11:1 Amplified

> "Now faith means putting our full confidence in the things we hope for, it means being certain of things we cannot see."
>
> —Hebrews 11:1 JB Phillips

The eleventh chapter of Hebrews is known as the "Hall of Faith", and also the "Faith Hall of Fame". Faith links us with God and is the assurance that the revealed things promised in the future are true, and with faith, we know the unseen things are real!

Faith makes us certain that what God says will happen, must happen. The future and the unseen can be made real for men by faith. It is not the kind of hope which looks forward with wistful

Faith Toward God

longing; it is the kind of hope which looks forward with utter certainty and expectancy. It is not the hope which takes refuge in "perhaps"; it is the hope which is founded on a conviction. Hope is not wishing; it is living, and active, and it is a certainty. Hope is directed toward the future, but faith is in the present and ongoing. Hope is primarily in the realm of the mind; faith is primarily in the realm of the heart.

The Walvoord and Zuck comment on page 807 beautifully states: "The author of Hebrews sets forth three fundamental considerations about faith:

1. Its basic nature ("assurance")
2. The honor associated with it ("of things hoped for")
3. Its way of seeing things ("conviction of things not seen")

How Important Is Faith?

A. One cannot be saved without faith in God

> "He who has believed and has been baptized shall be saved; but he who has disbelieved shall be condemned."
>
> —Mark 16:16

The word "condemned" in the King James Version is translated "damned."

> "Now the parable is this: the seed is the word of God. And those beside the road are those who have heard; then the devil comes and takes away the word from their heart, so they may not believe and be saved."
>
> —Luke 8:11-12

> "For since in the wisdom of God the world through its wisdom did not come to know God, God was well-pleased through the foolishness of the message preached to save those who believe
>
> —1 Corinthians 1:21

> "For by grace you have been saved through faith; and that not of yourselves, it is the gift of God."
>
> —Ephesians 2:8

B. You cannot please God without faith in Him

> "And without faith it is impossible to please Him, for he who comes to God must believe that He is, and that He is a rewarder of those who seek Him."
>
> —Hebrews 11:6

The goal of this lesson is to help build a strong foundation of faith in the believer's life so that each believer may show the same diligence as those great men and women of faith who went before us. As a result, the believer will not become sluggish, but will be an imitator of those who, through faith and patience, inherit the promises and press on to maturity in God.

What Is The Extent Of Our Involvement in Believing God's Word?

A. The mind must be informed.

> "So faith comes from hearing, and hearing by the word of Christ."
>
> —Romans 10:17

The Greek word for hearing in this verse is *"akoe"*. It is the sense of hearing – more accurately meaning "come to the ears". Faith comes to the ears through preaching, counseling, prophecy, teaching, reading out loud and singing.

> "Lord, who has believed our report?"
>
> —John 12:38

A report informs the mind. The result was:

> "But many of those who had heard the message believed."
>
> —Acts 4:4

> "But when they believed Philip preaching the good news about the kingdom of God and the name of Jesus Christ, they were being baptized, men and women alike."
>
> —Acts 8:12

> "But this I admit to you, that according to the Way which they call a sect I do serve the God of our fathers, believing everything that is in accordance with the Law, and that is written in the Prophets."
>
> —Acts 24:14

> "You believe that God is one. You do well, the demons also believe, and shudder."
>
> —James 2:19

B. The emotions are stirred

1. Godly Sorrow: In repentance one experiences the emotion of "godly sorrow and remorse."

This is understandable since repentance results from heartfelt sin which has estranged us from God and wrought havoc in our lives. In faith we experience peace, hope and joy through all the storms of life. This is the effect of God's grace since, through faith, we enter into all rich blessings of His great salvation.

> "For the sorrow that is according to the will of God produces a repentance without regret, leading to salvation; but the sorrow of the world produces death."
>
> —2 Corinthians 7:10

Faith Toward God

    2. Joy: In faith we experience joy and gladness.

> "So then, those who had received his word were baptized; and there were added that day about three thousand souls."
>
> —Acts 2:41

Read from verses 41 to 47 for further faith-building in joy.

In the eighth chapter of the Book of Acts we read, "Philip went down to the city of Samaria and began proclaiming Christ to them" (vs 5). Signs and wonders followed his preaching and the result was:

> "And there was much rejoicing in that city."
>
> —Acts 8:8

This same verse translated in the King James Version reads "And there was great joy in that city."

> "You also became imitators of us and of the Lord, having received the word in much tribulation with the joy of the Holy Spirit."
>
> —1 Thessalonians 1:6

> "….having received the word in much affliction with the joy of the Holy Spirit."
>
> —1 Thessalonians 1:6 KJV

> "And though you have not seen Him, you love Him, and though you do not see Him now, but believe in Him, you greatly rejoice with joy inexpressible and full of glory."
>
> —1 Peter 1:8

> "….you greatly rejoice with joy unspeakable and full of glory."
>
> —1 Peter 1:8 KJV

> "And the one on whom seed was sown on the rocky places, this is the man who hears the word, and immediately receives it with joy; yet he has no firm root in himself."
>
> —Mathew 13:20-21

In the above verse, this person *informed* his mind (heard) and then *stirred* his emotions (joy), but he did not *command* his will; therefore, he did not move into obedience.

> "Through whom we received grace and apostleship in order that there may be obedience to the Faith among all Gentiles in behalf of His Name, among whom you also are divinely summoned belonging to Jesus Christ, to all who are in Rome, God's loved ones, called saints. Grace to you and peace from God our Father and our Lord Jesus Christ."
>
> —Romans 1:5-7 KS Wuest

We are the "called ones", meaning "those divinely summoned by Him." Denny says, "We belong to Him because we have heard and obeyed the gospel." We are God's loved ones, "saints of God". The word "saint" is God's designated name for a believer. It is Jesus who has given us eternal life.

    C. The will is commanded - God wants to bring all nations into obedience.

> "For I will not presume to speak of anything except what Christ has accomplished through me, resulting in the obedience of the Gentiles by word and deed."
> —Romans 15:18

> "Now to Him who is able to establish you according to my gospel and the preaching of Jesus Christ, according to the revelation of the mystery which has been kept secret for long ages past, but now is manifested, and by the Scriptures of the prophets, according to the commandment of the eternal God, has been made known to all the nations, leading to obedience of faith."
> —Romans 16:25-26

Yielding to obedience of faith toward God is yielding to the highest of all obedience, that He might be glorified. This act of faith is commanding the will in obedience to God.

Who Is The Bible Example Of Faith?

"There is one man in the Bible who is referred to as "the father of all who believe." Romans 4:11 and "the father of us all" Romans 4:16. His name is Abraham. Believers are those who "follow in the steps of the faith of our father Abraham" (Isaac and Jacob) Romans 4:12, and they are spoken of as "sons of Abraham" Galatians 3:7. "And if you belong to Christ, then you are Abraham's offspring" Galatians 3:29.

When Paul wanted to illustrate saving, justifying faith, he recounted Abraham's relationship to God. The manner in which Abraham manifested faith is our example.

Paul's reference to Abraham's faith is found in Romans 4:

    A. He heard the word

> "For the promise to Abraham or to his descendants that he would be heir of the world was not through the Law, but through the righteousness of faith." (vs 13)

> "And being fully assured that what He had promised, He was able also to perform." (vs 21)

Faith Toward God

    B. He did not consider his hopeless condition

> "In hope against hope he believed, in order that he might become a father of many nations, according to that which had been spoken. 'So shall your descendants be.' And without becoming weak in faith he contemplated his own body, now as good as dead since he was about a hundred years old, and the deadness of Sarah's womb." (vss 18-19)

    C. He embraced the hope expressed in the Divine promise

> "In hope against hope he believed, in order that he might become a father of many nations, according to that which had been spoken, "so shall your descendants be." (vs 18)

    D. He didn't waver in his commitment

> "Yet, with respect to the promise of God, he did not waver in unbelief, but grew strong in faith, giving glory to God." (vs 20)

    E. He rejoiced in the Word as the accomplished fact

> "Yet, with respect to the promise of God, he did not waver in unbelief, but grew strong in faith, giving glory to God." (vs 20)

Does Good Works Have Anything To Do With Faith?

Faith has everything to do with good works or it is dead works. Before choosing to accept Jesus as Lord over our life, every work, deed, word, or thought was a dead work in the eyes of God because it did not include <u>trust in</u> and <u>dependence on</u> God, through His Son, Jesus, to accomplish that goal.

Let's look at some unusual good works.

    1. Abraham

> 2 For if Abraham was justified by works, he has something to boast about, but not before God.
> 3 For what does the Scripture say? "and *Abraham believed God, and it was reckoned to him as righteousness.*"
>
>   —Romans 4

What was Abraham's good work? Could it possibly be that to just believe God is considered a good work? Is it possible it's just that easy? It appears so. Therefore, believing God when He gives a directive is, therefore, a good work. Abraham did not use natural efforts or legal obedience. If natural efforts or legal obedience were the ground of Abraham's justification, he would have reason to boast, but in the eyes of God he was not justified by his works, but by his faith in God and his complete obedience to the call. Faith is in direct opposition to works in the matter of justification. (See vss 4 & 5.) It is not the mere act of believing.

Eternal Life Principles & Beyond

- (a) Abraham had simple faith in the divine promise of the Christ (Genesis 12:3;15:5) as we believe in Christ (vs 3).

- (b) Abraham cast himself upon the mercy of Him who justifies those who deserve condemnation (vss 6-8).

- (c) Abraham was justified before he was circumcised so he could have no dependence upon that rite (vss 9-12).

- (d) When he had no ground for hope in his dead body and the deadness of Sarah's womb, he exercised expectant faith (4:19).

Read the complete chapter of Romans 4 to chapter 5:11. These things were not recorded as mere historical facts, but as illustrations for all time of God's method of justification by faith.

2. Many other Faith heroes are also recorded

The eleventh chapter of Hebrews records many Old Testament saints who performed many unusual justifying acts of faith. This chapter is often called the "Hall of Faith." It gives us a view of the history of Israel and also the New Testament church written in the blood of the saints. Read this chapter in its entirety and underline each verse that starts with the words "by *faith.*"

3. Joshua

Much attention is given to Moses in the parting of the Red Sea, Daniel in a den of lions and Elijah calling down fire from heaven, and other than Joshua's involvement in the walls of Jericho falling down, little notice is given to Yahweh's other mighty feats through His many chosen prophets. After Moses' death, the Lord spoke to Joshua saying, "I will be with you; I will not fail you or forsake you. Be strong and very courageous. Do not tremble or be dismayed, for the Lord your God is with you where ever *you* go." (Joshua 1:1-9). With these words, Joshua:

- (a) — commanded the priests to carry the Ark to the borders of the Jordan River. The waters which were flowing down from above stood and rose up in one heap. The waters were completely cut off so all the people of Israel crossed to the opposite side on dry ground.

- (b) — commanded his men of war, the priests and all the people to silently circle the city of Jericho. On the seventh day he ordered them to shout and blow trumpets and the wall of the city fell down flat!

- (c) — commanded his people to prepare to take the city of Ai along with its spoil and cattle, then burn the city.

- (d) — agreed to help the men of Gibeon against all the kings of the Amorites in the hill country. The Lord confounded the enemy before Israel and threw large stones down from heaven and killed them. Then, the most amazing thing occurred. Joshua asked the Lord for the sun to stand still at Gibeon and the

Faith Toward God

moon to stand still in the valley of Aijalon until they avenged their enemies. It is recorded the sun stopped in the middle of the sky and did not go down for a whole day.

(e) — hamstrung the horses and burned the chariots of the kings of the north, the south, the east and the west in the hill country.

It was Joshua who said, "as for me and my house, we shall serve the Lord." And he did and died a fulfilled life at the age of 110.

4. Jesus had something to say about good works.

The day after Jesus walked on the water, He said to His disciples, "Do not work for the food which perishes, but for the food which endures to eternal life, which the Son of Man shall give to *you*, for on Him the Father, even God, has set His seal." His disciples then asked him a rather simple, but serious, question to this statement. In John 6:28 it is recorded that they asked, "What shall we do, that we may work the works of God?" Jesus' reply was just as simple:

"This is the work of God, that you believe in Him whom He has sent."

These works are those divine things which God can approve. There is no employment more acceptable to God than acknowledging His Son Jesus as your Messiah and the Savior of a lost world. The work of faith is the work of God in your daily endeavors. Without faith, we cannot please God. But, how many times do we cry out, "Lord, I believe, help my unbelief."

Where Are Several Places You Can Misplace Your Faith?

A. Weapons

> "For I will not trust in my bow, nor will my sword to save me."
>
> —Psalm 44:6

B. In wealth

> "So is the man who lays up treasure for himself, and is not rich toward God."
>
> —Luke 12:21

C. In oppression or extortion

> "Do not trust in oppression, and do not vainly hope in robbery; if riches increase do not set your heart upon them."
>
> —Psalm 62:10

D. In human greatness

"Do not trust in princes, in mortal man, in whom there is no salvation."

—Psalm 146:3

E. In one's self

"He who trusts in his own heart is a fool, but he who walks wisely will be delivered."

—Proverbs 28:26

F. In idols

"They shall be turned back and be utterly put to shame, who trust in idols, who say to molten images, 'You are our gods.'"

—Isaiah 42:17

G. In false prophets

"Do not trust in deceptive words, saying, 'This is the temple of the Lord, the temple of the Lord, the temple of the Lord.'"

—Jeremiah 7:4

"Behold you are trusting in deceptive words to no avail."

—Jeremiah 7:8

Some do not think we can also misplace our faith by joining organizations that are contrary to the Word of God such as the Masons, Silva Mind Control, and Scientology. The power of positive thinking, eclectic religions, spiritism, astrology, secular news reports, and the fence of denominations are all but a few examples that are also contrary to God's truths.

Consider the following Scriptures:

Jesus said:

"For where your treasure is, there will your heart be also."

—Matthew 6:21

Where is your heart?
What are your desires?
What are your passions and affections?

Additional Notes:

The doctrine title of this lesson is *Faith Toward God*. Faith must not be in those we admire, such as friends, family, or ministers, which is a misconception about faith, for even Jesus did not trust in man, for he knew what was in him. (See John 2:24-25). Faith and trust are directed toward Father God in Jesus' name. The question is, who is your God? How do you identify your God?

Faith Toward God

We will briefly address the importance of these questions because we live in a day and age when all absolutes are under attack and are being destroyed in the hearts and minds of this present generation. Since the Reformation of the 16th century, there have been numerous different religions and denominations, but most of us believe in the same God. The founding fathers of our great country based the Declaration of Independence, Constitution, the Bill of Rights, the Preamble and our Judicial Law on the Bible as their source of truth. Their personal writings, their songs and their lives reflected that their hearts were committed to the Lord, Jesus the Christ.

Since the hippie revolution of the 60's and the infiltration of Eastern religions and their practices in America, the need to identify the true God is vitally important.

The following is not a discourse on apologetics, nor do we want to stray from the purpose of this book, which is the study of New Testament doctrine; however, there are times we get stuck for answers when evangelizing or witnessing.

It is imperative to rely on the role of the Holy Spirit during times of objections or wrong notions. It is common to hear many say, "I worship god" or "we all have the same god" when we share the plan of salvation. These comments are a clue that you and they are not on the same page. The following is helpful toward exposing these false teachings and false notions. From there, the Holy Spirit will empower the Believer to witness the truth (Acts 1:8).

Buddha – The Buddha god is made of stone by human hands. Buddha does not have ears that hear, or eyes to see or a mouth that speaks. (Read Deuteronomy 4:28; Psalm 115:4-8 and Psalm 135:15-18).

Allah – Muhammad is supposedly Allah's prophet and is dead and did not rise from his grave. Muhammad's gospel promotes violence not peace.

Pantheism – Believes the doctrine that the whole universe is God. When, in truth, God is the creator of the whole universe and all the creations in the universe. (Read the Gospel of John 1:1-3).

Mormonism – believes their god was once as we are now and is an exalted man. Joseph Smith is their prophet and Adam is their father and their God. Jesus, is the son of Adam-God and Mary. The Holy Spirit is an ethereal substance diffused through space and is the purest, most refined of substances.

Unity – God is a Principle, not a person; Jesus was not the Christ and the Holy Spirit is not the Author of the Bible.

Christian Science – God is not a person. God is infinite mind, spirit, soul and principle. Jesus, the Christ, is not God but a divine ideal. Jesus' resurrection was spiritualization of thought—material belief yielding to spiritual understanding. The Comforter is Divine Science, therefore, when the Science of Christianity appears it will lead you into all truth.

Jehovah's Witness – The Godhead is Trinitarian nonsense. God is a solitary being from eternity unrevealed and unknown. No one has existed as His equal to reveal Him and Jesus is forever dead.

Eternal Life Principles & Beyond

These gods have no interest in a loving and personal relationship with their worshipers. For believers of Yahweh/Emmanuel/Elohim their prayers become an act of worship. It's an intimate spiritual relationship between a bride and their Groom (Christ). No other religion attempts to pray at this level. Ours is the "heavenly lover" of our souls. (Read John 4:21-24).

When you are asked to identify your God, are you prepared with a Biblical answer?

It is important that you point to the genealogy of our ancestors, for they said, "He, Yahweh, is the God of Abraham, Isaac and Jacob" (Matthew 22:32). He is the Father of His only-begotten Son named Immanuel, the same Jesus, the Messiah, who died for the sin of the world and rose from the dead on the third day. He is alive. He hears. He sees. He speaks and He is a rewarder of those who seek Him. There is only one way to God. For Jesus said, "I am the Way, the Truth and the Light." He also said, "I am the Door."

The Good News written by the Apostle John, as spoken by Jesus, appears in chapter ten:

> "I am the Door; if anyone enters through Me, he shall be saved and shall go in and out, and find pasture" (vs 9).

The reverse appears in John 10:1

> "Truly, truly, I say to you, he who does not enter by the door into the fold of the sheep, but climbs up some other way, he is a thief and a robber."

To those who say, "all roads lead to God", Jesus, who was God in the flesh, would disagree for He said, *I am the way,* and the truth, and the life; *no one* comes to the Father; *but through Me."* (John 14:6). He also warned, "Enter by the narrow gate; for the gate is wide, and the way is broad that leads to destruction, and many are those who enter by it. For the gate is small, and the way is narrow that leads to life, and few are those who find it." (Matthew 7:13-14).

There is great assurance and peace when one can point to and proclaim God's absolutes and live by them. Always remember it is Yahweh who has chosen to write our names in the Lamb's Book of Life. Therefore, faith in anyone or anything else for our existence, guidance, our daily provisions, or for our joy and peace of mind, is futile. No other god can write our name in the Lamb's Book of Life and no other god has such a book. More on the Lamb's Book of Life is discussed in the doctrine on "Eternal Judgment".

Faith Toward God
Lesson Study Review 6

1. Can a Believer have a genuine saving faith in Christ without repentance? _____

    Acts 20:21 _____

2. Describe the relationship of faith and repentance as expressed in the Thessalonians Epistle.

    1 Thess.1:9 _____

    _____

    _____

    _____

3. What are the definitions of the words "faith" and "believe"?

    Faith _____

    _____

    _____

    Believe _____

    _____

    _____

4. What is Charles G. Finney's definition of faith?

    _____

    _____

    _____

    _____

5. Write out your Bible's definition of faith.

   Heb. 11:1 _____

   _____

   _____

   _____

6. One can be a born-again Believer without faith. _____ (True or False)
   Give Scriptural support for your answer:

   _____

   _____

   _____

7. Show from Scripture what part of man must be involved in the faith process.

   A. _____

   _____

   B. _____

   _____

   C. _____

   _____

8. Abraham was cited as an excellent example of faith. List the five reasons why this is so.

   A. Rom 4:13, 21 _____

   _____

   B. Rom. 4:18-19 _____

   _____

   C. Rom. 4:18 _____

   _____

   D. Rom. 4:20 _____

   _____

Lesson Study Review 6

E. Rom. 4:20 _____

_____

9. List each person/persons/actions or personal pronouns of faith as recorded in Hebrews 11 and their unusual/unthought-of heroic deed that God considered a good work.

   A. vs __2__ , _____ Deed: _____

   _____

   B. vs __3__ , _____ Deed: _____

   _____

   C. vs ____ , _____ Deed: _____

   _____

   D. vs ____ , _____ Deed: _____

   _____

   E. vs __7a__ , _____ Deed: _____

   F. vs __a__ , _____ Deed: _____

      vs __b__ , _____ Deed: _____

      vs __c__ , _____ Deed: _____

   _____

      vs __9 d__ , _____ Deed: _____

   G. vs ____ , _____ Deed: _____

   _____

   H. vs ____ , _____ Deed: _____

   _____

   I. vs ____ , _____ Deed: _____

   _____

   J. vs ____ , _____ Deed: _____

   _____

Eternal Life Principles & Beyond

K. vs ____ , _____ Deed: _____

_____

L. vs ____ , _____ Deed: _____

_____

M. vs ____ , _____ Deed: _____

_____

N. vs 24a , _____ Deed: _____

_____

    (a) _____

    (b) _____

    (c) _____

    (d) _____

    (e) _____

    (f) _____

    (g) _____

O. vs 30 , _____ Deed: _____

_____

P. vs ____ , _____ Deed: _____

_____

Q. vs 32 , _____ Deed: _____

_____

10. Jesus spoke of various kinds of faith. Can you name four and give their reference?

    A. _____

    B. _____

    C. _____

    D. _____

Lesson Study Review 6

11. There are several places where we can misplace our faith. What are they?

    Psalm 44:6 _____

    Luke 12:21 _____

    Psalm 62:10 A. _____

                     B. _____

                     C. _____

    Psalm 146:3 _____

    Proverbs 28:26 _____

    Isaiah 42:17 _____

    Jeremiah 7:4-8 _____

12. There are organizations and cults which are contrary to the Word of God. Name at least six.

    _____

    _____

    _____

    _____

    _____

    _____

DOCTRINE 3

THE DOCTRINE OF BAPTISMS 1

We Come Now To The Third Of The "First Principles"
Which Constitute The Believer's Foundation 92

The Meaning Of The Word "Baptize" 92

The First Reference To Water Baptism In The New Testament 95

John, The Baptizer 95

What Was The Significance Of John's Baptism? 97

What Did The Lawyers And Pharisees Reject? 99

What Was The Origin Of A Believer's Baptism? 100

How Did The Apostles Obey This Commission? 100

INSTRUCTION ABOUT WASHINGS II

What Is One Of God's Many Names In The Old Testament? 107

The Lord Jesus Christ Did Not Command His Disciples To Baptize
In The Collective Names (plural) Of The Father And Of The Son
And Of The Holy Spirit, But In The Name (singular) Of All Of
The Persons In The Godhead 108

Our Lord Had Said "name" Of The Father, Son And Holy Spirit 109

Why Did The Apostles Baptize In The Name Of The Lord Jesus Christ? 110

What Is Required To Qualify For Baptism? 110

When Were People Baptized In The Early Church? 111

Our Lord Promised His Disciples There Would Be New And More Complete
Revelation Given By The Holy Spirit 112

INSTRUCTION ABOUT WASHINGS III

- What Did The Apostles Teach About Baptism?..118
- Baptism In Water Has To Do With Cleansing..120
- We Are "Baptized Into Jesus Christ"..121
- We Are Baptized Into The Lordship Of Jesus Christ...122

BAPTISM IV

- Baptism And Circumcision...127
- The Meaning Of The Word "Circumcision"?..127
- At The Very Beginning Of Life, Circumcision Marked That Life As Deserving Of Death..127
- Paul Said That Outward Circumcision Alone Did Not Make A Real Jew...............128
- In The Beginning Of Life In God, The Repentant, Believing Sinner Does Not Submit To The Physical Rite Of Circumcision.....................................129
- Baptism In Water Demonstrates The Obedience Of A Good Conscience Toward Christ..130
- Rewards Of Water Immersion..132

The Doctrine of Baptisms I

1 "What shall we say then? Are we to continue in sin that grace might increase?

2 May it never be! How shall we who died to sin still live in it?

3 Or do you not know that all of us who have been baptized into Christ Jesus have been baptized into His death?

4 Therefore we have been buried with Him through baptism into death, in order that as Christ was raised from the dead through the glory of the Father, so we too might walk in newness of life.

5 For if we have become united with Him in the likeness of His death, certainly we shall be also in the likeness of His resurrection,

6 knowing this that our old self was crucified with Him, that our body of sin might be done away with that we should no longer be slaves to sin;

7 for he who has died is freed from sin.

8 Now if we have died with Christ, we believe that we shall also live with Him.

9 Knowing that Christ, having been raised from the dead, is never to die again; death no longer is master over Him.

10 For the death that He died, He died to sin, once for all; but the life that He lives, He lives to God.

—Romans 6

Baptism I

We Come Now To The Third Of The First Principles"
Which Constitute The Believer's Foundation
—Hebrews 5:12; 6:1-2

Usually, when we speak of Baptism, we are referring to water baptism, and that is what we will be studying in this lesson. However, we must understand the word "baptism" before we can proceed.

New Testament references regarding baptism have several applications based on the happenings taking place just before and after Jesus' scourging, death and resurrection. In this lesson two of the baptisms, namely "B" and "D" below, will receive our attention as they are two major occurrences and are directly related to our study.

Let's first begin this lesson by understanding the word baptism as it is mentioned three times in the opening Scripture

The Meaning Of The Word "Baptize"

This word is not initially an English word, but rather an Anglicized Greek word. By definition and usage, the word means *"to put into or under water so as to entirely immerse or submerge." The root word is* "baptizo", meaning to make fully wet, to purify by washing. The verb *"bapto"* means to cover wholly with a penetrable fluid. Its usage has a more specialized meaning. A good expression to explain this meaning is "dyed in the wool".

During the Great Depression of the 30's, neither fabric nor money for clothes was a priority; food was the priority. Industrious and ingenious wives used empty flour and sugar sacks to make aprons, towels and clothing for their family. They opened the seams, bleached out the advertising and then dyed the fabric. The dying process was simple, but care was required. A very large pot was put on to boil. Then the desired color of dye was added to the boiling water; it was then stirred with a large, long wooden homemade wooden spoon, stick or broom handle. After the dye dissolved, the sacks were added and <u>fully submerged</u> in the dye. Or we could say, the wool had to be fully submerged to be baptized in the dye. While the pot still on the fire, the sacks were continuously stirred so that every woof and warp of thread was completely saturated with the dye. When this stirring process was finished, the sacks were lifted out of the tub with a long wooden broom handle and the steaming sacks were slung over the clothesline. They waited till the fabric cooled just a little, and then quickly and neatly spread out the fabric along the line and tightly pinned it to dry. Pinning was an important step to avoid creases in the fabric that would cause unwanted shading.

Let's now move on to the various verses using the word baptism, which means "fully submerged", because we are "fully submerged into the Kingdom of God and into His charge". Being fully submerged into the kingdom of God brings about repentance in many areas of our life causing a separation of the cleansed from the uncleansed.

A. Baptized into His Death - Romans 6:1-10

This lesson's opening Scripture refers to spiritual death three times. What is spiritual death? It's death to the self-life and all its dead works and deeds. We have been sealed with the seal of heaven and we have been "fully submerged" into all the benefits and all the obligations of a Believer's discipleship in general, and of His death in particular. And since Christ was "made sin" and "a curse for us" (2 Corinthians 5:21 and Galatians 5:13) "bearing our sins in His own body on the tree" and "rising again for our justification" (chapter 4:25; & 1 Peter 2:24), our whole sinful nature and condition and is taken up in His person and has been brought to an end in His death. Then, whosoever has been baptized into Christ's death has formally surrendered his life of sin and has sealed himself to be the "righteousness of God in Christ," and becomes "a new creature". Here is one of our goals in life and that is to crucify all our sins on a daily basis and die to the self life. Dying to the big "I". "I want...", "I need.....", "I don't...", "I ....".

B. The baptism of repentance by John

> "As for me, I *baptize you with water* for repentance, but He who is coming after me is mightier than I, and I am not fit to remove His sandals; He will *baptize you with the Holy Spirit and fire.*"
>
> —Matthew 3:11

The baptism of repentance is a 180° turn from our sins. We are identifying with Christ's death, burial and resurrection.

Read also Mark 1:4-8; and Acts 19:4 however, notice the above verse mentions three baptisms - water, fire and the Holy Spirit. Water baptism is the first act of obedience after hearing the Gospel when each man is "convinced in his own mind". Repentance was fully discussed in the previous lesson and the baptism of fire is discussed below.

C. Baptized into Christ

> "For all of you who were baptized into Christ have clothed yourselves with Christ."
>
> —Galatians 3:27

At the point of salvation, we are sealed by the Holy Spirit and placed "fully immersed" into the Body of Christ (His church for fellowship).

D. Baptism of the Saints

> "And Peter said to them, 'Repent, and let each of you be *baptized* in the name of Jesus Christ for the forgiveness of your sins; and you shall receive the gift of the Holy Spirit."
>
> —Acts 2:38

Verse 41 states "....those who had gladly received the Word and were *baptized*". These particular believers were coming out of a Jewish background and here they are so full of joy that

Baptism I

they devoted their time to the Apostles' teachings and to prayer. They also sold their property and possessions and shared them with anyone who might have a need. They also "met daily in the temple, breaking bread from house to house and took their meals together with gladness and sincerity of heart." They were "fully submerged" in the Holy Spirit and its safe to say they overflowed with the fruit of the Holy Spirit. (See Galatians 5:22-23.)

    E. Baptism with the Holy Spirit

> "And I remembered the word of the Lord, how He used to say, 'John baptized with water, but you shall be *baptized* with the Holy Spirit.'"
>
> —Acts 11:16

Also see Mark 1:8

This Scripture refers to Peter, who now is in Jerusalem, explaining to the other Apostles what had happened in Caesarea. And what had happened was, Peter was called by God to go into Caesarea and preach the Gospel to the Gentiles. At first he refused because he believed Gentiles were unclean, but the Lord put him into a trance and showed him clean and unclean animals and then said that he should not call any man unholy or unclean (Acts 10:28). "So Peter went to Caesarea and while he was speaking (to the Gentiles), the Holy Spirit fell upon all those who were listening to his message (Acts 10: 44) and the gift of the Holy Spirit was poured out upon the Gentiles also, for they (those who accompanied Peter) heard them speaking with tongues and exalting God." Peter continued explaining "Surely no one can refuse water for these (Gentiles) to be baptized ("fully submerged") who have received the Holy Spirit just as we did, can he?" And he ordered them to be baptized ("fully submerged" in water) in the name of Jesus Christ" (Acts 10: 46-48).

    F. Baptism of fire

> "As for me, I baptize you with water for repentance, but He who is coming after me is mightier than I, and I am not fit to remove His sandals; He will baptize you with the Holy Spirit and fire."
>
> —Matthew 3:11

The spirit of God is represented here as that similar to fire as He invigorates and illuminates the soul of man until we assimilate the image of God before others for His glory as a servant of Christ. We can only assimilate the image of God as we go through the process of various trials and tribulation, for that is when He "fully submerges" us in the refining fire same as a refiner of gold removes the dross. If we would be fully immersed with the Holy Spirit how do we sin? Does this mean we are not fully immersed in God? And if not, why not?

The second meaning of fire in this verse has to do with a future event when our Lord separates the wheat from the chaff. This subject is fully discussed and clarified in the lessons on Doctrine 6, Eternal Judgment.

Eternal Life Principles & Beyond

G. The Lord's baptism of suffering

"But I have a *baptism* to undergo, and how distressed I am until it is accomplished!"

—Luke 12:50

The King James Version uses the word "straitened". Strong's concordance #4912 explains it to mean "strained, burdened, to be in a strait". Also read Matthew 20:20-23, Mark 10:38, and 1 Peter 4:12-19. No man on earth has ever been so fully submersed in a baptism of suffering as that likened to Jesus. Let's look a little deeper at His last hours on earth before His crucifixion. As Jesus identified with our sins and suffered the penalty of sin, He was "fully immersed" in His distresses while praying in the garden of Gethsemane and sweat drops of blood. After dying to "self" He said, "Not my will but Thine, Oh Father." Shortly thereafter He was betrayed by Judas, one of His very own disciples. This was followed by His immediate arrest by the ruthless Roman soldiers. He would appear before the high priest where the elders and scribes had gathered to judge him. Rapidly, many phony witnesses came forth to give false testimony and discredit Him. He was slapped, punched with fists and many spit in His face. Soon afterward he would experience a horrible scourging and crowning of thorns. He was strapped to a whipping post and whipped across his back with a cat of nine tails tearing into His flesh producing excruciating pain and bleeding. He was stripped naked and a purple robe was placed upon his shoulders. His humiliation was great and punishment unimaginable! The roar of lies and jeers from the crowd was nothing less than hateful. And lastly He was nailed to a cross. He was "fully immersed" in His crucifixion. Surely, Jesus underwent a "baptism of suffering" that few ever experience.

What do all of the above Scriptures have in common? Death to the self-life. Therefore, if death to the self-life is experienced doesn't this mean the result is the lack of desire to move in dead works, dead words and deeds? Was not the "old man" crucified? Have we put away our sinful nature of "I want…", "I need…", I don't…", "I cant…."?

The First Reference To Water Baptism In The New Testament

"As for me, I (John) *baptize* you with water for repentance."

—Matthew 3:11a

Who is this John whom Jesus referred to as the greatest prophet of all prophets? Where did his boldness and authority come from? Who called him to perform this act of water baptism, something that had never been done before in all of Israel's history.

John, The Baptizer

A. He was the son of Zacharias the High Priest, and Elizabeth, a daughter of the High Priest Aaron.

"In the days of Herod, king of Judea, there was a certain priest named Zacharias, of the division of Abijah; and he had a wife from the daughters of Aaron, and her name was Elizabeth."

—Luke 1:5

Baptism I

> "But the angel said to him, 'Do not be afraid, Zacharias, for your petition has been heard, and your wife Elizabeth will bear you a son and you will give him the name John.'"
>
> —Luke 1:13

B. He was the greatest of the prophets

> "I (Jesus) say to you, among those born of women, there is no one greater than John; yet he who is least in the kingdom of God is greater than he."
>
> —Luke 7:28

Read Jesus' tribute to John in Matthew 11:7-15

Let's talk about John the immerser for a moment. He is one of the most neglected characters of the Bible. He is a unique individual and was immensely important to changing Old Testament law as well as a most amazing and obedient servant of the Most High God, regardless of cost. He truly laid down his life. We can safely say, he was not politically correct but God correct and absolutely dead to self. It's obvious he is single focused and does not care what the neighbors think for he is about His Father's business. He was not influenced by peer pressure nor was he indebted to the religious leaders of his day. His only focus was to be obedient to the call Yahweh had ordained. He walked in confidence, strength and power looking neither left nor right. Did it cost him his life at a very early age? We know it did. John was "fully immersed" in God's will and dead to the self-life.

John was unique in clothing, wearing a garment of camel's hair and a leather belt (Matthew 3:4). His dietary habits were unique, eating only locusts and wild honey (Matthew 3:4). He was also unique in personality; publicly and boldly calling the Pharisees and Sadducees "You brood of vipers!" as they contemptuously watched the water baptism (Matthew 3:7). The pious Pharisees believed they were ceremonially clean, therefore, not in need of water cleansing and were there to judge John of heresy. John boldly told Herod the Tetrarch, "You are living with your brother's wife. It is not lawful for *you* to have her!" (Matthew 3:19-20). And as most prophets, He was also very direct in his speech.

The highly documented (Luke 1:61-66) uniqueness of his life started immediately after his birth. Elizabeth informed their family and friends her baby's name would be John. This announcement removed everyone out of their comfort zone and sent them into a commotion (vs 61). They immediately went to the head of the family, the father of the baby, and inquired of him (vs 62). Zacharias, the high priest, took a tablet and confirmed his wife's announcement by writing, "His name is John" (vs 63). In the Middle East, and in most of Europe, it is customary to name babies after their parents and/or grandparents to identify tribes and the family lineage. The Lord restructured the heritage of Zacharias' lineage by giving his son a name that had never been used in the history of their ancestors. When Zacharias' tongue was loosed he was then able to articulate the destiny of his house, which in turn, would greatly affect Israel and eventually the rest of the world (Luke 1:64-79).

Eternal Life Principles & Beyond

C. He was sent to introduce Jesus, single handedly, to Israel

"And I (John) did not recognize Him, but in order that He might be manifested to Israel, I came *baptizing in water*."
—John 1:31

"For this is the one referred to by Isaiah the prophet, saying, 'The voice of one crying in the wilderness, make ready the way of the Lord, make His paths straight!'"
—Matthew 3:3

"And you, child, will be called the prophet of the Most High; For you will go on before the Lord to prepare His ways; To give to His people the knowledge of salvation by the forgiveness of their sins."
—Luke 1:76-77

What Was The Significance Of John's Baptism?

A. He was divinely sent to baptize

"And I (John) did not recognize Him (Jesus), but He (God) who sent me to *baptize in water* said to me, 'He upon whom you see the Spirit descending and remaining upon Him, this is the one who baptizes in the Holy Spirit.'"
—John 1:33

It was God Himself who chose and ordained water baptism as the physical means whereby to introduce His son Jesus to Israel. It was The Father who called John and anointed him to proclaim, "Behold the Lamb of God."

B. His ministry marked the beginning of a new age

Jesus said, "The law and the Prophets were proclaimed until John; since then the gospel of the kingdom of God is preached, and everyone is forcing his way into it."
—Luke 16:16

We also must put great significance in John's ministry and water baptism.

C. His ministry marked a new order of divine requirement

"....in the (time of the) high priesthood of Annas and Caiaphas, the word of God came to John, the son of Zacharias, in the wilderness. And he came into all the district around the Jordan, preaching baptism of repentance for the forgiveness of sins."
—Luke 3:2-3

It is interesting to note that Father God deems it important to document the time, place and season of John's ministerial calling.

Baptism I

    D. It was "the counsel (purpose, will) of God" for that time

        "But the Pharisees and the lawyers rejected God's purpose for themselves, not having been baptized by John."

        —Luke 7:30

        "But the Pharisees and the lawyers (of the Mosaic Law) annulled and rejected and brought to nothing God's purpose concerning themselves by (refusing and) not being *baptized* by (John)."

        —Luke 7:30 Amplified

    E. Those who were baptized, "justified God" (Declared God to be right in His demands)

        "And when all the people and the tax gatherers heard this, they acknowledged God's justice, having been baptized with the *baptism* of John."

        —Luke 7:29

        "And all the people who heard Him, even the tax collectors, acknowledged the justice of God (in calling them to repentance and pronouncing future wrath on the impenitent), being baptized with the baptism of John"

        —Luke 7:29 Amplified

    F. John's baptism was superseded by the Believer's baptism

        4 "And Paul said, 'John baptized with the baptism of repentance, telling the people to believe in Him who was coming after him, that is in Jesus."
        5 "And when they heard this, they were *baptized* in the name of the Lord Jesus."

        —Acts 19

        4 "And Paul said, 'John baptized with the baptism of repentance, continually telling the people that they should believe on the One Who was to come after him, that is, in Jesus (having a conviction full of joyful trust that He is Christ, the Messiah, and being obedient to Him.)
        5 "On hearing this, they were baptized (again, this time) in the name of the Lord Jesus.'"

        —Acts 19 Amplified

Before we move on to our seventh point, let's ask ourselves a few questions.

What qualified John to do these things? (The answer is in Luke 3:2-3 in the previous page.)

What significant changes did John bring about?

How could the people recognize who gave him this authority? John was making some seemingly rather rash statements. John was breaking a 3,000 year tradition! He was changing a 3,000 year commandment! His message was radical! Let's take a look at these changes.

Eternal Life Principles & Beyond

> John said, "REPENTANCE IS THE WAY FOR FORGIVENESS OF SINS!"

Repentance for salvation! The not-so-obvious truth was that soon the crucifixion would endorse the Lamb of God as the last spotless sacrificial animal for the remission of the sin of the world. An animal (lamb or goat) was no longer necessary for the atonement of sins.

> John said, "WATER BAPTISM IS THE WAY FOR FORGIVENESS OF SINS!" Some said, "This has never been done before!"

This is another radical message because water baptism does not exclude women!

> John was also proclaiming, "WATER BAPTISM REPLACES THE COVENANT OF CIRCUMCISION!"

Circumcision set God's people apart from the Gentiles. The covenant of circumcision was given to Abraham by Yahweh and was to be continued as an ordinance later given to God's great prophet, Moses.

What was another radical message introduced by John? Is water baptism to include women, of all things, since Israel, the Middle East and most of Europe were a patriarchal society?

> John also declares, "THERE WILL BE NO MORE BLOOD SACRIFICES. NO MORE BULLS! NO MORE GOATS! NO MORE LAMBS!" Because now the Messiah is here on earth walking among us!

JOHN – SOLITARILY – INTRODUCED – JESUS – HIS COUSIN – AS THE MESSIAH!

Too much cannot be said about this prophet of God for the importance of the role he played in the life of Israel, the life of the believers on the scene at the time, and for the preparation of their hearts to accept their Messiah. He was also preparing his followers for the acceptance of the coming New Agreement between God and His people. He could not have done it without the anointing. Imagine the awesome anointing that was on this man's life! Imagine the persecution! (Sadly, the anointing caused division among the Jewish leaders, which trickled down to certain people and John was eventually beheaded.)

What Did The Lawyers And Pharisees Reject?

A. The will of God

> "Go therefore and make disciples of all the nations, baptizing them in the name of the Father and the Son and the Holy Spirit."
>
> —Matthew 28:19

> "He who has believed and has been baptized shall be saved; but he who has disbelieved shall be condemned."
>
> —Mark 16:16

Baptism I

What Was The Origin Of A Believer's Baptism?

B. Jesus commanded the great commission

> "Go therefore and make disciples of all the nations, baptizing them in the name of the Father and the Son and the Holy Spirit."
>
> —Matthew 28:19

Christ instituted water baptism after His resurrection. In His three part commission He charged His disciples that while going, to first evangelize, then to baptize in water those who were made disciples *"into the name of the father and of the son and of the Holy Spirit"* and then to instruct them in the ways of God. That is, into a special relationship with the triune God that they may know and seek the purpose of their life here on earth.

> "He who has believed and has been baptized shall be saved; but he who has disbelieved shall be condemned."
>
> —Mark 16:16

Those who have disbelieved are condemned because they have rejected the only provision that could be effectual to their soul's salvation. Here water baptism is the external signature of man's inner faith of the heart. It is also an outward manifestation of the fruit of faith.

How Did The Apostles Obey This Commission?

> "….Repent and let each of you be baptized in the name of Jesus Christ for the forgiveness of your sins; and you shall receive the gift of the Holy Spirit."
>
> —Acts 2:38

Repentance is necessary for the forgiving of our sins. Another way of saying it is: Repentance is necessary so that "your sins may be forgiven". This fits with Peter's proclamation in Acts 10:43 in which the same expression "sins may be forgiven" occurs. Twice Luke writes that repentance results in remission of sins, first in his gospel chapter 24 verse 47 & Acts 5:31.

> "So then, those who had received his word were baptized, and there were added that day about 3,000 souls."
>
> —Acts 2:41

> "And when they heard this, they were baptized in the name of the Lord Jesus."
>
> —Acts 19:5

> "For He had not yet fallen upon any of them; they had simply been baptized in the name of the Lord Jesus."
>
> —Acts 8:16

In the above verse (Acts 8:16), Peter and John were praying for those in Samaria that they might receive the Holy Spirit.

Eternal Life Principles & Beyond

Additional Notes:

Below is an overview of the diverse translations by different translators of the doctrine title "baptism". Each author conveyed the importance of the original Greek as we have noticed in this lesson.

    "the teaching of baptism"   —JB Phillips
    "instructions about the different kinds of baptism"   —Ronald Knox
    "by instruction about cleansing rites"   —The New English Bible
    "of teaching of immersion"   —John A. Broadus
    "or of teaching about ceremonial washings"   —Richard F. Weymouth

Baptism I

Lesson Study Review 7

1. Name three main usages of baptism mentioned in this lesson? Give a short Scriptural illustration of each and document your answer.

   A. _____

   _____

   B. _____

   _____

   C. _____

   _____

2. Define the word "baptize."

   _____

   _____

   _____

3. Where is water baptism first recorded in the New Testament?

   _____

4. Who was John the Baptizer?

   A. _____

   B. _____

   C. _____

Eternal Life Principles & Beyond

5. Was water baptism John's own idea? _____ (Yes or No). Explain:

   A. John 1:33

   B. Luke 16:16

   C. Luke 3:2-3

   D. Luke 7:30

   E. Luke 7:29

   F. Acts 19:4-5

6. What did the lawyers and the Pharisees reject in refusing to be baptized with John's baptism?

7. What mandated the church's practice of the Believer's baptism?

   Matt. 28:19 & Mk. 16:16.

8. How did the practice of the apostles in administering water baptism seem to contradict the Great Commission as contained in Matthew 28:19

   Acts 2:38, 41
   Acts 8:16
   Acts 19:5

Baptism I: Lesson Study Review 7

9. Also, for an interesting and challenging research there are many passages of Scripture that describes "fully immersed" and none are in water. Ask the Holy Spirit to help you to recall at least eight of the 12 incidences starting in the Book of Genesis.

1._____

2._____

3._____

4._____

5._____

6._____

7._____

8._____

Instruction About Washings II

22 "Men of Israel, listen to these words: "Jesus the Nazarene a man attested to you by God with miracles and wonders and signs which God performed through Him in your midst, just as you yourselves know—

23 this man, delivered up by the predetermined plan and foreknowledge of God, you nailed to a cross by the hands of godless men and put Him to death.

24 "And God raised Him up again, putting an end to the agony of death, since it was impossible for Him to be held in its power.

25 "For David says of Him,

> 'I WAS ALWAYS BEHOLDING THE LORD IN MY PRESENCE; FOR HE IS AT MY RIGHT HAND, THAT I MAY NOT BE SHAKEN.

26 THEREFORE MY HEART WAS GLAD AND MY TONGUE EXULTED; MOREOVER MY FLESH ALSO WILL ABIDE IN HOPE;

27 BECAUSE THOU WILT NOT ABANDON MY SOUL TO HADES, NOR ALLOW THY HOLY ONE TO UNDERGO DECAY.

28 THOU HAS MADE KNOWN TO ME THE WAYS OF LIFE; THOU WILT MAKE ME FULL OF GLADNESS WITH THY PRESENCE.'

29 "Brethren, I may confidently say to you regarding the patriarch David that he both died and was buried, and his tomb is with us to this day.

30 "And so, because he was a prophet, and knew that GOD HAD SWORN TO HIM WITH AN OATH TO SEAT ONE OF HIS DESCENDANTS UPON HIS THRONE,

31 he looked ahead and spoke of the resurrection of the Christ, that He was NEITHER ABANDONED TO HADES, NOR DID His flesh SUFFER DECAY.

32 "This Jesus God raised up again, to which we are all witnesses.

33 "Therefore having been exalted to the right hand of God, and having received from the Father the promise of the Holy Spirit, He has poured forth this which you both see and hear.

34 "For it was not David who ascended into heaven, but he himself says:

> 'THE LORD SAID TO MY LORD, "SIT AT MY RIGHT HAND,
>
> **35** UNTIL I MAKE THINE ENEMIES A FOOTSTOOL FOR THY FEET."'

36 "Therefore let all the house of Israel know for certain that God has made Him both Lord and Christ this—Jesus whom you crucified."

37 Now when they heard this, they were pierced to the heart, and said to Peter and the rest of the apostles, "Brethren, what shall we do?"

38 And Peter said to them, "Repent, and let each of you be baptized in the name of Jesus Christ for the forgiveness of your sins; and you shall receive the gift of the Holy Spirit.

39 "For the promise is for you and your children, and for all who are far off, as many as the Lord our God shall call to Himself."

40 And with many other words he solemnly testified and kept on exhorting them, saying, "Be saved from this perverse generation!"

41 So then, those who had received his word were baptized; and there were added that day about three thousand souls.

42 And they were continually devoting themselves to the apostles' teaching and to fellowship, to the breaking of bread and to prayer.

—Acts 2

Eternal Life Principles & Beyond

What Is One Of God's Many Names In The Old Testament

The Hebrew name of God "YWH" was considered too holy to be uttered by the people of God in the Old Testament. We also know this name translated in German is "JHVH" and later Jehovah. However, the Israelites substituted "YWH" God for the word LORD "Adonai". The American Standard Version translated the "Incommunicable name" Jehovah, instead of following the practice of using "Lord". To pronounce the Hebrew name YHWH vowels were taken from the name Adonay and became YAH or Yahweh (Jehovah in German) meaning "He is"— "He exists" — "He is present"— "I am because I am"— "I WILL BE WHAT I WILL BE". God has many descriptive titles, but there is no question as to His name.

> "God spoke further to Moses and said to him, "I am the Lord; and I appeared to Abraham, Isaac, and Jacob, as God Almighty, but by My name, Lord, I did not make Myself known to them.'"
>
> —Exodus 6:2-3 NAS

> "I am the Lord, that is My name; I will not give My glory to another, nor My praise to graven images."
>
> —Isaiah 42:8

> "Our Redeemer, the Lord of hosts is His name, The Holy One of Israel."
>
> —Isaiah 47:4

> "Our Redeemer, Jehovah of hosts is His name, The Holy One of Israel."
>
> .—Isaiah 47:4 ASV

A. The revelation of God in Christ

1. "He who was revealed in the flesh." —1 Timothy 3:16

   "Jesus Christ was God manifested in the flesh." —1 Timothy 3:16 KJV

The writer to the Hebrews tells us that the God of the Old Testament was the God who:

2. "....spoke long ago to the fathers in the prophets in many portions and in many ways, in these last days has spoken to us in His Son, whom He appointed heir of all things, through whom also He made the world....having become as much better than the angels. As He has inherited a more excellent name than they."

   —Hebrews 1:1-2, 4

3. "And she will bear a Son; and you shall call His name Jesus, for it is He who will save His people from their sins."

   —Matthew 1:21

Instruction About Washings II

> "Behold, the virgin shall be with child, and shall bear a son, and they shall call his name Immanuel, which translated means, 'God with us.'"
>
> —Matthew 1:23

4. "....namely, that God was in Christ reconciling the world to Himself, not counting their trespasses against them,...."

—2 Corinthians 5:19

The name "Lord" which the Old Testament saints used for Jehovah is now given to Jesus, the Christ. This indicates that God is in Christ.

> "Therefore let all the house of Israel know for certain that God has made Him both Lord and Christ."
>
> —Acts 2:36

The Lord Jesus Christ Did Not Command His Disciples To Baptize In The Collective Names (plural) of The Father And Of The Son, And Of The Holy Spirit, But In The Name (singular) Of All Of The Persons Of The Godhead

The Spirit of Truth, according to the Scriptures, revealed to the apostles and disciples and to the church the fact that the name of the Father, and of the Son, and of the Holy Spirit is the name for the "Lord". Therefore, the "redemptive name" of God, according to revelation is the Lord Jesus Christ:

> "For in Him all the fullness of Deity dwells in bodily form."
>
> —Colossians 2:9 NASB

> "In Him the whole fullness of Deity (the Godhead) continues to dwell in bodily form, giving complete expression of the divine nature."
>
> —Colossians 2:9 Amplified

> "For it is in Him that all the plenitude of the Godhead has its corporal home."
>
> —Colossians 2:9 Way

> "For it is in Christ that the fullness of God's nature dwells embodied."
>
> —Colossians 2:9 Weymouth

> "It is in Christ that the entire fullness of Deity has settled bodily."
>
> —Colossians 2:9 Moffatt

> "And He is the image of the invisible God, the firstborn of all creation. For it was the Father's good pleasure for all the fullness to dwell in Him...."
>
> —Colossians 1:15, 19 NAS

"He is the exact likeness of the unseen God, the visible representation of the invisible…For it hath pleased (the Father) that all the divine fullness, the sum total of the divine perfection, powers, and attributes – should dwell in Him permanently."

—Colossians 1:15, 19 Amplified

Father, Son and Holy Spirit are not mere names; they are titles describing the office work of each person of the Godhead.

A. The Father has a name

"I (Jesus) have come in My Father's name."

—John 5:43

B. The Holy Spirit has a name

"….the Holy Spirit whom the Father will send in My name."

—John 14:26

C. The Son has a name - Jesus

"Therefore let all the house of Israel know for certain that God has made Him both Lord and Christ."

—Acts 2:36

D. It is the only name that saves

"And there is salvation in no one else; for there is no other name under heaven that has been given among men, by which we must be saved."

—Acts 4:12

And in no other is the great salvation to be found; for, in fact, there is no second name under heaven that has been given among men through which we are to be saved.

—Acts 4:12 Weymouth

Our Lord Had Said "Name" Of The Father, Son And Holy Spirit

18 "And Jesus came up and spoke to them, saying, "All authority has been given to Me in heaven and on earth.
19 "Go therefore and make disciples of all the nations baptizing them in the name of the Father and the Son and the Holy Spirit,
20 "Teaching them to observe all that I commanded you and lo, I am with you always, even to the end of the age."

—Matthew 28

Instruction About Washings II

Why Did The Apostles Water Baptize In The Name Of The Lord Jesus Christ?

Our Lord commissioned His disciples to baptize "in the name of the Father and the Son and the Holy Spirit" (Matthew 28:19). They obeyed and fulfilled His command by baptizing "in the name of the Lord Jesus Christ."

To say that this is unimportant, and that it doesn't matter how we baptize, is to ignore and miss the vital truths revealed to the apostles for our blessing, protection, and spiritual growth. There were other reasons for the apostolic action.

What Is Required To Qualify For Water Baptism?

A. Hearing and heeding His Word

> "Now when they heard this, they were pierced to the heart, and said....'Brethren, what shall we do?'"
> "And Peter said to them, "Repent," and let each of you be baptized in the name of Jesus Christ for the forgiveness of your sins;"
> —Acts 2:37-38

> "So then, those who had (gladly KJV) received his word were baptized."
> —Acts 2:41

> "And a certain woman named Lydia....the Lord opened her heart to respond to the things spoken by Paul....she and her household had been baptized."
> —Acts 16:14-15

> "And when they heard this, they were baptized...."
> —Acts 19:5

If you were to ask me, "What should we do?" It would be important how I answered you. Notice in 16:14-15 Lydia "heard", and in 19:5 they "heard", and in 2:37 they "heard", and "they were pricked in their hearts." Do we understand that hearing and heeding the Word is the commandment? I call this the Peter Package. Our needs are the impetus to make the will run.

The principles that come forth from these verses are:

```
INFORM THE MIND    —   THEY HEARD
STIR THE EMOTIONS  —   THEY WERE CONVICTED IN THEIR HEART
COMMAND THE WILL   —   WHAT SHALL WE DO?
```

Also, Peter's answer recorded by Luke in the Book of Acts 2:38 is important for all times. Further along into this lesson is an explanation of the difference between Peter's answer and Jesus' commandment.

Eternal Life Principles & Beyond

B. Conviction

"Now when they heard this, they were pierced to the heart, and said…'Brethren, what shall we do?'"

—Acts 2:37

C. Repentance

"*Repent,* and let each of you be *baptized….*"

—Acts 2:38

D. Faith

"He who has believed and has been baptized shall be saved."

—Mark 16:16

"But when they believed Philip preaching the good news about the kingdom of God and the name of Jesus Christ, they were being baptized, men and women alike."

—Acts 8:12

"Look! Water! What prevents me from being baptized?" And Philip said, "If you believe with all your heart, you may."

—Acts 8:36-37

"Believe in the Lord Jesus, and you shall be saved, you and your household…And he took them that very hour of the night and washed their wounds, and immediately he was baptized, he and all his household."

—Acts 16:31, 33

E. Obedience

"….but rise, and enter the city, and it shall be told you what you must do."

—Acts 9:6

Doing has to do with that part of our being called the "will." As Paul journeyed on the road to Damascus, he was focused on persecuting more Christians. His will was set; therefore, the Lord dealt strongly with him. Paul heard the Lord say, "….but rise, and enter the city, and it shall be told you what you must do." (Acts 9:6)

When Were People Baptized By Water In The Early Church?

A. The same day

"So then, those who had received his (Peter's) word were baptized; and there were added that day about 3,000 souls."

—Acts 2:41

Instruction About Washings II

B. When they believed

"But when they believed….they were being baptized.…"

—Acts 8:12

"And Philip said, 'If you believe with all your heart, you may. 'And he answered and said, 'I believe that Jesus Christ is the Son of God.' And he ordered the chariot to stop; and they both went down into the water….and he baptized him.'"

—Acts 8:37-38

"…. and many of the Corinthians when they heard were believing and being baptized."

—Acts 18:8

C. The same hour

"And he took them that very hour of the night and washed their wounds, and (immediately) he was baptized, he and all his household."

—Acts 16:33

Some believers think hours of teaching should come before baptism; however, in the "Great Commission" Jesus put teaching after baptism. Matthew records Jesus as saying, "All authority has been given to Me in heaven and on earth. Go therefore and make disciples of all the nations, baptizing them in the name of the Father and the Son and the Holy Spirit, teaching them to observe all that I commanded you; and lo, I am with you always, even to the end of the age." (Mt. 28:18-20)

Our Lord Had Promised His Disciples There Would Be New And More Complete Revelation Given By The Holy Spirit

"I have many more things to say to you, but you cannot bear them now. But when He, the Spirit of truth, comes, He will guide you into all the truth."

—John 16:12-13

"But the Helper, the Holy Spirit, whom the Father will send in My name, He will teach you all things, and bring to your remembrance all that I said to you."

—John 14:26

When Jesus states, "I have many more things to say to you", He clearly shows that the later revelation (which was going to be deposited in written form in Acts, the epistles, and the book of Revelation) was His own work. Therefore, the manner in which the disciples baptized was due to the promised revelation of Jesus Christ through the newly-given Holy Spirit. We cause offense and insult to God's will and purpose in revelation if we treat this lightly or carelessly. We would not need to belabor this point if men had not chosen to ignore the progress of revelation as promised by our Lord, and decided to make "their" choice as to how to baptize. We quote from the *Dictionary of the Apostolic Church*:

"The practice of baptizing into the name of Jesus continued into the third century when Pope Stephen, in opposition to Cyprian and the Apostolic Canons, declared such baptism to be invalid" (Dictionary of the Apostolic Church, Vol. 2 Page 73).

Summary:

Words Spoken At the Time of Baptism

It is unfortunate that many see a discrepancy between Matthew 28:19 and the references to water baptism in the Acts of the Holy Spirit by the Apostles. It is my view that there is no discrepancy, but rather a divine intention, as I have tried to show.

In conversing with some fellow servants of the lord on the subject of Baptism, one of them quite emphatically stated the he would baptize only "in the Name of the Father and of the Son and of the Holy Spirit," since that was the way the Lord had commanded it be done.

However, that raises the question as to who was responsible for the record of the Acts of the Apostles. Did not the same Lord Jesus Christ who spoke in Matthew 28:19 superintend the revelation of the Acts? I believe so. Therefore, our friend's position does not resolve the apparent problem.

Since it is the clear teaching of the New Testament that "in Him all the fullness of the Godhead dwells in bodily form" (Colossians 2:9), does it not then follow that, when one is "baptized into the Lord Jesus, the Christ" he is baptized into the "fullness of the Godhead" – Father, Son, and Holy Spirit?

The Lord Jesus, the Christ is that One of the Holy Three Who has come forth to relate to men in their nature and need. Through baptism, they in turn may relate to the Godhead through Him.

As Neander wrote:

> "....the full import of baptism could not be realized until the process which began with Christ's death and resurrection, and the glorified Redeemer, had displayed His triumphant power in the outpouring of the Holy Spirit."

The first repentant, believing sinners who came to the Savior in the first days of this Gospel age, in being baptized into the name of the Lord Jesus, the Christ, understood that they were being baptized into Jesus, the Christ (Romans 6:3). By being baptized in this manner, they were not denying the nature of God's Being as consisting of Father,

Son, and Holy Spirit, but were recognizing that the Lord Jesus, the Christ was their Savior, and the one through whom they entered into a living relationship with the Triune God.

We consider it unnecessary to argue against the matter of formula. Not that formula is unimportant, for it should bear a direct relationship to what is happening in the act of baptism. But, if the meaning and intent of baptism is not understood by the one being baptized, then whatever is said matters not at all.

There is no magic in the words spoken. The vital element in baptism is the new relationship with God through Jesus, the Christ, being declared and sealed in this divinely-ordained act of faith and obedience.

Since baptism is analogous (similar in function) to a marriage ceremony (as well as a burial), we may see a relationship between what is said at the time of baptism and the vows exchanged at a wedding. The words spoken in the wedding ceremony will be meaningless if there is not a genuine love relationship between the participants.

This is also true in baptism. The words can be meaningless if there is not a relationship of love between the sinner and his Savior, based on a repentance-faith-obedience response to the Christ. It is the vital relationship expressed in the act that is important, which relationship is articulated in the words spoken by the baptizer, i.e., "in the name of the Father, the Son and the Holy Ghost," which we refer to as "formula".

Must sides be taken on the matter? There are many good men and women who are staunch believers in the threeness of God, who baptize in the name of the Lord Jesus, the Christ and there are other equally fine men and women who believe in the oneness of God and baptize in the Name of the Father and of the Son and of the Holy Spirit. If Matthew 28:19 and Acts 2:38 are to be considered as formulas, we do no service to truth and unity by considering them to be irreconcilable. We do not believe them to be mutually contradictory, but when rightly related, to be divinely intended, as I have attempted to prove.

Would it not be consistent with the total teaching of the Scriptures on baptism, and at the same time do much to bring about unity in this area, if a formula incorporating the command of our Lord and the practice of the apostles be used? This is not unity at the cost of compromise, for what would one be compromising?

I, along with many others, have found the following formula to be agreeable to the total scriptural teaching on baptism:

> "Upon the ground of the confession of your faith: To the glory of God, Father, Son and Holy Spirit: We baptize you into the name of our Lord Jesus, the Christ."

Instruction About Washings II
Lesson Study Review 8

1. Did Our Lord Jesus Christ impart all revelation before He returned to Heaven?

    _____ (YES or NO).   Justify your answer.

    John 16:12 _____

    _____

2. What did Christ promise His apostles concerning further revelation of truth?

    _____

    _____

    _____

    _____

3. What did God declare His Name to be in the Old Testament?

    _____

    _____

4. Where does the Threeness of God reside bodily?

    Col. 2:9 _____

    _____

5. What is the significance of baptism into the Name of the Lord Jesus, the Christ?

    Rom. 6:3 _____

    _____

    _____

Instruction About Washings: Lesson Study Review 8

6. What are those things which qualify one for water baptism?

    A. _____

    B. _____

    C. _____

    D. _____

    E. _____

7. In the New Testament, how soon were repentant, believing sinners baptized?

    A. Acts 2:41 _____

    B. Acts 8:12, 37-38, 18:8 _____

    C. Acts 16:31-33 _____

Instruction About Washings III

We will now get into the doctrinal aspects of water baptism. Some Bible translations correctly translate the Greek word "*baptismos*" as "instruction about washings" instead of "instruction about baptism" for a reason. It has significance deeper than being sprinkled, dunked or dipped. *Strong's Exhaustive Concordance of the Bible* translates "baptismos" referred to in Hebrews 6:2 and 9:10 as the act of "dipping, washing/washings, ceremonially washed and to sink".

In this lesson, we will have some repetition in our Scriptures because each Scripture says more than one thing. Bible colleges incorporate a course into their curriculum called "Hermeneutics". Hermeneutics is the laws and study of interpreting the Bible profitable for doctrine. One of the first laws of interpreting the Bible is — "All that the Scripture has to say on any one given subject is the doctrine of that subject." Therefore, if Peter said on the day of Pentecost, "repent and be baptized for the remission of your sins", then that is part of your data.

We know that the Blood of Jesus remits all sin, but for this lesson, let's remain focused on the doctrine of baptism and to the "law of interpretation" of it. There are five things to be said about "remission".

1. Christ came to make remission possible. (See Acts 5:31; 13:38, and Col. 1:14).

    "In Him we have redemption (deliverance and salvation) through His blood, the remission (forgiveness) of our offenses (shortcomings and trespasses) in accordance with the riches and generosity of His gracious favor."

    —Ephesians 1:7 Amplified

2. Legally, only the Blood remits sin. (See Eph. 1:7; Col. 1:14 and Matt. 26:28).

    "(In fact) under the Law almost everything is purified by means of blood, and without the shedding of blood there is neither release from sin and its guilt nor the remission of the due and merited punishment for sins."

    —Hebrews 9:22 Amplified

3. Faith and Trust

    "To Him all the prophets testify (bear witness) that everyone who believes in Him (who adheres to, trusts in, and relies on Him, giving himself up to Him) receives forgiveness of sins through His name."

    —Acts 10:43 Amplified

    "To this One all the prophets bear testimony, that through His Name everyone who places his trust in Him receives remission of the penalty of sins."

    —Acts 10:43 K. Wuest

Instruction About Washings III

    4. John came preaching repentance for the remission of sins. (See Luke 3:3)

> "John the Baptist appeared in the wilderness (desert), preaching a baptism (obligating) repentance (a change of one's mind for the better, heartily amending one's ways, with abhorrence of his past sins) in order to obtain forgiveness of and release from sins."
>
> —Mark 1:4 Amplified

> "There came upon the human scene John the Baptizer, in the uninhabited region, making a public proclamation with that formality, gravity, and authority which must be heeded and obeyed, of a baptism which had to do with a change of mind relative to the previous life an individual lived, this baptism being in view of the fact that sins are put away."
>
> —Mark 1:4 K. Wuest

Now you see why Acts 2:38 is not in conflict with Matthew 28:19. It is just another aspect of the doctrine "Repent" and be "baptized" in the "Name of the Lord Jesus Christ" for the remission of sins.

    5. The importance that baptism is made available

> "And that repentance (with a view to and as the condition of) forgiveness of sins should be preached in His name to all nations, beginning from Jerusalem."
>
> —Luke 24:47 Amplified

Luke 24:47 shows us how important it is that baptism is made available to everyone right from the beginning. It is part of what God wants preached as we go from place to place and around the world.

What Did The Apostle Teach About Baptism?

    A. Baptism in water is the Bible-required act of obedience that testifies of genuine repentance and faith.

> "Repent, and let each of *you* be baptized in the name of Jesus Christ."
>
> —Acts 2:38

> "So then, those who had received his word were *baptized*...."
>
> —Acts 2:41

When God visited Cornelius and his household, Peter "*commanded*" (ordered) them to "*be baptized in the name of Jesus Christ*" (Acts 10:48). The order is no less valid today. Water baptism is *not optional*! It is ordained of God. It ought to follow salvation as a first step of obedience and identification with the Christ. The early believers needed to separate themselves from the religions of the day. Outward profession of your faith through a water baptism ceremony definitely accomplishes that. This most humbling act is before God; as we are transferring our trust from self to our Savior and Lord, Jesus, the Christ. Again, we come back to Peter's response to their question, "what must we do to be saved?" The people asked, they heard, and 3,000 souls gladly obeyed! (Read also Acts 22:16, which is Paul's defense when standing in court before the Jews).

B. Baptism in water has to do with the remission of sins

"Repent, and let each of you be baptized in the name of Jesus Christ for the forgiveness of your sins;....."

—Acts 2:38

"Repent and be baptized every one of you in the name of Jesus Christ for the forgiveness of and release from your sins."

—Acts 2:38 Amplified

In the NAS translation of the Bible, the Hebrew word *"shemittah"* translated "remission" means: "forgiveness, deliverance, liberty, a sending-away, to throw down, a letting-go." It is only found in the Old Testament and not in the New Testament; and is used only in the book of Deuteronomy chapter 15 verses 1-2; 9; and 31:10, and only associated with debts.

In the NKJ version of the Bible, the word *"aphesis"* translated "remission" is found only in the New Testament and not in the Old Testament. It also means "pardon", "deliverance", "forgiveness" and "liberty".

1. Christ came to make remission possible

"He is the One whom God exalted to His right hand as a Prince and a Savior, to grant repentance to Israel, and forgiveness of sins."

—Acts 5:31

To understand remission more fully, also read Acts 13:38, Ephesians 1:7 and Colossians 1:14

2. The legal ground of remission is Our Savior's blood

"....for this is My blood of the Covenant, which is poured out for many for forgiveness of sins."

—Matthew 26:28

"....without shedding of blood, there is no forgiveness."

—Hebrews 9:22

Actually, if Jesus tasted death for every man, and is the propitiation for the whole world legally, then Jesus' Blood has made it possible for how many people to experience forgiveness? Is it not everyone? However, does everyone experience forgiveness? Sadly, no. Therefore, there is a difference between legal remission and actual or experiential remission.

Instruction About Washings III

> 3. Faith and Trust in the Savior is essential to receive remission
>
>> "....through His name everyone who believes in Him receives forgiveness of sins."
>>
>> —Acts 10:43

Can *you* have your sins remitted if *you* don't repent and believe? Not according to the above verse. Then we see here that, if the Blood is legal remission from our sins, it is still not available to us apart from "faith" and "trust" in our Savior.

> 4. Water Baptism is the divinely-ordained way of expressing such faith
>
>> "*Repent,* and let each of you be *baptized* in the name of Jesus Christ for the forgiveness of your sins."
>>
>> —Acts 2:38

(See Mark 1:4, Luke 3:3)

> 5. The message of remission is to be preached universally
>
>> "....and that repentance for forgiveness of sins should be proclaimed in His name to all the nations, beginning from Jerusalem."
>>
>> —Luke 24:47

It is important to mention here that one must believe that it is the Blood which provides remission of sins to receive salvation. (Also see Acts 13:38, Ephesians 1:7 and Colossians 1:14).

Baptism In Water Has To Do With Cleansing

> "And now why do *you* delay? Arise, and be baptized, and wash away your sins, calling on His name."
>
> —Acts 22:16

Also see 1 Peter 3:21

> A. We are washed by the Blood of Our Lord Jesus
>
>> "To Him who loves us, and released us from our sins by His blood."
>>
>> —Revelation 1:5

We are legally cleansed and purified from our sins by the Blood of Christ, a purification that is essential in the symbolism of baptism.

> B. We are cleansed by the Word of God
>
>> "You are already clean because of the word which I have spoken to you."
>>
>> —John 15:3
>
> C. Our cleansing from sin is signified in Baptism

The blood of our Savior, Jesus Christ, washes us from our sins legally. The Word cleanses us from our sins in practice as we "keep it according to" (Psalm 119:9). In water baptism, the purpose of God in washing and loosing us from our sins is signified and made real to the repentant, believing, obedient sinner. It is the confession of our desire to be clean from sin of every kind. Purification that is essential is in the symbolism of baptism.

We Are "Baptized Into Jesus Christ"

"For all of *you* who were baptized into Christ have clothed yourselves with Christ."

—Galatians 3:27 NAS

"All of *you* who were BAPTIZED *"INTO CHRIST"* have put on the family likeness of Christ."

—Galatians 3:27 JB Phillips

"For all of *you* who had yourselves *baptized into Christ* have taken on the character of Christ."

—Galatians *3:27* Moffatt

"All of *you* who have by *baptism* passed into union *with Messiah* have clothed yourselves with Messiah's personality."

—Galatians 3:27 Way

"Or do you not know that all of *us* who have been *baptized into Christ Jesus* have been baptized into His death? Therefore, we have been buried with him through baptism into death, in order that as Christ was raised from the dead through the glory of the Father, so we too might walk in newness of life."

—Romans 6:3-4 NAS

"Have you forgotten that all of us who were *baptized in Jesus Christ* were, by that very action, sharing his death? We were dead and buried with Him in baptism, so that just as He was raised from the dead by that splendid revelation of the Father's power so we too might rise to life on a new plane altogether.

—Romans 6:3-4 JB Phillips

"Do you not comprehend that all of us, who passed by *baptism into union with Messiah Jesus,* were by baptism made sharers in His death? Well then, if that baptism made us share His death, it must have made us share His burial, too. It must follow that, as Messiah was raised from among the dead by the means of the descent of the Father's glory, so we, too, who rose with Him, are to be employed wholly in the activities of the New Life."

—Romans 6:3-4 Way

Instruction About Washings III

We have seen that, in the beginning, repentant and believing sinners were baptized "the same day"— "when they believed" —"the same hour". Baptism was an accepted fact of normal New Testament procedure and life. Sinners "believed and were baptized."

Repentance, faith, and baptism should never be separated. They were not in the beginning, as we learned from the preaching of Peter on the day of Pentecost. It also was not a problem for Paul, as a basis for his teachings, making it applicable to all future Followers of Christ.

At the time of conversion of the early Believers through repentance, faith and baptism, there was a divine response and some wonderful things happened to them. They experienced the *passing* of the old and the *emergence* of the new way of life in Christ which brought power for daily living, peace, hope and joy as mentioned in Lesson II of "Laying-On-Of-Hands".

> "Therefore if any man is in Christ, he is a new creature; the *old things passed away;* behold, *new* things have come."
>
> —2 Corinthians 5:17

Baptism not only speaks of our identification with Christ in His death, and burial, but also of His resurrection. In the natural realm, when we die we are buried and that is the end of the matter. However, "being buried *with Him by baptism into death"*, we can expect the same Spirit who raised Christ from the dead to resurrect our spirits that we, too, might walk in newness of life. (See Romans 6:4-11)

So, *"like as Christ was raised* up....even *so we!"*

> "For if we have become united with Him in the *likeness of His death,* certainly we shall be also *in the likeness of His resurrection."*
>
> —Romans 6:5

> "For if we have become one with Him by *sharing a death like Him,* we shall also be one with Him in *sharing His resurrection* (by a new life lived for God)."
>
> —Romans 6:5 Amplified

Can we have newness of life without spiritual death? Since spirit baptism occurs once and for all at the point of salvation, then wouldn't it be prudent to follow with water baptism as an outward sign of an inward transaction? The answer is "Yes!" One's position in Christ before God should be manifested in one's position in Christ before the world."

We Are Baptized Into The Lordship Of Jesus Christ

> "For I do not want you to be unaware, brethren, that our fathers were *all* under the cloud, and *all* passed through the sea; and *all were baptized into Moses* in the cloud and in the sea."
>
> —1 Corinthians 10:1-2

"Everyone of them (allowed himself too) to be baptized into Moses in the cloud and in the sea, that is, they were thus brought under obligation to the law, to Moses and to the covenant, consecrated and set apart to the service of God."

—1 Corinthians 10:2 Amplified

By this their baptism in the cloud and in the sea, *they pledged themselves to follow Moses.*

—1 Corinthians 10:2 Way

Paul said, "Those things happened as types for us" (vs 6). Moses is a type of our Lord Jesus. In the baptism of the sea (water) and the baptism of the cloud (Spirit). So we, in our water baptism and reception of the Holy Spirit, declare *Jesus, the Christ, as Lord*! We will follow Him into the fullness of the land of rest!

Additional Notes:

Two Things About Cleansing:

First, does this mean that the Word cleans apart from the Blood? No, it does not. The Blood is the legal basis for cleansing. It is the Word of God that brings our lives into line with the Will of God. The Holy Spirit and the Word are also "agents" of cleansing and equally important as there are three witnesses, the Father, the Son and the Holy Spirit. The Spirit and the Word cleans a man on the basis of his repentance and faith in the work of the Blood of Christ.

And second, when we accept Jesus Christ as our Lord, we not only have our sins dealt with, but we also have our "self" dealt with. For every time the Bible mentions Jesus as Savior, it mentions Jesus as Lord 27 times. In examining the NAS *Exhaustive Concordance*, "Savior" is recorded 27 times (includes Old Testament and New Testament), but "Lord" records 25 full pages. Understandable in the Old Testament section, lord also referred to husbands and masters. In the New Testament section, the Lord refers to Jesus and there are one and a half pages!

To say that you are saved by accepting Christ as your Savior is not really accurate – Paul said, "we are saved by accepting Him as Savior-Lord". By title and position, Christ is Lord and Savior. Lordship is the key factor and, until we accept Him as Lord, He cannot legally do anything for us. We have to accept Him as Lord and it is the Lordship that allows Him to be our Savior. Lordship and His work as Savior are inseparable. Here is where some Followers of Christ have a problem because Lordship is accountability. When we come up out of the water we are saying, "I am your bonded slave." The new Believer continually chooses whether or not to let Christ "do" His lording. Yes, Christ saves us from the past penalty of sin, present power over sin, and future presence of sin, but Christ is Lord by title no matter if we allow Him to be Lord or not.

Instruction About Washings III

Baptism should not be optional – the Lord commanded it. We must not try to get to God on our terms; we must meet God on His terms.

Part of my calling is what I call "restoration". I love the word, "restoration". You hear much about renewal and revival these days. The question is renewal and revival to what? When I speak of restoration, I simply mean there is a deep and dire need for us to go back to the foundation principles and do things in the light of the Bible blueprint. We should have the courage to change and to accommodate Him when the Word of God rebukes us. When this takes place in our hearts, then and only then, will renewal and revival take place.

Do we have the right to do anything in the Name of Christ that is not supported by the Word of Christ? No. It's just that so many of us are in turmoil because of being "shot through" with violations of God's Word.

God's Own, who thirst after Him, will try to conform to Christ's teachings in thought, word and deed. Those of you who have chosen to undertake this study have put joy in my heart because I know that through you we can help correct this ritualistic stream of Bible confusion.

I am not teaching things to be controversial, but I hope them to be purgative and restorative. What I teach is not at all popular with Satan. It is not popular with modern-day Sadducees and Pharisees who don't want the status-quo upset. We must ask ourselves, is our view of the Scriptures the same as His view? We should not say or do anything that does not line up with the Word of God.

As we confer with those of like mind, we are comfortable. But, when we move outside of this company, we are uneasy. When Peter got out of jail, he headed directly for his own fellow believers.

Can you imagine what went through Peter's head on the day of Pentecost as he raised his voice to declare to those outside the upper room what had just happened? There were no Gentiles there. He had never experienced this before. All he knew was that he was supposed to have the "keys". It is not recorded if Jesus had a 40-day seminar before His ascension. Can you visualize Peter standing there asking, "What now Lord?" And Jesus says, "the keys Peter, the keys."

Is it important to have the right key? The Holy Ghost came upon Peter and he said, "repent and be baptized." You mean it was a one shot deal? Yes, I call it "The Peter Package." Preach, repent, faith, baptism — all in one day! Of course, others came, but not right away. Often the planted seed needs time to grow. For some, their understanding is not immediately adequate and some wait until they understand the importance of baptism and some wait until they are convinced in their own minds. Repentance often comes long after the hearing.

Eternal Life Principles & Beyond

Water baptism relates to cleansing:

>Actually – Acts 22:16
>Legally – Revelation 1:5b
>Positionally – John 15:3 (Psalm 119:9)
>Experientially – Luke 24:47 (Acts 2:38; 3:19)

Amen and Amen

Comment:

It appears water baptism is a prerequisite to the gift of the Holy Spirit (Acts 2:38).

Worthy of mention is Acts 11:14-17. The Holy Spirit fell upon those in Caesarea, as Peter began to speak the words of salvation, baptizing them just as He did the 120 in the upper room on the day of Pentecost.

Instruction About Washings III
Lesson Study Review 9

1. Explain the Scripture that relates water baptism and sin.

   Acts 2:38 _____

   _____

   _____

   _____

2. Does water baptism relate to cleansing? _____ (Yes or No).

   If so, how?

   A. Acts 22:16 _____

   B. Rev. 1:5b _____

   C. John 15:3 _____

   D. Luke 24:47 _____

3. According to Romans 6, what is this baptism (placed into the body of Christ) telling us?

   vss 3-5 _____

   _____

   _____

   _____

4. Should repentance, faith, and baptism be separated? _____ (Yes or No).

   Why or why not? _____

   _____

   Explain 1 Cor. 10:1-2 _____

   _____

   _____

   _____

   _____

Baptism IV

Baptism And Circumcision:
Baptism In Water As It Relates
To The Old Testament Covenant Of Circumcision

11 "....In Him you were also circumcised with a circumcision made without hands, in the removal of the body of the flesh by the circumcision of Christ."

12 "....Having been buried with Him in baptism, in which you were also raised up with Him through faith in the working of God, who raised Him from the dead."

—Colossians 2

The Word "Circumcision" Means "the Cutting Around".
When Spoken Of As A Physical Rite In The Bible,
It Refers To "the Cutting Off Or Around Of The Foreskin In Males".
God Instituted It As A "Token Of The Covenant" Between Himself And Abraham.

"This is My covenant, which you shall keep, between Me and you and your descendants after you; *Every male among you shall be circumcised.*

And *you* shall be circumcised in the flesh of your foreskin, and it shall be the sign of the covenant between Me and you.

—Genesis 17:10-11

God instituted circumcision as a token of the "covenant" between Himself and Abraham and then carried it through as part of the Mosaic law. (Read Genesis 17:1-21 and 21:4). In the New Testament, circumcision is a "spiritual cutting off" of the flesh of the heart.

At The Very Beginning Of Life,
Circumcision Marked That Life As Deserving Of Death.
By The Mutilation It Practices On The Organ Of Generation,
It Points To Corruption In Its Source
As Adhering To The Very Being And Birth.

Israel was to be a people "cut off" from sin and pollution. The rite of circumcision was intended to be a permanent sermon declaring God's desire that Israel be His peculiar and holy people. Moses and the prophets understood this and so urged it upon the people.

"Circumcise then your heart, and stiffen your neck no more."

—Deuteronomy 10:16

Baptism IV

> "Moreover the LORD your God will circumcise your heart and the heart of your descendants, to love the LORD your God with all your heart and with all your soul, in order that you may live."
>
> —Deuteronomy 30:6

> "Circumcise yourselves to the LORD and remove the foreskins of your heart, men of Judah and inhabitants of Jerusalem, lest My wrath go forth like fire and burn with none to quench it, because of the evil of your deeds."
>
> —Jeremiah 4:4

At the beginning of life — at the birth of a male child — circumcision marked that boy's life as deserving of death. There is the shedding of blood. By the mutilation it practices on the organ that produces life — it points to corruption in the heart of man — from the very beginning of life — which is at his birth.

Paul Said That Outward Circumcision Alone Did Not Make A Real Jew, But It Was An Inward Token Of A Heart Attitude Toward God And Sin.

> "For he is not a Jew who is one outwardly; neither is circumcision that which is outward in the flesh. But he is a Jew who is one inwardly, and circumcision is that which is of the heart, by the Spirit, not by the letter, and his praise is not from men, but from God."
>
> —Romans 2:28-29

> "For in Christ Jesus neither circumcision nor uncircumcision means anything, but faith working through love."
>
> —Galatians 5:6

In his letter to the Believers in Rome, Paul instructs that circumcision is of the heart and to make an immediate and firm decision to repent and circumcise the flesh. Listed below are weaknesses of the flesh needing repentance.

bitterness	stealing	stiff neck
manipulation	nasty remarks	gossip
idle conversation	foolish talking	envy
control/dominance	worldly jokes	sarcasm
causing of divisions	dissension	striving
degrading passions	arrogance	boastfulness
defiance	mocking	ill will
selfishness	accusations	aggression
revealing of secrets	immaturity	immorality
masturbation	fear	uncooperativeness
holding grudges	indecent acts	bragging
deceitfulness	causing strife	slander
untrustworthiness	cursing	disrespect
betrayal	smearing	lying
greed……..		

disobedience to parents , guardian, employer or local laws and things that are not proper. If our five senses are unbridled, they will cause much upheaval in our daily lives.

In The Beginning Of Life In God,
The Repentant, Believing Sinner Does Not Submit
To The Physical Rite Of Circumcision. He Does, However,
Experience A "Circumcision Not Made With Hands"
Which Paul Calls "A Spiritual Circumcision Performed By Christ"
Which Involves The "Putting Off The Body Of The Flesh"

This circumcision or cutting off of the old life and burial in baptism are spoken of together. "Thus you were circumcised when you were buried with Him in your baptism."

—Colossians 2:11-12

11 In Him also you were circumcised with a circumcision not made with hands, but in a [spiritual] circumcision [performed by] Christ by stripping off the body of the flesh (the whole corrupt, carnal nature with its passions and lusts).

12 [Thus you were circumcised when] you were buried with Him in [your] baptism, in which you were also raised with Him [to a new life] through [your] faith in the working of God [as displayed] when He raised Him up from the dead.

13 And you who were dead in trespasses and in the uncircumcision of your flesh (your sensuality, your sinful carnal nature), [God] brought to life together with [Christ], having [freely] forgiven us all our transgressions, ...

—Colossians 2: 11-13 Amplified

Circumcision of the flesh was the shadow of the substance to come that was satisfied through Christ. In Christ, all the substances of the ceremonial laws were fulfilled. We are complete in Christ, not in ceremonial laws that were defective and imperfect. It is not cutting off a part of the flesh, but a putting off the body the "sins of the flesh" through the circumcision of Christ. Jesus, the Christ, by His grace and Spirit, underwent and performed all rites necessary to qualify Him to be the Mediator between God and Man. The gospel requires circumcision of the heart in which all fleshly desires dwell. It is His circumcision that is the source of our sanctification and not any rite. It is imputed for all Believers for our justification to die to the self-life.

Baptism IV

Baptism In Water Demonstrates
The Obedience Of
A Good Conscience Toward Christ

"….who once were disobedient, when the patience of God kept waiting in the days of Noah, during the construction of the ark, in which a few, that is, eight persons, were brought safely through the water. And corresponding to that, baptism now saves you — not the removal of dirt from the flesh, but an appeal to God for a good conscience — through the resurrection of Jesus Christ."

—1 Peter 3:20-21

"….a few people, actually eight in number, were saved through water. And baptism, which is a figure (of their deliverance), does now also save you (from inward questionings and fear), not by the removing of outward body filth (bathing), but by (providing you with) the answer of a good and clear conscience (inward cleanness and peace) before God, (because you are demonstrating what you believe to be yours) through the resurrection of Jesus Christ."

—1 Peter 3:20b-21 Amplified

Water baptism is not for the purpose of cleansing the physical body from "filth". It is that act of obedience that demonstrates the reality of our repentance and faith and the desire to have "a good conscience before God".

Coincidentally, John the Baptizer also prepared the way for Peter's call and ministry for Peter was headstrong and legalistic and after Pentecost, God's calling on his life was to the Jews, a patriarchal nation. Peter's anointing now carried with it the understanding that water baptism included women.

Additional Notes:

We will touch for a moment on the subject of infant and child baptism.

Infant Baptism

The New Testament contains no command to baptize infants and does not record a single instance of it.

Children's Baptism

The New Testament contains no command to baptize children yet this does not prove it unbiblical. Child baptism is not based on a single passage of Scripture, but on a series of considerations. It may be considered a parental commitment to raise the child in godly ways.

Eternal Life Principles & Beyond

The covenant made with Abraham was primarily a spiritual covenant, though it also had a national aspect. The words of this covenant are discussed by Paul in his writings to the Galatians in chapter 3:8-9 and 14 and in the book of Romans.

> 16 "For this reason it is by faith, that it might be in accordance with grace, in order that the promise may be certain to all the descendants, not only to those who are of the Law, but also to those who are of the faith of Abraham, who is the father of us all,
> 17 (as it is written, "A FATHER OF MANY NATIONS HAVE I MADE YOU") in the sight of Him whom he believed, even God, who gives life to the dead and calls into being that which does not exist.
> 18 In hope against hope he believed, in order that he might become a father of many nations, according to that which had been spoken, "SO SHALL YOUR DESCENDANTS BE."
>
> —Romans 4

This covenant is still in force and is essentially the same as the "new covenant" of the present age found in Romans 4:13-18, Galatians 3:15-18, and Hebrews 6:13-18. Children shared in the blessings of the covenant, received the sign of circumcision, and were reckoned as part of the congregation of Israel, 2 Chronicles 20:13 and Joel 2:16.

In the New Testament we read in Acts 2:39 and Colossians 2:11-12 that adult baptism is substituted for circumcision as the sign and seal of entrance into the covenant.

> 38 "And Peter said to them, "Repent" and let each of you be baptized in the name of Jesus Christ for the forgiveness of your sins; and you shall receive the gift of the Holy Spirit.
> 39 For the promise is for you and your children, and for all who are far off, as many as the Lord our God shall call to Himself.
>
> —Acts 2

The "New Covenant" is represented in Scripture as more gracious than the old, (Isaiah 54:13, Jeremiah 31:34, Hebrews 8:11), and therefore, would hardly exclude children. This is also unlikely in view of such passages as Matthew 19:14, Acts 2:39, and 1 Corinthians 7:14. Since, whole households were baptized, it is unlikely that these contained no children. (See Acts 16:15, 33; 1 Corinthians 1:16).

> 15 "And when she (Lydia) and her household had been baptized....
>
> 31 (Paul and Silas speaking to the jailer). And they said, "Believe in the Lord Jesus, and you shall be saved, you and your household."
> 32 And they spoke the word of the Lord to him together with all who were in his house.
> 33 And he took them that very hour of the night and washed their wounds, and immediately he was baptized, he and all his household."
>
> —Acts 16

Baptism IV

If the question is raised, as to how child baptism can function as a means of grace to strengthen spiritual life, the answer is that it can, at the very moment of the rite. The child must be of an age when he/she can fully understand the foundation truths as it strengthens the regenerate life, and can strengthen faith later on when the significance of baptism is more clearly understood. This varies from child to child, but must be evident. Its operation of importance is not necessarily limited to the very moment of its administration.

Reward Of Water Immersion

"And Peter said to them, "Repent" and let each of you be baptized in the name of Jesus Christ for the forgiveness of your sins: and you shall receive the <u>gift</u> of the Holy Spirit.

—Acts 2:38

Baptism IV

Lesson Study Review 10

1. What are the four things signifying the relationship between Old Testament circumcision and New Testament water baptism?

   (Colossians 2:11-12)

   A. _____

   B. _____

   C. _____

   D. _____

(See Genesis 17:10-11 and Romans 2:28-29)

2. Describe the relationship between Israel, Moses and water baptism.

   1 Cor. 10:1-2 _____

The pillar of fire that hovered over the Ark by night and the cloud that hovered over the Ark by day means they were led of the Holy Spirit during their trip. As the Israelites passed through the sea, which was a sign of Yahweh's miraculous deliverance, they saw the faces of the Egyptians no more. They closed the door to their past and water baptism can close the door to your past. And as they passed through the sea, they were baptized into Moses as Yahweh united them with their spiritual head.

3. Does water baptism have anything to do with the conscience? _____ (Yes or No)

   Explain your answer: 1 Peter 3:20b-21 _____

Baptism IV: Lesson Study Review 10

4. Research and write a 50-word essay giving reference to the responsibility of parents toward baby dedication in the New Testament and Old Testament.

Eternal Life Principles & Beyond

Mid-Summary Review

1. _____ and _____ toward God are inseparable in effecting a genuine conversion.

2. What is the summary definition of Repentance?

   A. _____

   B. _____

   C. _____

3. Scripture says, "We are _____ into His Lordship."

4. Give the meaning of the word "Repentance" in 50 words or more and give a short description of any typical experience.

   _____
   _____
   _____
   _____
   _____
   _____
   _____
   _____
   _____
   _____
   _____
   _____
   _____

5. Name the six foundation stones God has provided as a solid foundation before we go on to maturity.

   _____   _____
   _____   _____
   _____   _____

Mid-Summary Review

6. Baptism had to do with cleansing according to Acts 22:16, but the Word reveals we are not only cleansed by the water, but we are also cleansed by _____ and by the _____ and by _____.

7. A. Describe John the Baptizer's calling and why it was so significantly different than that of the Prophets of the OT and that of the Apostles of the NT.

_____
_____
_____
_____
_____
_____

B. Describe the changes in custom and law he was bringing to the people

_____
_____
_____
_____
_____
_____

8. The foundation of a building determines the maximum height of the building. So, when the winds blow and the rains fall, peace is not freedom from the storm, but there is _____ in the midst of the storm.

9. Do the elementary principles in Hebrews 6:1-2 give us what we need in a storm? In 25 words give support for your answer. _____ (Yes or No)

_____
_____
_____
_____

DOCTRINE 4

LAYING-ON-OF-HANDS I

    What Does The Old Testament Say About "Laying-On-Of-Hands"? 141

    What Does The New Testament Say About "Laying-On-Of-Hands"? 143

LAYING –ON-OF-HANDS II

    Laying-On-Of-Hands And The Reception Of The Holy Spirit 151

    The Significance Of The Laying-On-Of-Hands 151

    The Appointment Of The First Deacons 152

    The Ordination Of Ministers 152

    Separation To A Specific Work 153

    Care Should Be Taken In The Laying-On-Of-Hands For Ordination 153

    Who Should Lay-On-Hands? 154

My Inspirations, Challenges & Revelations:

Laying-On-Of Hands I

1 Now it came about after these things that Joseph was told, "Behold, your father is sick." So he took his two sons Manasseh and Ephraim with him.

2 When it was told to Jacob, "Behold, your son Joseph has come to you," Israel collected his strength and sat up in the bed.

3 Then Jacob said to Joseph, "God Almighty appeared to me at Luz in the land of Canaan and blessed me,

4 and He said to me, 'Behold, I will make you fruitful and numerous, and I will make you a company of peoples, and will give this land to your descendants after you for an everlasting possession.'

5 And now your two sons, who were born to you in the land of Egypt before I came to you in Egypt, are mine; Ephraim and Manasseh shall be mine, as Reuben and Simeon are.

6 But your offspring that have been born after them shall be yours; they shall be called by the names of their brothers in their inheritance.

7 Now as for me, when I came from Paddan, Rachel died, to my sorrow, in the land of Canaan on the journey, when there was still some distance to go to Ephrath; and I buried her there on the way to Ephrath (that is, Bethlehem)."

8 When Israel saw Joseph's sons, he said, "Who are these?"

9 And Joseph said to his father, "They are my sons, whom God has given me here". So, he said, "Bring them to me, please, that I may bless them."

10 Now the eyes of Israel were so dim from age that he could not see. Then Joseph brought them close to him, and he kissed them and embraced them.

11 And Israel said to Joseph, "I never expected to see your face, and behold, God has let me see your children as well."

12 Then Joseph took them from his knees, and bowed with his face to the ground.

13 And Joseph took them both, Ephraim with his right hand toward Israel's left and Manasseh with his left hand toward Israel's right, and brought them close to him.

14 But Israel stretched out his right hand and laid it on the head of Ephraim, who was the younger, and his left hand on Manasseh's head, crossing his hands, although Manasseh was the first-born.

15 And he blessed Joseph, and said,
"The God before whom my fathers Abraham and
Isaac walked, The God who has been my shepherd
all my life to this day,

16 The angel who has redeemed me from all evil,
Bless the lads;
And may my name live on in them.
And the names of my fathers Abraham and Isaac;
And may they grow into a multitude in the midst of
the earth."

17 When Joseph saw that his father laid his right hand on Ephraim's head, it displeased him; and he grasped his father's hand to remove it from Ephraim's head to Manasseh's head.

18 And Joseph said to his father, "Not so, my father, for this one is the first-born. Place your right hand on his head."

19 But his father refused and said, "I know, my son, I know; he also shall become a people and he also shall be great. However, his younger brother shall be greater than he, and his descendants shall become a multitude of nations."

20 And he blessed them that day, saying,
"By you Israel shall pronounce blessing, saying,
'May God make you like Ephraim and Manasseh!'"
Thus he put Ephraim before Manasseh.

21 Then Israel said to Joseph, "Behold, I am about to die, but God will be with you, and bring you back to the land of your fathers.

22 And I give you one portion more than your brothers, which I took from the hand of the Amorite with my sword and my bow."

—Genesis 48

Eternal Life Principles & Beyond

The doctrine of "laying-on-of-hands" is the fourth of the "First Principles" which form "the foundation" of the Believer's life.

Laying-on-of-hands occurs a number of times in the Bible, and we shall consider most of these. However, as an elementary Biblical doctrine it specifically refers to the reception of the Holy Spirit. The act of laying-on-of-hands signifies "*transference, transmission, impartation* and *identification.*"

What Does The Old Testament Say About "Laying-On-of-Hands"?

A. Jacob laid his hands on his grandchildren and blessed them

> 14 But Israel stretched out his right hand and laid it on the head of Ephraim, who was the younger, and his left hand on Manasseh's head crossing his hands, although Manasseh was the first-born.
> 15 And he blessed Joseph, and said, "The God before whom my fathers Abraham and Isaac walked, the God who has been my Shepherd all my life to this day,
> 16 The angel who has redeemed me from all evil, Bless the lads and may my name live on in them, And the names of my fathers Abraham and Isaac; And may they grow into a multitude in the midst of the earth."
>
> —Genesis 48

This is the first occurrence of the laying-on-of-hands for the purpose of symbolizing the *transmission of spiritual benefit.* With his hands laid on the heads of Ephraim and Manasseh, Israel prayed "The Angel which redeemed me from all evil, *bless the lads!*" Thus, in this first instance of the laying-on-of-hands, and the transference of a blessing, we are taught something of its symbolic meaning.

In verse 14 Joseph was questioning his father's authority of not adhering to the "Law of the First Born". Since a 'first born' usually is endowed with the temperament of taking on responsibilities of the younger siblings and property issues they usually have leadership qualities, and knowing that his father was almost blind he felt the right to question him. But Jacob was following Yahweh's Will.

B. The Israelite and his sacrificial offering

> "And he shall lay his hand on the head of the burnt offering, that it may be accepted before the Lord."
>
> —Leviticus 1:4

> "And he shall lay his hand on the head of his offering and slay it at the doorway of the tent of meeting, and Aaron's sons the priests, shall sprinkle the blood around on the alter."
>
> —Leviticus 3:2

Laying-On-Of-Hands I

God required the Israelites to bring an animal sacrifice (an unblemished lamb) to the door of the Tabernacle which was directly in front of the Brazen Alter. Before the sacrificial animal was slain and offered, the Israelite was required to "lay his hand on the head of the burnt offering", with the accompanying promise that it "may be accepted for him to make atonement on his behalf".

In putting his hand on the head of the sacrificial animal, the Israelite was indicating the transference of his sin and guilt to the victim, and by this symbolic act implying, "This animal is now myself, and its life is my life, thereby bearing my sin and guilt."

This Old Testament symbolical act of impartation was temporary, while Jesus' decision to take on the sin of the world is permanent.

We must take into account the intimacy involved and the responsibility taken by each man for the death of the animal which points to the Romans' responsibility for the execution of Jesus, but also the Jews whose hands on Him were culpritable.

As Jacob's act symbolized the transmission of blessing, the Israelite's act symbolized the *transmission or transference of sin and guilt.*

This is further seen in the sacrificial ceremony on the Day of Atonement. On this great day of national contrition, Aaron, the High Priest, represented the people. The goat represents the nation.

> "Then Aaron shall lay both of his hands on the head of the live goat, and confess over it all the iniquities of the sons of Israel, and all their transgressions in regard to all their sins; and he shall lay them on the head of the goat and send it away into the wilderness by the hand of a man who stands in readiness."
>
> —Leviticus 16:21

Here *transmission* and *transference* are clearly symbolized as Aaron confesses all the sins of the children of Israel over the goat. We cannot begin to conclude the number of hours this may have taken. Certainly those in his hearing range were convicted of their sins.

    C. The children of Israel and the Levites

> (At the tent of meeting) "....present the Levites before the Lord, and the sons of Israel shall lay their hands on the Levites."
>
> —Numbers 8:10

> "Then after that the Levites may go in to serve the tent of meeting."
>
> —Numbers 8:15

The Levites were ordained by God to "serve the tent of meeting" (vs 15), purporting to do the service of the Tabernacle. In this service they represented the congregation. The "laying-on-of-hands signified that the obligation of the Levites was to personally assist in the service of the sanctuary, and at that time the sins of the congregation were *transferred* from the whole congregation to the Levites." In doing so, the responsibility of the service of the tabernacle was transferred. So, again, we see the principle of *transference* and *identification* symbolized in the laying-on-of-hands.

D. Moses and Joshua, Numbers 27:15-23, Deuteronomy 34:9

In appointing a successor to Moses, God instructed the greater leader to "Take Joshua the son of Nun, a man in whom is the Spirit, and lay your hand on him." In so doing, God said, "and *you* shall put some of your authority on him." That there was also at that time an *impartation* of spiritual *enablement* is indicated in the Deuteronomy passage, which says that "Joshua the son of Nun was filled with the spirit of wisdom, for Moses had laid his hands on him." Here honor is being *transferred*. The leader, being the greater, is bestowing honor on his successor. Moses is saying, "I approve of this young man."

I encourage *you* to take your concordance and research the word "honor". The whole structure of God supports the honor system. And Jesus has put His honor on us in the Great Commission.

The Scripture in Deuteronomy indicates the *imparting* of a spiritual enablement. It tells us "Joshua was full of the Spirit of Wisdom."

What Does The New Testament Say About "Laying-On-of-Hands"?

A. Jesus and His earthly ministry of healing

"....He laid His hands upon a few sick people and healed them."
—Mark 6:5

"And while the sun was setting, all who had any sick with various diseases brought them to Him; and laying His hands on everyone of them, He was *healing* them."
—Luke 4:40

"And He (Jesus) laid His hands on her; and immediately she was made erect again, and began glorifying God."
—Luke 13:13

There is a significant contrast between Mark 6:5 and Luke 4:40. In His own country (Mark 6:1) where His relations lived and during one of His earlier visits when He was in danger of His life, He could only heal "a few sick people" because of their persistent unbelief. Only a few in this village had faith to come to Him for healing. But in Capernaum, a city in Galilee, (Luke 4:40) it is interesting to observe He spent almost

Laying-On-Of-Hands I

the whole day and night healing all those who came to Him because of their faith. Recorded in Luke 13:13 is the story of the women who pressed through the crowd for her healing. She was bent over for 18 years!

B. Jesus imparting a blessing to little children

> 13 "Then some children were brought to Him so that He might lay His hands on them and pray:
>
> 15 "....laying His hands on them...."
>
> —Matthew 19

C. The Great Commission and healing

> "....they will lay hands on the sick, and they will recover."
>
> —Mark 16:18

D. The fulfillment of the Great Commission

> "And at the hands of the apostles many signs and wonders were taking place among the people."
>
> —Acts 5:12

> "And Ananias departed and entered the house, and after laying his hands on him said, 'Brother Saul, the Lord Jesus, Who appeared to you on the road by which you were coming, has sent me so that you may *regain your sight,* and be *filled with the Holy Spirit.*'"
>
> —Acts 9:17

Here we see Paul received a double blessing through the laying-on-of-hands.

> "Therefore they spent a long time there speaking boldly with reliance upon the Lord, who was bearing witness to the word of His grace, granting that *signs and wonders* be done by their hands."
>
> —Acts 14:3

> "And God was performing extraordinary *miracles* by the hands of Paul."
>
> —Acts 19:11

> "And it came about that the father of Publius was lying in bed afflicted with recurrent fever and dysentery; and Paul went in to see him and after he had prayed, he laid his hands on him and *healed* him."
>
> —Acts 28:8

The above Scriptures speak of four benefits transferred to Believers after the laying-on-of-hands.

Comments:

The laying-on-of-hands is a meaningful act. It is used almost exclusively as a sign that something is being given. When we talk about "first principles," we are talking about the reception of the Holy Spirit. No man should minister without knowing all the proper spiritual benefits with the laying-on-of-hands. There is an impartation of God taking place. We are not placing empty hands on an empty head, nor is it symbolic. It is a vital part of Biblical ministry and we are transferring blessings to another person's wellbeing.

A lesser spiritual significance we express today, yet the same principle is shaking hands when greeting a friend. We are touching. We are saying, "I'm reaching out to you with a warm greeting". The same principle is communicated when we touch a grieving person. Sometimes words fail and, in offering compassion and comfort, we put our hand on their arm or shoulder or take their hand. We are saying, "I'm reaching out to you. I am taking part in your grief. My heart is relating to your loss." It goes beyond empathy and sympathy.

We impart concern when rubbing the back of a crying baby or rubbing a body part that has been injured and is in pain. Something is being given.

Hebrews 5:8-12 forever informs us that First Principles are an ongoing invitation to us. These Elementary Principles are meaningful and have been given to the Believer exclusively! They are our privilege as an heir in the Kingdom of God.

Laying-On-Of-Hands I

Lesson Study Review 11

1. Listed are the Old Testament occurrences of laying-on-of-hands. Tell what is actually taking place.

   Gen. 48:14-16 _____

   Lev. 1:4 & 3:2 _____

   Lev. 16:21 _____

   Nu. 8:9-11 _____

   Nu. 27:15-23 _____

   Deut. 24:9 _____

2. For what purpose did our Lord lay on hands during His earthly ministry?

   A. Mark 5:5 _____

      Luke 4:40 _____

      Luke 13:13 _____

   B. Matt. 9:18,25 _____

   C. Matt. 19:13, 15 _____

   D. Mark 16:18 _____

3. What does the act of laying-on-of-hands in the New Testament signify?

   A. _____

   B. _____

   C. _____

   D. _____

Eternal Life Principles & Beyond

4. The following Scriptures are the fulfillment of the Great Commission. Write by whom and what happened

Acts 5:12 _____

Acts 9:17 _____

Acts 14:3 _____

Acts 19:11 _____

Acts 28:8 _____

My Inspirations, Challenges & Revelations:

Laying-On-Of-Hands II

1 And Saul was in hearty agreement with putting him to death. And on that day a great persecution arose against the church in Jerusalem; and they were scattered through out the regions of Judea and Samaria, except the apostles.

2 And some devout men buried Stephen, and made loud lamentation over him.

3 But Saul began ravaging the church, entering house after house; and dragging off men and women, he would put them in prison.

4 Therefore, those who had been scattered went about preaching the word.

5 And Philip went down to the city of Samaria and began proclaiming Christ to them.

6 And the multitudes with one accord were giving attention to what was said by Philip, as they heard and saw the signs which he was performing.

7 For in the case of many who had unclean spirits, they were coming out of them shouting with a loud voice; and many who had been paralyzed and lamed were healed.

8 And there was much rejoicing in that city.

9 Now there was a certain man named Simon, who formerly was practicing magic in the city, and astonishing the people of Samaria, claiming to be someone great;

10 and they all, from smallest to greatest, were giving attention to him, saying, "This man is what is called the Great Power of God."

11 And they were giving him attention because he had for a long time astonished them with his magic arts.

12 But when they believed Philip preaching the good news about the kingdom of God and the name of Jesus Christ, they were being baptized, men and women alike.

13 And even Simon himself believed; and after being baptized, he continued on with Philip; and as he observed signs and great miracles taking place, he was constantly amazed.

14 Now when the apostles in Jerusalem heard that Samaria had received the word of God, they sent them Peter and John,

15 who came down and prayed for them, that they might receive the Holy Spirit.

16 For He had not yet fallen upon any of them; they had simply been baptized in the name of the Lord Jesus.

17 Then they began laying their hands on them, and they were receiving the Holy Spirit.

18 Now when Simon saw that the Spirit was bestowed through the laying on of the apostles' hands, he offered them money,

19 saying, "Give this authority to me as well, so that everyone on whom I lay my hands may receive the Holy Spirit."

20 But Peter said to him, "May your silver perish with you, because you thought you could obtain the gift of God with money!

21 "You have no part or portion in this matter, for your heart is not right before God.

22 "Therefore repent of this wickedness of yours, and pray the Lord that if possible, the intention of your heart may be forgiven you.

23 "For I see that you are in the gall of bitterness and in the bondage of iniquity."

24 But Simon answered and said, "Pray to the Lord for me yourselves, so that nothing of what you have said may come upon me."

25 And so, when they had solemnly testified and spoken the word of the Lord, they started back to Jerusalem, and were preaching the gospel to many villages of the Samaritans.

—Acts 8:1-25

Eternal Life Principles & Beyond

Laying-On-Of-Hands And The Reception Of The Holy Spirit

There are five recorded instances of receiving the Holy Spirit in the Book of the Acts of the Holy Spirit by the Apostles. Two of them describe immediate or direct reception and three describe mediate or indirect reception.

On the Day of Pentecost, the Holy Spirit was given immediately, or directly, without any laying-on-of-hands. This was also true of Cornelius' household. Thus, the Holy Spirit was immediately and directly given to the Jews at Pentecost and to the Gentiles at Cornelius' house. The other three instances describe receiving the Holy Spirit immediately or indirectly, with the laying-on-of-hands.

The Significance Of The Laying-On-Of-Hands

A. Samaria – Read Acts 8:5-17

> 5 "Philip went down to the city of Samaria, and preached *Christ* unto them."

Philip's preaching was accompanied with astounding healings and deliverances, causing "great joy in that city" (vs 8).

> 12 "When they believed Philip preaching the things concerning the kingdom of God, and the name of Jesus Christ, *they were baptized,* both men and women.

Verse 13 says, "they beheld great miracles and signs, deliverance was taking place, healings were taking place and there was great joy. And a convert, Simon, accompanied Philip on his mission."

> 14 Now when the Apostles in Jerusalem heard that Samaria had received the word of God, they sent them Peter and John
> 15 who came down and prayed for them, that they might receive the Holy Spirit.
> 16 However, for He [the Holy Spirit] had not yet fallen upon any of them; they had simply been baptized in the name of the Lord Jesus.
> 17 "Then they [Peter, John & Phillip] *began laying their hands on them, and they were receiving the Holy Spirit!*"

B. Saul of Tarsus – Read Acts 9:1-19

> 17 "And Ananias went his way and entered the house; and *laying his hands on him* he said, "Brother Saul, the Lord Jesus, who appeared to you on the road as you came, has sent me that you may receive your sight and *be filled with the Holy Spirit.*"

This Saul of Tarsus, later called Paul, received a double blessing. He received his sight and was filled with the Holy Spirit at the same time.

Laying-On-of-Hands II

C. Ephesus – Read Acts 19:1-7

In Ephesus, Paul found "certain disciples" standing in front of the synagogue who knew about Jesus, but only in terms of John the Baptist's message. The distinctive spiritual life of a New Covenant community was lacking, causing Paul to ask,

> 2 "Did you receive the Holy Spirit when *you* believed?" To which they replied, "We have not so much as heard whether there is a Holy Spirit."

Paul then brought them up-to-date, presenting the full message of the Lord Jesus Christ.

> 5 "When they heard this, they were baptized in the name of the Lord Jesus."
> 6 "And when *Paul had laid hands on them, the Holy Spirit came upon them, and they spoke with tongues and prophesied*".

The Appointment Of The First Deacons

– Read Acts 6:1-6

> 6 "….whom (seven qualified men) they set before the apostles and when they had prayed, *they laid hands on them.*"

The purpose of appointing deacons was for daily ministration to the Hellenistic widows as well as the Hebrew widows. The office of deacon is a high and holy work of caring for the distress existing among the members of the church. It is always a high and holy work to care for those in the Body of Christ. But the foremost high and holy work is the fulfillment of that specific "call" which the Most High places on one's life. We must set everyone free, to perform their call, from everything except prayer.

The Ordination Of Ministers

> "Do not neglect the gift that is in you, which was given to you by prophecy with the *laying on of the hands of the eldership."*
>
> —1 Timothy 4:14

> "Therefore I remind *you* to stir up the gift of God which is in you *through the laying on of my hands."*
>
> —2 Timothy 1:6

Paul, along with the presbyters, ordained Timothy.

Simply put, presbyters are elders, a superintendent or an overseer. They are the guides of each church, the senior persons, the shepherds of the people. They determine the will of God for their specific assembly. It must be noted that a pastor is not exempt from accountability to any pre-selected committee or authority in the local assembly.

The Deacons in Acts 6:1-6, on the other hand, are a group of men chosen by the people (vs 3) who are designated certain responsibilities. The requirements being they were of good reputation, full of the Spirit and of wisdom. Scripture does not indicate they ever laid hands on anybody. They were responsible for the widows and had a hands-on ministry in the community. These men were from their locality and were picked by the village/town's people. As communities go, the people obviously knew of their virtues.

Although the deacons chosen in Acts 6:1-6 were all men, the word "servant" found in Romans 16:1 describing Pheobe is *"diaconos"* the same Greek word translated "deacons" in those verses. Paul met Pheobe while ministering in Cenchrea and in Romans 16:1, we notice he called her *"our sister* who is a *servant* of the church in Cenchrea" and in vs 2, he called her "a *helper of many as well as myself"*. Whether she was called a servant/deacon before he arrived we do not know. However, it was obvious he recognized the call upon her life and that she carried the necessary qualifications for the office of deacon, thereby conferring this title upon her as he did Timothy, Titus and others.

When Paul stated that she has "helped him" the verse speculates that he may have been ill when he arrived at Cenchrea and she may have nursed him back to health. In any case, as he observed her heart during this time, he considered her to be trustworthy and dependable to carry his letter from Corinth which would become a record to all the churches she visited along the way to Rome. When he chose her to be his private messenger to deliver the epistle to Rome, he also expressed his trust in her by bestowing this great honor upon her. Pheobe would have to travel a great distance by foot, by animal and/or by boat and each mode of transportation could be dangerous. Paul asked the Roman Christians to ".... receive her in the Lord in a manner worthy of being in the company of the saints, and that you help her in whatever matter she may have need of you....". In other words, he wanted her to be received with confidence and respect, and he expected that they would aid her to the utmost of their power (Romans 16:2).

Separation To A Specific Work

"As they ministered to the Lord and fasted, the Holy Spirit said, 'Now separate to Me Barnabas and Saul for the work to which I have called them.' Then, having fasted and prayed, and *laid hands on them,* sent them away.'"

—Acts 13:2-3

The separation to a specific work was after they heard from the Holy Spirit. Notice verse 4 says that they are being sent out by the Holy Spirit and not by man.

Care Should Be Taken In The Laying-On-Of-Hands For Ordination

"Do not lay hands on anyone hastily!" —1 Timothy 5:22

"Do not be in a hurry in *the laying on of hands!"* —1 Timothy 5:22 Amplified

"Never be in a hurry to ordain a man!" —1 Timothy 5:22 JB Phillips

Laying-On-of-Hands II

A new Believer's faith has not been tested or put into the fire. All events strengthen or weaken our faith. The Holy Spirit is pivotal in our efforts if we choose righteousness over the flesh. The candidate must be well-proved before being appointed to the sacred ministry. Elders who are rash in ordaining will make themselves partakers in other men's sins.

Who Should Lay-On-Hands?

The laying-on-of-hands is not to be practiced indiscriminately. The Scriptures are quite explicit as to the kinds of people who should participate in this God-ordained action. Let us consider further the permission and restrictions as indicated in the Scriptures.

    A. Believers may lay on hands for healing   —Mark 16: 17-19

> 17 "And these signs will follow *those who believe:....*"
> 18 *They will lay hands* on the *sick,* and *they will recover.*

It is profitable to read the context of this quotation and note what these believers believed. Since faith is measurable, some believe more than others. The Bible speaks of "no faith", "little faith", "mustard seed faith", and "great faith". The basis of faith is the Word of God. We have a tendency to measure our own faith by our knowledge of, and trust in, the Word.

    B. Apostles and disciples laid on hands for the reception of the Holy Spirit

    1. Apostles

> "And when Simon saw that through the *laying on of the apostles' hands the Holy Spirit was given....*"
>
> —Acts 8:18

There is little need for us to discuss the qualifications of the 12 Apostles chosen by Christ before His death, resurrection and ascension. These were men appointed and anointed of God, whose lives and ministries were committed and spiritually vital.

However, let's digress for just a moment. The Apostle Paul wrote a letter to the Jews living in Rome around 55-56 AD during his third missionary journey. We know that Paul was not one of the 12 original Apostles chosen by Jesus while he walked on earth so let's talk about apostleship for a second. Many believers assume there were only 12 apostles and some imagine there were perhaps 14 or 15 with Paul being the 15th or even the 16th. However, a closer study of the Book of Acts and a few of Paul's epistles, reveal there are a total 24 apostles. 23 are named and one is not named. And in Romans 16:7 the Apostle Junias may just be a female. The point is that — the office of the Apostle scanned many years well beyond the first century church. One other point worthy of mention is in Revelation 21 as John describes the New Jerusalem that comes down out of heaven, he mentions in verse 14 that — "The wall of the city had twelve foundation stones, and on them were the twelve names of the <u>twelve apostles of the Lamb</u>." The Scriptures do not give us a clue as to who is the twelfth apostle. If God always is, and always was, and always will be, can we not have apostles here on earth today?

    2. Disciples Acts 9:10-18

> 10 "Now there was a certain *disciple,* named Ananias....
> 11 And the Lord said to him, "Arise and go the street called Straight....
> 12 and lay hands on him, so that he might regain his sight."
>
> 17" ....(and Ananias) *laying his hands* on him (Paul) said, *"regain your sight, and be filled with the Holy Spirit!"*

Let us also carefully notice the qualifications of Ananias the disciple. As a disciple, he was 1) subject to the disciplines of the Lord Jesus Christ. He was a 2) devout (reverential, pious) man having a 3) good testimony with all the Jews who dwelt at Damascus (Acts 22:12). When the Lord called him, he replied, "Here I am, Lord." (Acts 9:10), implying he was 4) a ready man! When the Lord instructed him to go on what appeared to be a dangerous and unpleasant task, he went, showing that he was an 5) obedient man.

    3. Apostles and elders laid on hands for ordination

> "....the *laying-on-of-hands* of the *eldership."*
>
>   —Timothy 4:14
>
> "....the gift of God which is in *you through the laying on of my (*Paul) *hands."*
>
>   —2 Timothy 1:6

The qualifications of the apostle has been previously addressed.

There is a high standard set for elders and bishops in the following Scriptures:

>   1 It is a trustworthy statement: if any man aspires to the office of overseer, it is a fine work he desires to do.
>   2 An overseer, then, must be above reproach, the husband of one wife, temperate, prudent, respectable, hospitable, able to teach,
>   3 not addicted to wine or pugnacious, but gentle, uncontentious, free from the love of money,
>   4 He must be one who manages his own household well, keeping his children under control with all dignity
>   5 (but if a man does not know how to manage his own household, how will he take care of the church of God?)
>   6 and not a new convert, lest he become conceited and fall into the condemnation incurred by the devil.

Laying-On-of-Hands II

> 7 And he must have a good reputation with those outside the church, so that he may not fall into reproach and the snare of the devil.
>
> —1 Timothy 3:1-7

The office of Bishop is a divine appointment and not of human invention. It requires diligence and application, a work of the greatest importance. He should look to their work more than to the honor and advantage of their office.

The term "Bishop" is an Anglo-Saxon term coming from the Greek word "*episcopes*" and the Latin "*episcous*" meaning to "look over" or "inspect over" signifying one who has the inspection or oversight of a place, person or business such as a superintendent.

> 5 "and appoint elders in every city as I directed you,
>
> 6 namely, if any man be above reproach, the husband of one wife, having children who believe, not accused of dissipation or rebellion.
>
> 7 For the overseer must be above reproach as God's steward, not self-willed, not quick-tempered, not addicted to wine, not pugnacious, not fond of sordid gain,
>
> 8 but hospitable, loving what is good, sensible, just, devout, self-controlled,
>
> 9 holding fast the faithful word which is in accordance with the teaching, that he may be able both to exhort in sound doctrine and to refute those who contradict."
>
> —Titus 1:5-9

Laying-On-Of-Hands II
Lesson Study Review 12

1. What is the significance of the laying-on-of-hands in terms of foundation principles? Tell what happened.

    A. Acts 8:12-17 _____

    B. Acts 9:1-8 _____

    C. Acts 19:1-7 _____

2. Why did the Apostles lay hands on the deacons?

    _____

    _____

3. What accompanied the laying-on-of-hands in the ordination of ministers?

    A. 1 Tim 4:14 _____

    B. 2 Tim 1:6 _____

4. Are there special purposes for the laying-on-of-hands?

    Acts 13:2-3 _____

5. Should care be taken by the elders in the laying-on-of-hands for ordination?

    _____ (Yes or No)   Why?

    1 Tim 5:22a _____

    _____

    _____

6. Who is qualified to minister with the laying-on-of-hands?

    A. Mk 16:17-18 _____

    B. Acts 8:18 _____

    C. 1 Tim 4:14 _____

157

Lesson Study Review 12

7. Was the "laying-on-of-hands" to be practiced after Christ returned to heaven? Support your answer in 50 words or more.

___

Give a short example of your experience, if applicable.

___

DOCTRINE 5

RESURRECTION OF THE DEAD I

What Are The Three Resurrections In The New Testament To Which Our Faith Must Relate?..162

What Is The Meaning Of The Word "Resurrection"?..162

Did Jesus, The Christ, Rise From The Dead?...162

Was Jesus, The Christ, Seen After His Resurrection?..162

Did He Rise With The Same Body That Was Crucified?...163

Did The Old Testament Speak About The Resurrection Of Christ?..........................165

Is It Necessary To Believe In The Resurrection Of The Lord Jesus Christ?.............165

What Does The Resurrection Of Jesus, The Christ Declare?....................................166

RESURRECTION OF THE DEAD II

In The Present, What Is The Spiritual Resurrection Of The Believer In Jesus, The Christ?..172

Does Water Baptism Signify A "Divine Order"?..174

How Is The Resurrection Signified?..175

What Are The Evidences Of This Resurrection..175

RESURRECTION OF THE DEAD III

When Is The Future Resurrection To Take Place?..179

How Many Shall Be Raised In The Resurrection?..181

Who Does The Raising?...181

Did The Apostles Preach The Resurrection?..182

What Kind Of Bodies Will Believers Have?...182

What Effect Should The Resurrection Have On A Believer's Conduct?..................184

What Scripture Refers To A Body Like That Of Our Risen Lord?...........................185

My Inspirations, Challenges & Revelations:

The Resurrection Of The Dead I

1 Now after the Sabbath, as it began to dawn toward the first day of the week, Mary Magdalene and the other Mary came to look at the grave.

2 And behold, a severe earthquake had occurred, for an angel of the Lord descended from heaven and came and rolled away the stone and sat upon it.

3 and his appearance was like lightning, and his garment as white as snow;

4 and the guards shook for fear of him, and became like dead men.

5 And the angel answered and said to the women, "Do not be afraid; for I know that you are looking for Jesus who has been crucified.

6 "He is not here, for He has risen, just as He said. Come, see the place where He was lying.

7 "And go quickly and tell His disciples that He has risen from the dead; and behold, He is going before you into Galilee, there you will see Him; behold, I have told you."

8 And they departed quickly from the tomb with fear and great joy and ran to report it to His disciples.

9 And behold, Jesus met them and greeted them. And they came up and took hold of His feet and worshipped Him.

10 Then Jesus said to them, "Do not be afraid; go and take word to My brethren to leave for Galilee, and there they shall see Me."

—Matthew 28

"Resurrection of the dead" is the fifth of the six principles referred to as "foundational" in Hebrews 6.

A commitment in heart and mind to the revelation of the Word of God concerning "resurrection" is essential to a sound foundation. Error or weakness here will affect the whole structure of a Believer's life. What do I mean? It is through faith in a resurrected Christ that allows you to know Jesus is sitting in the heavenlies at the right hand of the Father and that gives meaning to certain hope of the resurrection of our own bodies in the future. In fact, Paul says, "if you do not believe in a resurrection your faith is in vain." (1 Corinthians 15:13-14)

What Are The Three Resurrections In The New Testament To Which Our Faith Must Relate?

1. The resurrection of Jesus Christ – Past
2. The spiritual resurrection of the believer in Jesus Christ through baptism – Present
3. The ultimate resurrection of "all that are in the graves" - Future

What Is The Meaning Of The Word "Resurrection"?

The Greek word *"anastasis"* means "a raising-up again or rising-up again". In its verb form it means, "to cause to stand up or rise; to raise up; to raise from sleep and from the dead, standing up again, raised to life again, rising again and moral recovery from spiritual truth." It is used in the past, present and future tense. (Strong's #386)

Did Jesus, The Christ Rise From The Dead?

The angel who is speaking to the two named Mary said.

> "He is not here, for *He has risen*, just as He said. Come; see the place where He was lying."
>
> —Matthew 28:6

> "But now *Christ has been raised from the dead.*"
>
> —1 Corinthians 15:20

There are about 104 references to the resurrection of Christ in the New Testament. The resurrection was the foundation for apostolic preaching and practically every sermon in the Book of Acts refers to it.

Also see – Acts 2:24; 3:26; 4:10; 5:30; 13:33-34, 37; Romans 4:24; 8:11, 34; 1 Corinthians 6:14; 2 Corinthians 4:14; Galatians 1:1; Ephesians 1:20; 1 Thessalonians 1:10; 2 Timothy 2:8.

Was Jesus, The Christ, Seen After His Resurrection?

> "To these (120) He also presented Himself alive, after His suffering, by many convincing proofs, appearing to them over a period of forty days, and speaking of the things concerning the kingdom of God."
>
> —Acts 1:3

> "After His suffering He showed Himself alive to them in many convincing ways, and appeared to them repeatedly over a period of forty days talking to them about the affairs of the kingdom of God."
>
> —Acts 1:3 JB Phillips

"....and that He appeared to Cephas, then to the twelve. After that He appeared to more than five hundred brethren at one time, most of whom remain until now, but some have fallen asleep; then He appeared to James, then to all the apostles; and last of all, as it were to one untimely born, He appeared to me also."

—1 Corinthians 15:5-8

Also see – Matthew 28:6, 9, 17; Mark 16:1-5, 6, 7, 9, 12, 14; Luke 23:54-56; 24:1-3, 6, 12, 16-38; John 20:14-20; 21:14; Acts 1:22; 2:32; 3:15; 4:33; 10:40-41; 13:30-31; 1 Timothy 3:15-16.

From these passages, we see that Jesus was careful to give His disciples the clearest evidence that, after His resurrection, He had a real body, and that His body was the same that had been crucified.

Did He Rise With The Same Body That Was Crucified?

The answer is "yes" and "no". The Bible does not address this issue. We can only speculate from the natural because the natural comes before the spiritual. Yes, it was the same body, but it was also raised a spiritual body and completely glorified. His post-resurrection appearances were also a body in transition. His body saw no corruption. Logically, bodies do not walk through walls, at least not bodies that contain blood. That can be frightening. Since the disciples thought He was a ghost, it is possible it was because He had no blood. Blood gives color to the countenance. When Jesus rose from the dead, He was not in gaseous form. He was visible and tangible and was identified by the wounds of Calvary. He was "glorified" and was recognizable by His wounds and His features.

> "Jesus answered and said to them, 'Destroy this temple, and in three days I will raise it up.' The Jews therefore said, 'It took forty-six years to build this temple, and will You raise it up in three days?' But He was speaking of the temple of His body. When therefore He was raised from the dead, His disciples remembered that He said this...."
>
> —John 2:19-22

> "Now the women who had come with Him out of Galilee followed after, and saw the tomb and how His body was laid. And they returned and prepared spices and perfumes. And on the Sabbath they rested according to the commandment. But on the first day of the week, at early dawn, they came to the tomb, bringing the spices, which they had prepared. And they found the stone rolled away from the tomb, but when they entered, they did not find the body of the Lord Jesus."
>
> —Luke 23:55 - 24:3

Luke 23 states that the women who went to His grave did not find the body, meaning His physical, visible body.

Resurrection of the Dead I

> "And while they were telling these things, He himself stood in their midst. But they were startled and frightened and thought that they were seeing a spirit. And He said to them, "Why are you troubled, and why do doubts arise in your hearts? See My hands and My feet, that it is I Myself;...."
>
> —Luke 24:36-40

The Lord's body was no longer subject to the limitations of a mortal body in this present world order. Jesus could now appear or disappear at will; He could enter a closed room; He could pass between earth and heaven, and He could pass between earth and Hades. However, making allowances for these changes, it was still in other respects the same body that had been crucified.

> "See My hands and My feet, that it is I Myself; touch Me and see, for a spirit does not have flesh and bones as you see that I have.' [And when He had said this, He showed them His hands and His feet. He had flesh and bones.]
>
> —Luke 24:39-40

In Luke 24, notice Jesus did not say, "for a spirit does not have flesh and blood...."

> "Then He said to Thomas, 'Reach here your finger, and see My hands; and reach here your hand, and put it into My side; and be not unbelieving, but believing.' Thomas answered and said to Him, 'My Lord and my God!'"
>
> —John 20:27-28

In John 20, Thomas truncated (stopped short) in his thinking. We must never stop short in our thinking, but give time for the Holy Spirit to reveal the things of God to us. Always think of Jesus in His fullness from "incarnation" to "glorification".

From these passages above, we see that Jesus immediately reassured them, and gave them positive proof of His identity and of the reality of His body. He had a real body, and His body was the same that had been crucified. The evidence of this was in His hands and feet and in His side, which still bore the marks of the nails and of the spear.

Not to be redundant, it's very important and necessary to re-emphasize the following verses from the previous page:

Luke 23:55 to 24:3 states, that the women who went to His grave did not find the body, meaning His physical, visible body.

In Luke 24:40, notice Jesus did not say, "....for a spirit does not have flesh and blood" He said, "....for a spirit does not have flesh and bones." [This means an angel does not have flesh and bones].

In John 20:27-28 Thomas truncated in his thinking. We must never stop short in our thinking, but give time for the Holy Spirit to reveal the things of God to us.

Again, we must always think of Jesus in the fullness of His "incarnation" to His "glorification".

Did The Old Testament Speak About The Resurrection Of Christ?

"And so, because he (David) was a prophet and knew that God had sworn to him with an oath to seat one of His descendants upon His throne, he looked ahead and spoke of the resurrection of the Christ."
—Acts 2:30-31

"Being, therefore, a prophet (David), and knowing that God had sworn with an oath to him, that of the fruit of his loins he would set one upon his throne; he foreseeing this spake of the resurrection of the Christ...."
—Acts 2:30-31 ASV

The message of Calvary without the "resurrection" is not sufficient for salvation. The sacrifice for sin would not have been adequate. In the Book of Acts, the preachers never finished their message at the cross and you are not telling the Good News if you stop at the cross. Giving half a story is falsehood and is not partial truth.

Is It Necessary To Believe In The Resurrection Of The Lord Jesus Christ?

"That if you confess with your mouth Jesus as Lord, and believe in your heart that God raised him from the dead, you shall be *saved*."
—Romans 10:9

"If thou shalt confess with thy mouth Jesus as Lord, and shalt believe in thine heart that God raised him from the dead, thou shalt be saved."
—Romans 10:9 ASV

"Now I make known to you, brethren, the gospel which I preached to you, which also you received, in which also you stand, by which also you are saved, if you hold fast the word which I preached to you, unless you believed in vain. For I delivered to you as of first importance what I also received, that Christ died for our sins according to the Scriptures, and that He was buried, and that He was raised on the third day according to the Scriptures, and that He appeared to Cephas, then to the twelve."
—1 Corinthians 15:1-5

"But let me recall to you, brethren, the Good News which I brought you, which you accepted, and on which you are standing, through which also you are obtaining salvation if you bear in mind the words in which I proclaimed it—unless indeed your faith has been unreal from the very first. For I

Resurrection of the Dead I

repeated to you the all-important fact which I had been taught, that Christ died for our sins in accordance with the Scriptures; that He was buried, and was seen by Peter, and then by the Twelve."

—1 Corinthians 15:1-5 Weymouth

What Does The Resurrection Of Jesus Christ Declare?

A. Jesus Christ "is" the Son of God (not "was")

"Who was *declared* (openly designated) *the son of God* with power by the *resurrection from the dead*, according to the Spirit of holiness, Jesus Christ our Lord."

—Romans 1:4

"And (as to His divine nature) according to the Spirit of holiness, was *openly designated the son of God* in power — in a striking, triumphant and miraculous manner — by His *resurrection from the dead*, even Jesus Christ our Lord, the Messiah, the Anointed One."

—Romans 1:4 Amplified

B. Death is defeated because of the resurrection

"....knowing that *Christ*, having *raised* from the dead, is never to die again; death *no longer* is *master over Him.*"

—Romans 6:9

"We can be sure that the *risen Christ* never dies again — death's power to touch Him is *finished!*"

—Romans 6:9 JB Phillips

C. Jesus Christ is supreme over all created beings because of the resurrection

"And Jesus came up and spoke to them, saying, '*all authority* has been given to Me *in heaven and on earth!*'"

—Matthew 28:18

"....which He brought about in Christ, *when He raised Him from the dead,* and *seated* Him at His right hand in the heavenly places, *far above* all rule and authority and power and dominion and *every name that is named,* not only in this age, but also in the one to come. And *He put all things in subjection under His feet,* and gave Him as *head over all things* to the *church,* which is His body, the fullness of Him who fills all in all."

—Ephesians 1:20-23

Eternal Life Principles & Beyond

"That power is the same divine energy which was demonstrated in Christ *when He raised Him from the dead* and gave Him the *place of supreme honor* in Heaven — a place that is *infinitely superior* to any conceivable command, authority, power or control, and which carries with it a *name far beyond any name* that could ever be used in this world or in the world to come. *God has placed everything under the power of Christ* and has set Him up as *head of everything* for the *church*. For the Church is His Body, and in that body lives fully the one Who fills the whole wide universe."

—Ephesians 1:20-23 Amplified

Again, never stop short in your thinking in the middle of the miracle. Always think of Jesus in His fullness from incarnation to glorification.

    D. There is a Man on the Throne of the universe because of the resurrection

"....but *He*, having offered one sacrifice for sins for all time, *sat down at the right hand of God.*"

—Hebrews 10:12 NKJ

"But this man, after He had offered one sacrifice for sins forever, *sat down at the right hand of God.*"

—Hebrews 10:12 ASV

    E. Believers are justified because of the resurrection

"He who was delivered up because of our transgressions, and *was raised because of our justification.*"

—Romans 4:25

    F. There is a new life source for men because of the resurrection

"Blessed be the God and Father of our Lord Jesus Christ, who according to His great mercy *has caused us to be born again to a living hope through the resurrection of Jesus Christ from the dead.*"

—1 Peter 1:3

    G. Future judgment is assured because of the resurrection

"....because He has fixed a *day in which He will judge the world in righteousness* through *a man* whom He has appointed, having furnished proof to all men *by raising Him from the dead.*"

—Acts 17:31

"Because He has fixed a *day when He will judge the world righteously* (justly) by a *man* Whom He has destined and appointed for that task, and He has made this credible and given conviction and assurance and evidence to everyone *by raising him from the dead.*"

—Acts 17:31 Amplified

Resurrection of the Dead I

Summary:

Without Christ's death, burial and resurrection, we have nothing. The resurrection of Christ separates Christianity from religions that serve a dead god. All other world religions are built upon the teachings of their founders, who are dead, or will die. Christianity alone is built upon the death, burial and resurrection of Jesus, the Christ, the Founder. Without the resurrection of Christ, Christianity is reduced to the level of other religions.

Christ's death was a voluntary act (John10:17-18), a manifestation of His Divine Love (1 John 3:16) for the whole world (John 3:16).

For us, it is the power of God.

> "But if the Spirit of Him who raised Jesus from the dead dwells in you, He who raised Christ Jesus from the dead will also give life to your mortal bodies through His Spirit who indwells you."
>
> —Romans 8:11

Life in Christ can only bring about health to our spirit, soul and body for He is "Christ in me the hope of glory."

Resurrection Of The Dead I

Lesson Study Review 13

1. What are the three resurrections that relate to our salvation?

    1. _____

    2. _____

    3. _____

2. What is the meaning of the word "resurrection"?

    _____

    _____

    _____

3. Did Jesus rise from the dead? _____ (Yes or No)

    Mathew 28:6 _____

    Acts 2:24 & 4:10 _____

    1 Cor. 15:20 _____

4. Was Jesus Christ visible after His resurrection? _____ (Yes or No)

    A. Acts 1:3 _____

    B. 1 Cor. 15:5-8 _____

    C. Matt. 28:16-17 _____

5. Was the body raised the same one which was crucified? _____ (Yes or No)

    A. Luke 23:55 to 24:3
    B. Luke 24:36-40
    C. John 20: 27-31

Resurrection of the Dead: Lesson Study Review 13

6. What does the Old Testament say about the resurrection of Christ?

   Acts 2:30-31 _____

   _____

7. Must one believe in the resurrection of Jesus Christ to be saved? _____ (Yes or No)

   Rom. 10:9 _____

   _____

8. List the seven things insured by the resurrection of Jesus Christ

   1. Rom. 1:4 _____

   2. Rom. 6:9 _____

   3. Matt 28:18 & Eph 1:20-23 _____

   4. Heb 10:12 _____

   5. Rom. 4:25 _____

   6. 1 Pet 1:3 _____

   7. Acts 17:31 _____

The Resurrection Of The Dead II

20 If you have died with Christ to the elementary principles of the world, why, as if you were living in the world, do you submit yourself to decrees, such as,

21 "Do not handle, do not taste, do not touch!"

22 (which all refer to things destined to perish with the using) —in accordance with the commandments and teachings of men?

23 These are matters which have, to be sure, the appearance of wisdom in self-made religion and self-abasement and severe treatment of the body, but are of no value against fleshly indulgence.

1 If then you have been raised up with Christ, keep seeking the things above, where Christ is, seated at the right hand of God.

2 Set your mind on the things above, not on the things that are on earth.

3 For you have died and your life is hidden with Christ in God.

4 When Christ, who is our life, is revealed, then you also will be revealed with Him in glory.

5 Therefore consider the members of your earthly body as dead to immorality, impurity, passion, evil desire, and greed, which amounts to idolatry.

6 For it is on account of these things that the wrath of God will come,

7 and in them you also once walked, when you were living in them.

8 But now you also, put them all aside; anger, wrath, malice, slander, and abusive speech from your mouth.

9 Do not lie to one another, since you laid aside the old self with its evil practices,

10 and have put on the new self who is being renewed to a true knowledge according to the image of the One who created him

11 —a renewal in which there is no distinction between Greek and Jew, circumcised and uncircumcised, barbarian, Scythian, slave and freeman, but Christ is all, and in all.

—Colossians 2 & 3

Resurrection of the Dead II

In our first lesson on the "Resurrection of the Dead", we pointed out that there are three resurrections in the New Testament to which our faith must relate. They are:

1. The resurrection of Jesus, The Christ – Past
2. The spiritual resurrection of the Believer in Jesus Christ – Present
3. The ultimate resurrection of "all that are in the graves" – Future

Having dealt with the first of these in our last lesson we now proceed to consider the second one.

In The Present, What Is The Spiritual Resurrection of The Believer In Jesus Christ?

A. In what sense are Believers now raised?

> "And *you were dead* in your trespasses and sins,"....even when *we were dead* in our transgressions, *made us alive* together with Christ (by grace you have been saved), and *raised us up* with Him, and seated us with Him in the heavenly places, in Christ Jesus,...."
>
> —Ephesians 2:1, 5-6

> "And you (*He made alive*), when *you were dead* (slain) by (your) trespasses and sins, ...even when *we were dead* (slain) by (our own) shortcomings and trespasses, *He made us alive* together in fellowship and in union with Christ. He gave us "*the very life of Christ Himself,*" *the same new life* with which He quickeneth Him,.... And *He raised us up together* with Him and made us sit down together—giving us joint seating with *Him*—in the heavenly sphere,...."
>
> —Ephesians 2:1, 5-6 Amplified

> "Now if we *have died* with Christ, we believe that we shall also *live* with Him."
>
> —Romans 6:8

It should be noted that while we have had a spiritual resurrection, we must wait for the resurrection of the body. There is nothing "vile" about our bodies, but a better translation would be "the body of my humiliation". The body is not yet conditioned to experience all of its spiritual experiences. We have in us now the "spirit of resurrection".

> "And when you were dead in your transgressions and the uncircumcision of your flesh, He made you alive together with Him, having forgiven us all our transgressions."
>
> —Colossians 2:13

172

"And to you—dead as you once were in your transgressions and in the uncircumcision of your natural state—He has nevertheless given life with Himself, having forgiven us all our transgressions."
—Colossians 2:13 Amplified

"For through the Law I died to the Law, that I might live to God. I have been crucified with Christ; and it is no longer I who live, but Christ lives in me; and the life which I now live in the flesh I live by faith in the Son of God, Who loved me, and delivered Himself up for me."
—Galatians 2:19-20

"For I through the Law—under the operation (of the curse) of the Law—have (in Christ's death for me) myself died to the Law and all the Law's demands upon me, so that I may (henceforth) live to and for God. I have been crucified with Christ—(In Him) I have shared His crucifixion; it is no longer I who live, but Christ, the Messiah, lives in me; and the life I now live in the body, I live by faith—by adherence to and reliance on and (complete) trust—in the Son of God, Who loved me and gave Himself up for me."
—Galatians 2:19-20 Amplified

14 "For the love of Christ controls us, having concluded this, that One died for all, therefore *all died*;

15 and He died for all, that *they who live* should no longer live for themselves, but for Him Who died and *rose again on their behalf.*"

17 "Therefore if any man is in Christ, he is a *new creature*; the old things passed away; behold, *new things have come.*"
—2 Corinthians 5

14 "For the love of Christ controls and urges and impels us, because we are of the opinion and conviction that (if) One died for all, then *all have died*;

15 and He died for all, so that *all those who live* might live no longer to and for themselves, but to and for Him Who died and *was raised again for their sake.*

17 Therefore, if any person is (engrafted) in Christ, the Messiah, he is (*a new creature altogether*), *a new creation*; the old (previous moral and spiritual condition) has passed away. Behold, the *fresh and new has come!*"
—2 Corinthians 5 Amplified

Resurrection of the Dead II

God has a plan and purpose for His Elect and has placed His people on the earth to represent Him as:

- Ambassadors – Wherever you go. Whether the job, grocery store, social event or family gathering
- Bondslave – By doing His Will at all times
- Walking epistles – Being a ready witness of the Word
- Problem solvers – Sharing your knowledge of the Word and helping psychologically, physically or monetarily when possible and appropriate
- Healers – You shall "lay hands on the sick and they shall recover"
- Deliverers – "Those who believe shall cast out demons"
- Givers – Feeding the poor, helping the widows and orphans, and supporting ministries and the fellowships, and etc.
- Humble of heart – Going the extra mile
- Lamplighters – Shedding light in areas of darkness
- Living stones – For we all are fitly framed together for we are being built up as a spiritual house for a holy priesthood.
- Peacemakers – For they shall be sought after

We are to be walking in His fullness, authority, power and dominion. Ephesians 1:18-21 says we are not only to be representing Him in this age, but also in the age to come. Angels are not running the universe. God is, and Jesus has delegated that responsibility to His Beloved. But there is a short circuit here because there is a gulf between what we believe and how we act. To quote Peter Lord, "We live what we believe; all the rest is just religious talk."

Does Water Baptism Signify A "Divine Order"?

"....buried with Him in baptism, in which you also were raised with Him
through faith in the working of God, Who raised Him from the dead."
—Colossians 2:12

Water baptism, administered at the proper time, is the foundation of "resurrection". The Jamieson, Faussett and Brown Commentary gives a more accurate translation — "Having been buried with Him in your baptism." Baptism is regarded as the burial of the old carnal life by immersion. Raised with Him through the faith of, by means of, your faith in the operation of God. "Faith of" for "faith in". Faith in God's mighty operation in raising up Jesus from the grave, is saving faith. Believing is the act of the soul, but the grace, or power to believe, comes from God Himself.

Eternal Life Principles & Beyond

How Is The Resurrection Signified?
Read Romans 6:1-23

> "Therefore we have been buried with Him through baptism into death, in order that as Christ was raised from the dead through the glory of the Father, so *we too* might walk in newness of life. For if we have become united with him in the likeness of his death, certainly we shall be also in the likeness of his resurrection."
>
> —Romans 6:4-5

> "We were buried, therefore, with Him by the baptism into death, so that just as Christ was raised from the dead by the glorious (power) of the Father, we too might habitually live and behave in newness of life. For if we have become one with Him by sharing in a death like his, we shall also be (one with Him in sharing) his resurrection (by a new life lived for God)."
>
> —Romans 6:4-5 Amplified

Buried, our conformity is complete. We profess to be cut-off from all commerce and communion with sin. As Christ was separate from sin, we rise again to a new life of faith and love. Newness of life supposes newness of heart and we choose to walk in new paths.

What Are The Evidences Of This Resurrection?

A. An attitude of faith is established and maintained

> "Even so consider yourselves to be *dead* to sin, but alive to God in Christ Jesus."
>
> —Romans 6:11

You also must regard yourselves as *dead* in relation to sin, but as *alive* in relation to God, because you are in Christ Jesus!

Christ is our spiritual life. We live for God through Him. He is the Mediator, our all in all. He who is dead cuts-off all communication with sin. If we are in Christ we will examine ourselves as to whether we be in the faith.

B. A new life is manifest

> "....so we too might walk in newness of life." —Romans 6:4

> "....We also should walk in newness of life!" —Romans 6:4 Weymouth

> "....rise to life on a new plane altogether!" —Romans 6:4 JB Phillips

> "....so we too might habitually live and behave in newness of life."
>
> —Romans 6:4 Amplified

Resurrection of the Dead II

Our new life consists in a body of saints, an assembly of saints, not a congregation with one saint. We were sanctified into a community.

>Community relates to communion and fellowship
>Community relates to closeness of God's people
>Community relates to sharing life together

   C. A new Master is obeyed

>"....that they who live should no longer live for themselves, but *for Him* who died and rose again on their behalf."
>
>—2 Corinthians 5:15

We need to set our minds on living for Christ and keep them set. What a man thinks, so is he. We govern our thought process. We shouldn't want to engage in thought patterns outside of Christ and live unto ourselves for that would be our final ruin.

   D. A new life purpose is embraced

>"If then you have been raised up with Christ, keep seeking the things above, where Christ is, seated at the right hand of God. Set your mind on the things above, not on the things that are on earth."
>
>—Colossians 3:1-2

>"If then you have been raised with Christ (to a new life, thus sharing His resurrection from the dead), aim at and seek the (rich, eternal treasures) that are above, where Christ is seated at the right hand of God. And set your minds and keep them set on what is above – the higher things – not on the things that are on earth."
>
>—Colossians 3:1-2 Amplified

Let your thoughts dwell on things above. Don't let them grovel on earthly things. We must put our faith in what God says about us. Legally, we are joint sharers with Christ. We are seated with Christ in the heavenly places. That's how God sees us and that's how we are to see ourselves. We must walk all the more closely with God. The world is in opposition to the things above and if we preference our affection to one, it proportionally weakens our affection to the other.

We Are What God Says We Are:

>Water Walkers – as He calls us forth
>Mountain Movers – by the power of the Word Spoken
>Living Letters – known and read by all men
>Serving Saints – becoming great in the Kingdom of God

>"But you are a chosen race, a royal priesthood, a holy nation, a people for God's own possession, that you may proclaim the excellencies of Him who has called you out of darkness into His marvelous light;"
>
>1 Peter 2:9

Summary:

Again, resurrection is a new life in Christ — it is not re-creation. When God saved us, He made us His own; He did not replace us. The Scriptures say He has quickened us to life. We have to develop our faith in Him. We also have to be willing to make ourselves receptive to His power so it may flow through us. We have to submit to the training directed by the Holy Spirit being aware of His nudges and the endowment of His gifts.

Believers have a past, present and future resurrection.

> Present – For some, their salvation was not an experience and, therefore, life is Blah and unrewarding of good fruit and good deeds; and on the other hand for some, the disciplines of God are overtaxing. No doubt about it, dying to the self-life is painful.
>
> Past – Born-again and baptized in water.
>
> Future – The resurrection of the body into the heavenlies.

Additional Notes:

A brief word about the times we struggle in our faith. Godly counselors have the responsibility to help us in renewing the mind in the area in which we have been hurt or injured. This is usually the area in which we struggle to trust in God. At the moment we recognize this need that is the exact time to ask Him to bring restoration to that part of our soulman that has been violated or injured. (See Psalm 23:3)

Another kingdom principle to faith is to die daily, and each time a part of us decreases, He increases.

For a true exhaustive list of names God has ordained to call us, Mike Shreve has written *Our Glorious Inheritance*. To order, visit www.shreveministries.org or call 423-478-2843.

Resurrection Of The Dead II
Lesson Study Review 14

1. Is there a present resurrection for the Saints?

    A. Eph. 2:1, 5-6 _____

    B. Rom. 6:1-9 (vs 8) _____

    C. Col 2:12-13 _____

    D. Gal. 2:19-20 _____

    E. 2 Cor. 5:14-15, 17 _____

2. What "Divine Ordinance" signifies the Believer's resurrection?

    Col 2:12 _____

3. How do we relate to the resurrection?

    Rom. 6: 4-5 _____

4. What things in a Believer's life would indicate he has experienced spiritual resurrection?

    A. Rom. 6:11 _____

    B. Rom. 6:4 _____

    C. 2 Cor 5:15 _____

    D. Col 3:1-2 _____

Note: We seek the eternal treasures that are above and not the temporal things this world offers.

The Resurrection Of the Dead III

> **21** For since by a man came death, by a man also came the resurrection of the dead.
>
> **22** For as in Adam all die, so also in Christ all shall be made alive.
>
> **23** But each in his own order; Christ the first fruits, after that those who are Christ's at His coming,
>
> **24** then comes the end, when He delivers up the kingdom to the God and Father, when He has abolished all rule and all authority and power.
>
> **25** For He must reign until He has put all His enemies under His feet.
>
> **26** The last enemy that will be abolished is death.
>
> **27** For HE HAS PUT ALL THINGS IN SUBJECTION UNDER HIS FEET. But when He says, "All things are put in subjection," it is evident that He is excepted who put all things in subjection to Him.
>
> **28** and when all things are subjected to Him, then the Son Himself also will be subjected to the One who subjected all things to Him, that God may be all in all.
>
> —1 Corinthians 15:22-28

This is our third study on the "Resurrection of the Dead", in which we examine the ultimate resurrection: of "all that are in the graves!" – Future

When Is The Future Resurrection To Take Place?

Jesus said,

> 39 And this is the will of Him who sent Me, that of all that He has given Me I lose nothing, but raise it up on the last day.
> 40 For this is the will of My Father, that everyone who beholds the Son and believes in Him, may have eternal life; and I myself will raise him up on the last day.
> 44 No one can come to Me, unless the Father who sent Me draws him; and I will raise him up on the last day.
> —John 6

The words "He has given Me" in verse 39 and the words "draws him" in vs 44 is a work of grace upon our will by the Father. It is not a force put upon our will but a work of grace.

> 54 He who eats My flesh and drinks My blood has eternal life, and I will raise him up on the last day.
>
> —John 6

The words "I will raise him up at the last day" are mentioned four times by John in this discourse. Surely He can do anything. Let our expectations be carried out toward a happiness reserved for the last day. The "raising up" not only includes our whole person, but all that belongs to us, i.e., our services and all our interests. All that He has is ours and all that we have is His.

> Jesus said to her, "Your brother (Lazarus) shall rise again." Martha said to Him, "I know that he will rise again in the resurrection on the last day."
>
> —John 11:23-24

> "But each in his own order: Christ the first fruits, after that those who are Christ's at His coming."
>
> —1 Corinthians 15:23

The words "each in his own order" is a rather unique statement. The Apostle Paul states that there will be an order observed in the resurrection. What that precisely will be we are not told. The first fruits are supposed to rise first and afterward all who are Christ's.

I would venture to guess "first fruits" could well mean those who walked with Christ before and after His resurrection, then those who bore the heat of the day, and lastly us. All of this will occur in the blinking of an eye. What an abruptly orchestrated event! At the Judgment Seat of Christ, though, I believe the first shall be last and the last shall be first. Here on earth, to be the last recipient of an award is of the highest honor. I have no idea if this protocol holds true in Heaven. But Paul did say, "the natural first, then the supernatural."

The Greek word *"tagma"* translated "order" means that which has been arranged in order, to draw up in order, specifically, a division, or rank. This is the only time *"tagma"* is used in the whole New Testament. We can liken it to a concrete image of troops "each in his own regiment".

> "Behold, I tell you a mystery; we shall not all sleep, but we shall all be changed, in a moment, in the twinkling of an eye, at the last trumpet; for the trumpet will sound, and the dead will be raised imperishable, and we shall be changed."
>
> —1 Corinthians 15:51-52

The last trumpet is God's trumpet. It is not one of the seven that will sound in Revelation chapters 8 and 9. The last trumpet in Revelation 9 will bring God's wrath immediately after we are raptured and after the half hour of silence.

> "For the Lord Himself will descend from heaven with a shout, and with the voice of the archangel, and with the trumpet of God; and the dead in Christ shall rise first."
>
> —1 Thessalonians 4:16

In verse 16 above the Lord's people alone are spoken of here. Believers of all ages from every generation are included. Then we will be with Him and one another forever never to be separated.

How Many Shall Be Raised In The Resurrection?

> "Do not marvel at this; for an hour is coming, in which all who are in the tombs shall hear His voice, and shall come forth; those who did the good deeds to a resurrection of life, those who committed the evil deeds to a resurrection of judgment."
>
> —John 5:28-29

> "Having a hope in God, which these men cherish themselves, that there shall certainly be a resurrection of both the righteous and the wicked."
>
> —Acts 24:15

The "righteous/just" shall rise by virtue of their union with Christ as their head; the "wicked/unjust" shall rise by virtue of Christ's dominion over them as their Judge.

Who Does The Raising?

A. God, the Father

> "Now God has not only raised the Lord, but will also raise us up through His power."
>
> —1 Corinthians 6:14

> "Indeed, we had the sentence of death within ourselves in order that we should not trust in ourselves, but in God who raises the dead."
>
> —2 Corinthians 1:9

> "Knowing that He who raised the lord Jesus will raise us also with Jesus and will present us with you."
>
> —2 Corinthians 4:14

B. The Son

> 37 "All that the Father gives Me shall come to Me, and the one who comes to Me I will certainly not cast out.
>
> 39 And this is the will of Him who sent Me, that of all that *He has given Me* I lose nothing, but *raise it up* on the last day.
>
> 40 I myself will raise him up on the last day...."

44 ....I will raise him up on the last day.

54 ....I will raise him up on the last day.

—John 6

Did The Apostles Preach The Resurrection?

1 And as they (Peter and John) were speaking to the people, the priests and the captain of the temple guard, and the Sadducees, came upon them,
2 being greatly disturbed because they were teaching the people and proclaiming in Jesus the resurrection from the dead."

33 And with great power the apostles were giving witness to the resurrection of the Lord Jesus, and abundant grace was upon them all.

—Acts 4

18 .... —because he (Paul) was preaching Jesus and the resurrection."

32 Now when they heard of the resurrection of the dead, some began to sneer, but others said, "We shall hear you again concerning this."

—Acts 17

But perceiving that one part were Sadducees and the other Pharisees, Paul began crying out in the Council, "Brethren, I am a Pharisee, a son of Pharisees; I am on trial for the hope and resurrection of the dead!"

—Acts 23:6

What Kind Of Bodies Will Believers Have?

A. A body according to the will of God

"But God gives it (the seed *you* sow) a body just as He wished, and to each of the seeds a body of its own."

—1 Corinthians 15:36-38

"God gives to it (the seed *you* sow) the body that He plans and sees fit, and to each kind of seed a body of its own."

—1 Corinthians 15:38 Amplified

B. A glorious body

"It (our body) is sown in dishonor, it is raised in glory; it is sown in weakness, it is raised in power."

—1 Corinthians 15:43

"It is sown in dishonor and humiliation; it is raised in honor and glory."

—1 Corinthians 15:43a Amplified

Eternal Life Principles & Beyond

C. A powerful body

"It is sown in infirmity and weakness; it is resurrected in strength and endued with power."

—1 Corinthians 15:43b Amplified

D. A spiritual body

"It is sown a natural body, it is raised a spiritual body. If there is a natural body, there is also a spiritual body."

—1 Corinthians 15:44

"It is sown a natural (physical) body, it is raised a supernatural (a spiritual) body. (As surely as) there is a physical body, there is also a spiritual body."

—1 Corinthians 15:44 Amplified

The "natural body" literally means "an animal body," a body molded in its organism of "flesh and blood" to suit the animal soul, which predominates in it. After the body is raised, the Spirit of God shall predominate and the animal soul will be duly subordinate.

E. An incorruptible and immortal body

42 "So also is the resurrection of the dead. It is sown a perishable body, it is raised an imperishable body...."

—1 Corinthians 15

"Now I say this, brethren, "that flesh and blood cannot inherit the kingdom of God; nor does the perishable inherit the imperishable. Behold, I tell you a mystery; we shall not all sleep, but we shall all be changed, in a moment, in the twinkling of an eye, at the last trumpet; for the trumpet will sound, and the dead will be raised imperishable, and we shall be changed. For this perishable must put on the imperishable, and this mortal must put on immortality."

—1 Corinthians 15:50-53

"(The body) that is sown is perishable and decays, but (the body) that is resurrected is imperishable—immune to decay, immortal.... But I tell you this, brethren, flesh and blood cannot (become partakers of eternal salvation and) inherit or share in the kingdom of God; nor does the perishable—that which is decaying—inherit or share in the imperishable (the immortal). Take notice! I tell you a mystery—a secret truth, an event decreed by the hidden purpose and the counsel of God. We shall not all fall asleep (in death), but we shall all be changed (transformed) in a moment, in the twinkling of an eye, at the (sound of the) last trumpet call. For a trumpet will sound, and the dead (in Christ) will be raised imperishable—free and immune from decay, and we shall be changed (transformed). For this perishable (part of us) must put on the imperishable (nature), and this mortal (part of us)—this nature that is capable of dying—must put on immortality (freedom from death)."

—1 Corinthians 15:42, 50-53 Amplified

F. body like that of Our Risen Lord

"And just as we have borne the image of the earthy, we shall also bear the image of the heavenly."

—1 Corinthians 15:49

What Effect Should The Resurrection Have On A Believer's Conduct?

A. It should keep us from sinful indulgence – negative

"If from human motives I fought with wild beasts at Ephesus, what does it profit me? If the dead are not raised, let us eat and drink, for tomorrow we die. Do not be deceived: "Bad company corrupts good morals." Become sober-minded as you ought, and stop sinning; for some have no knowledge of God. I speak this to your shame."

—1 Corinthians 15:32-34

"What do I gain if, merely from the human point of view, I fought with (wild) beasts at Ephesus? If the dead are not raised (at all), let us eat and drink, for tomorrow we will be dead. Do not be so deceived and misled! Evil companionships, (communion, associations), corrupt and deprave good manners, morals and character. Awake (from your drunken stupor and return) to sober sense and your right minds, and sin no more. For some of you have not the knowledge of God—you are utterly and willfully and disgracefully ignorant, and continue to be so, lacking the sense of God's presence and all true knowledge of Him. I say this to your shame."

—1 Corinthians 15:32-34 Amplified

B. It should cause us to be committed to intelligent service – positive

"Therefore, my beloved brethren, be steadfast, immovable, always abounding in the work of the Lord, knowing that your toil is not in vain in the Lord."

—1 Corinthians 15:58

"Therefore, my beloved brethren, be firm (steadfast, immovable), always abounding in the work of the Lord—that is, always being superior (excelling, and doing more than enough) in the service of the Lord, knowing and being continually aware that your labor in the Lord is not futile—never wasted or, to no purpose."

—1 Corinthians 15:58 Amplified

What Scripture Refers To A Body Like That Of Our Risen Lord?

"But now Christ has been raised from the dead, the first fruits of those who are asleep."

—1 Corinthians 15:20

Christ did rise from the dead, He was the first to be reaped of those who sleep in death.

—1 Corinthians 15:20 Moffatt

Messiah has been raised from the dead! He is the first sheaf of a great harvest!

—1 Corinthians 15:20 Way

"And just as we have borne the image of the earthy, we shall also bear the image of the heavenly."

—1 Corinthians 15:49

Just as we have been made like the material men, so we are to bear the likeness of the heavenly man.

—1 Corinthians 15:49 Moffatt

"Who will transform the body of our humble state into conformity with the body of His glory, by the exertion of the power that He has even to subject all things to Himself."

—Philippians 3:21

"Who will transform and fashion anew the body of our humiliation to conform to and be like the body of His glory and majesty, by exerting that power which enables Him even to subject everything to Himself."

—Philippians 3:21 Amplified

"Beloved, now we are children of God, and it has not appeared as yet what we shall be. We know that, when He appears, we shall be like Him, because we shall see Him just as He is."

—1 John 3:2

"Beloved, we are (even here and) now God's children, it is not disclosed (made clear) what we shall be (hereafter), but we know that when He comes and is manifested we shall (as God's children) resemble and be like Him, for we shall see Him just as He (really) is."

—1 John 3:2 Amplified

"And so, brothers of mine, stand firm! Let nothing move you as you busy yourselves in the Lord's work. Be sure that nothing you do for Him is ever lost or wasted.

—1 John 3:2 JB Phillips

Resurrection of the Dead III

Summary:

Not to be reiterating, one more mention must be made about reincarnation, which is also re-creation in which some people believe. Reincarnation is believed to be cycles of death and life. But this is a lie from the "father of lies." Some who believe they can come back as an animal do not understand that animals have no concept of the universe around them. Yahweh says, "We are made in His image". Man has a conscience which noticeably sets us apart, as we know right from wrong. Science and Scripture categorize us as part of the animal kingdom because of physical things, but we are not part of the animal kingdom in matters of the spiritual realm. Physically, man uses tools and instruments and operates machinery. Man uses a spoken language, has gifts, and some gifts provide an income; man is personal. After salvation, we are called to works of faith and the fruit of our labors live on for which we will be rewarded at the Judgment Seat of Christ.

Resurrection and glorification is a fact! Our bodies will be raised in the first resurrection of both those saints who are in their graves and those still alive. King David said, "What is man, that Thou dost take thought of him. Thou hast made him a little lower than God, and dost crown him with glory and majesty!"— Psalm 8:4-5.

The wisest man recorded on the face of the earth was Solomon and he said, "There is a time to give birth, and a time to die...." (Ecclesiastes 3:2). In verse 20 Solomon declares "....the body came from the dust and will return to the dust." After our body dies, our spiritman and soulman continue to live on. Death for the Believer is an event! It is part of our sojourn in life. Life then passes on from this world to an eternal Kingdom. There is no stopping in time, we simply move on, because its graduation time for us!

The writer of Hebrews said, "And inasmuch as it is appointed for men to die once and after this comes judgment (9:27).

Resurrection Of The Dead III

Lesson Study Review 15

1. When is the future resurrection to take place?

    John. 6:39, 44, 54

2. How many shall be resurrected at that time? _____

    John 5:28-29 ⎱
    Acts 24:15   ⎰

3. Who, according to the Scriptures, raises the dead?

    A. 1 Cor. 6:14

    B. John. 6:39-40, 44, 54

4. Was the future resurrection a prominent feature of the apostolic preaching?

    _____ (Yes or No)

    Acts 4:2

    Acts 17: 18, 32

5. How much information do we have about the kind of body that we will receive at the resurrection?

    A. 1 Cor. 15:38

    B. 1 Cor. 15:43a

    C. 1 Cor. 15:43b

    D. 1 Cor. 15:44

    E. 1 Cor. 15:42, 50-53

    F. 1 Cor. 15:49

6. Should the fact of the coming resurrection affect the conduct of The Called?

    _____ (Yes or No)

    A. 1 Cor. 15:32-34

    B. 1 Cor. 15:58

My Inspirations, Challenges & Revelations:

The author takes literary license in the following lessons to express deliberate emphases to secure the position of the doctrines. Words written in all capitals in these lessons are mostly mine.

Several of the following doctrines, because of their extreme emphasis on sin, hell and judgment, may move you out of your comfort zone. These doctrines have been white-washed by many teachers and pastors in an effort to not offend. No question about it, these lessons may be hard; therefore, some people take different points of view. Let the Holy Record speak for itself. I encourage you to become an "overcomer" and move on.

Originally, this book was developed for the Prison Correspondence Course Department of the Bible College. However, there are many saints worthy of their calling, with high profile ministries, that led a life of debauchery before salvation. Since the following three lessons on *Eternal Judgment*, coupled with the lesson on *Hell*, are hard words to receive, they can be internalized hurtfully. Therefore, I felt it necessary to bring to your remembrance verse 37 of John 6, "ALL that the Father gives Me shall come to Me, and the one who comes to Me I will certainly not cast out." Jesus' words are exceedingly emphatic. Never does He reject the humble and contrite prayers of the truly repentant, however grievous his crimes may have been. The Father has given you to Jesus and all that the Father has given Him shall unquestionably be given to Him! His errand on earth shall in no wise be defeated. The word "shall" expresses the glorious certainty of it. Welcome this word to your soul. The King James Revised uses a double negative—"I will not, no, I will not." Much favor is expressed here. It is a pure gospel promise. We all have reason to fear that He should frown upon us and cast us out, but He obviates these fears with assurance. He will not reject us though we have a sinful nature. He will receive us and give us our rewards at the Judgment Seat of Christ. Now, go on to your next lessons in peace.

It is also important to note the Scriptures are not specifically designed for the hereafter. The word of God to Israel in Deuteronomy 29:29 was, "The secret things belong unto the Lord our God: but the things which are revealed belong unto us and to our children forever, that we may do them...." The Sacred Records are given as a template to govern, chasten and instruct us while we exist on earth. After we leave this world, we no longer need the written Word. We will have perfect knowledge as we eternally behold the Living Word. Man must satisfy himself with the measure of truth concerning these doctrines as revealed in the Scriptures, not seeking to go beyond it, knowing that God will answer your questions in His own time.

My Inspirations, Challenges & Revelations:

DOCTRINE 6

ETERNAL JUDGMENT I
    Biblical Meaning Of Judgment..194
    What Is The Dictionary Meaning Of The Word Judgment?.......................194
    Why Must There Be Judgment?...194
    When Does Judgment Occur?..196
    Who Is The Judge?...200
    What Are The Principles Governing Divine Judgment?............................201
    Pivotal Judgments..213

ETERNAL JUDGMENT II
    What Is The Judgment Seat Of Christ?...215
    What Will Happen Just Before This Day?..215
    Where Shall This Judgment Take Place?..216
    What Are The First Things Christ Will Do?...216
    A Cleansing Of Fire...225
    The Bride Has Made Herself Ready..226
    Believers Will Be Rewarded..226
    The Rewards..227
    The Bible, Our Absolute Guideline For Rewards......................................227

ETERNAL JUDGMENT III
    What Is The Great White Throne Judgment?...233
    What Will Happen On This Day?...233
    Where Does This Judgment Take Place?..234
    When Does This Happen?...235
    What Does The Throne Room Look Like?...235
    What Will Happen At This Judgment?...238
    The Books..244
    New Heaven And New Earth..244

My Inspirations, Challenges & Revelations:

Eternal Judgment I

1 THEREFORE, you are without excuse, every man of you who passes judgment for in that you judge another, you condemn yourself; for you who judge practice the same things.

2 And we know that the judgment of God rightly falls upon those who practice such things.

3 And do you suppose this, O man, when you pass judgment upon those who practice such things and do the same yourself, that you will escape the judgment of God?

4 Or do you think lightly of the riches of His kindness and forbearance and patience, not knowing that the kindness of God leads you to repentance?

5 But because of your stubbornness and unrepentant heart you are storing up wrath for yourself in the day of wrath and revelation of the righteous judgment of God,

6 WHO WILL RENDER TO EVERY MAN ACCORDING TO HIS DEEDS;

7 to those who by perseverance in doing good seek for glory and honor and immortality, eternal life;

8 but to those who are selfishly ambitious and do not obey the truth, but obey unrighteousness, wrath and indignation.

9 There will be tribulation and distress for every soul of man who does evil, of the Jew first and also of the Greek

10 but glory and honor and peace to every man who does good, to the Jew first and also to the Greek.

11 For there is no partiality with God.

12 For all who have sinned without the Law will also perish without the Law; and all who have sinned under the Law will be judged by the Law;

13 for not the hearers of the Law are just before God, but the doers of the Law will be justified.

14 For when Gentiles who do not have the Law do instinctively the things of the Law, these, not having the Law, are a law to themselves,

Eternal Judgment I

> **15 in that they show the work of the Law written in their hearts, their conscience bearing witness, and their thoughts alternately accusing or else defending them,**
>
> **16 on the day when, according to my gospel, God will judge the secrets of men through Christ Jesus.**
>
> —Romans 2

The view generally held is that judgment is at the end of history, but this is not so. Yahweh is exercising moral judgment constantly and at the end of history His story will be finalized. Judgment at the end of the age is only part of its definition. Yahweh sat as King over the flood. Yahweh is King over history and Yahweh is govern-mentally active in our lives daily. He chastens, governs and instructs us here on earth with the purpose in mind of eternal quality to govern an eternal government. Eternal life is Yahweh's quality kind of life, which He will bestow on His Saints.

Biblical Meaning Of Judgment

In the Old Testament, the Hebrew words "*mishpat*" and "*shaphat*" and the Aramaic "*din*" translated "judgment" is used in two ways. It refers to the statutes, testimonies, and the Law of God and is usually in the plural. In both the Old and New Testament the word "judgment" is used in connection with "Yahweh's judgments on the affairs of men and nations both in history and at the end of history".

What Is The Dictionary Meaning Of The Word Judgment?

The word "to judge" means "to separate; to make a distinction between; to exercise judgment upon; to estimate; to assume a censorial power over; to call to account; to bring under question; to judge judiciously; to try as a judge; to bring to trial; to sentence; to be brought to account; to incur arrangement; to administer government over; to govern."

Why Must There Be Judgment?

A. Because of sin against Yahweh's law

> "For as many as have sinned without Law will also perish without Law,
> and as many as have sinned in the law will be judged by the law,"
> —Romans 2:12 AKJV

The Greek for the word "sinned" in this verse is "*hamartia*" meaning "to miss a mark, to be in error". See the lesson entitled "Sin" for a concise definition of the word "*hamartia*" and a complete list of categories of the different kinds of sins which appear in Scripture.

1. Because of ungodliness

   "But the present heavens and earth by His word are being reserved for fire, until the *"day of judgment"* and perdition (destruction) of *"ungodly"* men.
   —2 Peter 3:7

   "....to execute *judgment* on all, who are *ungodly* among them of all their *ungodly deeds* which they have committed in an *ungodly way,* and of all the harsh things which *ungodly* sinners have spoken against him."
   —Jude 15

   "....to execute *judgment* upon all, and to convict all the *ungodly* of all their works of *ungodliness* which they have *ungodly wrought,* and of all the hard things which *ungodly* sinners have spoken against him."
   —Jude 15 JB Phillips

2. Because of unrighteousness

   "....then the Lord knows how to rescue the godly from temptation, and to reserve the *unjust* (unrighteous) under punishment for the day of *judgment."*
   —2 Peter 2:9

3. Because of disobedience

   "And the angels who *did not keep their proper domain* but left their own abode, He has reserved in everlasting chains under darkness for the *judgment* of the great day.
   —Jude 6

   "And angels....those who *did not keep the position originally assigned to them,* but deserted their own proper abode—He reserves in everlasting bonds, in darkness, in preparation for the *judgment* of the great day.
   —Jude 6 The Way

4. Because of Unbelief

   "He who believes in Him is not condemned; but he *who does not believe is condemned already,* because *he has not believed* in the name of the only begotten Son of God."
   —John 3:18

Eternal Judgment I

> "He who believes on Him—who clings to, trusts in, relies on Him—is not judged (he who trusts in Him never comes up for judgment; for him there is no rejection, condemnation; he incurs no damnation), But *he who does not believe* (not cleave to, rely on, trust in Him), is *judged already*; (he has already been convicted; has already received his sentence), because *he has not believed on* and trusted in the name of the only begotten Son of God. He is condemned for refusing to let his trust rest in Christ's name."
>
> —John 3:18 Amplified

5. Because of trespass

> "Therefore, as through one man's *offense, judgment* came to all men, resulting in condemnation;...."
>
> —Romans 5:18

6. Because of evil deeds

> "And this is the *condemnation*, that the Light has come into the world, and men loved darkness rather than Light, because *their deeds were evil.*"
>
> —John 3:19

> "The (basis of the) judgment (indictment, the test by which men are judged, the ground for the sentence) lies in this: that the Light is come into the world, and people have loved the darkness rather than and more than the Light, for their works (deeds) were evil."
>
> —John 3:19 Amplified

Numbers 5 and 6 above also carry the understanding of immediate judgment, delayed judgment and the last judgment.

When Does Judgment Occur?

A. It has occurred

1. Satan

> "....the ruler (Satan) of this world has been judged."
>
> —John 16:11

> "....the ruler (prince) of this world (Satan) is judged *and condemned and sentence is already passed on him.*"
>
> —John 16:11 Amplified

In the twelfth chapter and verse 31 John writes, "*Now judgment is upon this world*; now shall the prince of this world be *cast out.*" Both verses above mean Satan's dominion over men or his power to enslave men to ruin them is destroyed. The death of Christ

Eternal Life Principles & Beyond

"judged" or judicially overthrew him and he was thereupon "cast out" or expelled from his usurped dominion. (See Hebrews 2:14 and 1 John 3:8). He was cast out of the souls of people by the grace of God working with the gospel of Christ. Since Satan has been subdued by Christ, we may be sure no other power can stand before him.

> "Having disarmed principalities and powers, He made a public spectacle of them, triumphing over them in it."
> —Colossians 2:15

> "God disarmed the principalities and powers raged against us and made a bold display and public example of them, in triumphing over them in Him and in it (at the cross)."
> —Colossians 2:15 Amplified

Yahweh does not allow sin to challenge Him. Do not mistake the long-suffering of Yahweh as indifference. As Victor, Jesus has the honor of an open triumph! The devil and all the powers of hell were conquered and disarmed by the dying Redeemer. Our Redeemer conquered all by dying.

2. The World

> "Now is the judgment of this world; now the ruler of this world will be cast out."
> —John 12:31 RKJV

By our Lord's death and resurrection, He passed sentence on the world and Satan. Satan's authority has been broken and he is allowed limited activity until his final imprisonment in the Lake of Fire. The world is a doomed city. God has passed judgment on it at Christ's cross and it has been decreed to end in fire.

3. Man

> "He who believes in Him is not condemned; but he who does not believe is condemned already, because he has not believed in the name of the only begotten Son of God."
> —John 3:18

> "Most assuredly, I say to you, he who hears My word and believes in Him who sent Me has everlasting life, and shall not come into judgment, but has passed from death into life."
> —John 5:24

> "....he does not have to face judgment!"
> —John 5:24 JB Phillips

> "Much more then, having now been justified by His blood, *we shall be saved from wrath through him.*"
> —Romans 5:9

Eternal Judgment I

> "Therefore, since we are now justified—acquitted, made righteous and brought into right relationship with God—by Christ's blood, how much more (certain is it that) we shall be saved by him from the indignation and wrath of God."
>
> —Romans 5:9 Amplified

> "There is therefore now no condemnation to those who are in Christ Jesus...."
>
> —Romans 8:1

> "Therefore (there is) now no condemnation—no adjudging guilty of wrong—for those who are in Christ Jesus...."
>
> —Romans 8:1 Amplified

  B. It is occurring

    1. Sinners

> 18 "For the wrath of God is *revealed from heaven against all ungodliness and unrighteousness* of men, who suppress the truth in unrighteousness...."
>
> —Romans 1:18-32

> 18 "For God's (holy) wrath and indignation *are revealed from heaven against all ungodliness and unrighteousness* of men, who in their wickedness repress and hinder the truth and make it inoperative."
>
> —Romans 1:18-32 Amplified

Continue reading in Romans 1:19-32.

Yahweh's righteousness will be vindicated in each person so that it shall be manifest to *all* His creatures and even to the conscience of the sinner himself. Godliness has to do with our attitude toward Yahweh. Unrighteousness applies to our attitude toward people and Yahweh. To be unrighteous to our neighbor is to show godlessness toward Yahweh. The God who gives joy, (Hebrews 12:2) governs us for our own good.

    2. Believers

> "For this reason many are weak and sick among you, and many sleep. For if we would judge ourselves, we would not be judged. But when we are judged, we are *chastened by the Lord,* that we may not be condemned with the world."
>
> —1 Corinthians 11:31-32

> "For if we searchingly examine ourselves — detecting our shortcomings and recognizing our own condition — we should not be judged and penalty decreed (by the divine judgment). But when we (fall short and) are

judged by the Lord, we are disciplined and chastened so that we may not (finally) be condemned (to eternal punishment along) with the world."

—1 Corinthians 11:31-32 Amplified

"If we were closely to examine ourselves beforehand, we should *avoid the judgment of God.* But when *God does judge us.* He disciplines us as His own sons, that we may not be involved in the general condemnation of the world."

—1 Corinthians 11:31-32 JB Phillips

Sin is rejecting what Yahweh said is sin. John Sandford says, *"The work of the cross cancels no sin that cancels the cross."* We will not only be judged for being a sinner, but Yahweh will judge the product that is the result of that sin. For example, a bastard has a birth, but it is not legitimate. When we bring a man to Christ, we must get the foundation right. We cannot tell anyone they are going to heaven after they are saved! But, we can tell them they will go to heaven *if* they *are* saved. Only you and Yahweh the Father know if you will be going to heaven.

C. When will it occur in the future?

1. After death

"And as it is appointed for men to die once, but *after this the judgment....*"

—Hebrews 9:27

2. The last day

"....the word that I have spoken will *judge* him in the *last day."*

—John 12:48

The JB Phillips translation of this verse is very beautiful.

"If anyone hears my sayings and does not keep them I do not judge him for I did not come to judge the world, but to save it. Every man who rejects me and will not accept my sayings has a judge — *on the last day, the very words that I have spoken will be his judge.* For I have not spoken on my own authority: the Father who sent me has commanded me what to say and how to speak. And I know that what He commands means eternal life. All that I speak only in accordance with what the Father has told me."

—John 12:47-50

3. The day

"*....in the day of judgment....*"

—Matthew 10:15

Eternal Judgment I

(Also read – Matthew 11:22, 24; 12:36; Acts 17:31; Romans 2:5; 1 Corinthians 3:13; 2 Thessalonians 1:10; 2 Peter 2:9, 3:7; 1 John 4:17)

Who Is The Judge?

A. Yahweh

"….because He (God) has appointed a day on which *He* will *Judge the world* in righteousness by the Man whom He has ordained.
—Acts 17:31

"He (God) has fixed a day when *He will judge the world* righteously (justly) by a Man Whom He has destined and appointed for that task…."
—Acts 17:31 Amplified

"….how will God *judge* the world?"
—Romans 3:6

"….to God *the judge* of all…."
—Hebrews 12:23

"They will give an account to *Him* (God) who is ready to *judge the living and the dead.*"
—1 Peter 4:5

"Judge" is one of Yahweh's names. He is the official authorized to bring execution upon sin. Yahweh, who is love, expresses this love in His paternal judgment. His righteousness is in contrast with sin, which brings about His holy wrath. The Greek word "orgen" is Yahweh's righteous anger against sin. Judging requires an authorized official to judge behavior and morals. Yahweh is our ultimate judge and He is also the judge of the universe, which includes principalities, dominions and powers.

B. The Son

The official capacity of judging has been further delegated as Yahweh has committed all future authority to His Son.

22 " For the Father judges no one, but has committed *all judgment to the son…."*

27 ….and He has given Him authority to execute *judgment* also, because He is the Son of man.
—John 5

22 "Even the Father judges no one; for He has given *all judgment* – the last judgment and the whole business of judging – entirely into the *hands of the son…."*

27 "And He has given *Him authority* and granted Him power to execute (exercise, practice) *judgment,* because He is the son of man (very man)."

—John 5 Amplified

"And He commanded us to preach to the people, and to testify that it is He who was ordained by God to be *Judge of the living and the dead."*

— Acts 10:42

"And He (now Jesus of Nazareth) charged us to preach to the people, and to bear solemn testimony that He is God-appointed and God-ordained Judge of the *living and the dead."*

—Acts 10:42 Amplified

C. The Saints

"Do you know that *the saints will judge the world?* And if the world will be judged by you, are you unworthy to judge the smallest matters? Do *you* not know that we *shall judge angels*? How much more, things that pertain to this life?"

—1 Corinthians 6:2-3

The church in Corinth boldly operated in the gifts of the Spirit more actively than any of the other churches under Paul's care, yet they also committed outrageous sins. Paul strongly chastised them in all three of his letters. The gifts of the Holy Spirit do not necessarily say we are walking in the will of Yahweh, nor does it indicate we are without sin.

The Corinthian church operated in all the gifts yet they took other Believers to court; they got drunk at the Lord's Table and one man fornicated with his father's wife, etc.

What Are The Principles Governing Divine Judgment?

A. Measure of Light and Privilege

"And whoever will not receive you nor hear your words, as you go out of that house or city, shake off the dust from your feet. Assuredly, I say to you, it will be *more tolerable for the land of Sodom and Gomorrah in the Day of Judgment* than for that city!"

—Matthew 10:14-15

Jesus is the way, the truth and the light. He also said, "we are the light of the world and that we are not to put our light under a bushel." When we go into "all the world" and preach His gospel, we are shedding His light to a darkened world. The light we bring is the measure by which they will be judged. The hearer is responsible for what he/she hears and knows whether it is accepted or not.

Eternal Judgment I

> Then He began to rebuke the cities in which most of His mighty works had been done, because they did not repent. "Woe to you, Chorazin! Woe to you, Bethsaida! For if the mighty works which were done in you had been done in Tyre and Sidon, they would have repented long ago in sackcloth and ashes. But I say to you, it will be more tolerable for Tyre and Sidon in the day of judgment than for you. And you, Capernaum, who are exalted to heaven will be brought down to Hades; for if the mighty works which were done in you had been done in Sodom, it would have remained until this day. But I say to you that it shall be more tolerable for the land of Sodom in the day of judgment than for you."
>
> —Matthew 11:20-24

> "The men of Nineveh will rise up in the judgment with this generation and condemn it; because they repented at the preaching of Jonah; and indeed a greater than Jonah is here. The queen of the South (the queen of Sheba) will rise up in the judgment with this generation and condemn it, for she came from the ends of the earth to hear the wisdom of Solomon; and indeed a greater than Solomon is here."
>
> —Matthew 12:41-42

Yahweh's people need to obey the Great Commission that we may change history once again. (See Acts 17:6)

B. Divine All-Knowledge

> "You judge according to the flesh; I judge no one. And yet if I do judge, my judgment is true; for I am not alone but I am with the Father who sent Me."
>
> —John 8:15-16 NKJV

> "You (set yourselves up) to judge according to the flesh by what you see; you condemn by external human standards. I do not (set myself up) to judge or condemn or sentence anyone. Yet even if I do judge, My judgment is true —My decision is right, for I am not alone (in making it), but (there are two of Us), I and the Father who sent Me."
>
> —John 8:15-16 Amplified

Yahweh is going to judge from His infinite knowledge in the light of the written Word on righteousness and holiness. The Scriptures are divine knowledge.

On a previous page the presented Scriptures indicated future judging was committed to Jesus. There is no contradiction here with the above listed Scriptures. Jesus is speaking about His time when on earth. He did not take advantage of His Deity while walking on earth. The first time He came to the world was as Savior, not as judge.

C. The Book of Life

> "And I saw the dead, small and great, standing before God, and *books* were opened. And another book was opened, which is *the book of Life*. And the dead were judged according to their works, by the things which were written in the *books*."
>
> —Revelation 20:12

> "And anyone not found written in the *book of Life* was cast into the lake of fire."
>
> —Revelation 20:15

D. The Book of Remembrance

> "Then those who feared (revered) the Lord spoke to one another, and the Lord gave attention and heard it, and a book of remembrance was written before Him for those who fear the Lord and who esteem His name."
>
> —Malachi 3:16

We do not know how many books were opened. But obviously one of the books contains infinite knowledge about each saint. David said:

> "My frame was not hidden from Thee, when I was made in secret, and skillfully wrought in the depths of the earth. Thine eyes have not seen my unformed substance. And in Thy books they were all written, the days that were ordained for me, when as yet there was not one of them."
>
> —Psalm 139:15-16

Although the book of Malachi is the last book in the Old Testament, it is interesting to note Moses, who wrote the first five books in the Old Testament, was willing to have his name removed from it (Exodus 32:32-33) and with which a number of psalmists were concerned. (See Ps 40:7 written by David and Ps 87:6 written by the sons of Korah).

E. The Word – Jesus

> "He who rejects Me, and does not receive *My words,* has that which judges him — *the word that I have spoken will judge him in the last day.* For I have not spoken on My own authority; but the Father who sent Me gave Me a command, what I should say and what I should speak."
>
> —John 12:48-49

F. Personal responsibility

Solomon, author of the book of Ecclesiastes shows from personal experience that all earthly goals and blessings, when pursued as ends in themselves, lead to dissatisfaction and emptiness. He learned in life that the highest good lies in reverencing and obeying Yahweh in all matters. Who as a man of faith was skeptical only of human wisdom and endeavor writes the following:

Eternal Judgment I

> "For God will bring every act to judgment, everything which is hidden, whether it is good or evil.
> —Ecclesiastes 12:14

The future judgment is the test of what "vanity" is, and what is solid, as regards to the most important good. Only He is in a position to judge every work whether it is good or evil and will announce His verdict at that time. Reverence toward the Lord is vital regarding our decisions whether they be righteous or unrighteous and in spite of all our good intentions, we must leave the end result to Him. Our responsibility is to be careful to observe His Word at all times.

Apostle Paul also admonishes:

> 10 For we shall all stand before the judgment seat of Christ.
>
> 12 So then each one of us *shall give an account of himself to God.*
> —Romans 14

> "Each of us then will *have to answer for himself* to God."
> — Romans 14 James Moffatt

> Therefore you are without excuse, every man of you who passes judgment, for in that you judge another, you condemn yourself; for you who judge practice the same things. "But we know that the *judgment of God is according to truth* against those who practice such things."
> —Romans 2:1-2

> *God's judgment,* we know, *is utterly impartial in its action* against such evil-doers.
> —Romans 2 JB Phillips

Personal responsibility is fully discussed in lesson II of Eternal Judgment.

    G. Personal conduct

> "For we must all appear before the *judgment seat of Christ,* that each one may receive the things done in the body, according to what he has done, whether good or bad."
> —2 Corinthians 5:10

Two things are important. (1) There will be no favoritism in the judgment and Jesus will reward the Believers. Jesus will not make an exception in your case. (2) There is a positive side at the judgment seat of Christ. The Believer will receive his/her rewards for the good deeds he/she has done.

> "Everyone of us will have to stand without pretense before *Christ our Judge,* and we shall be rewarded for *what we did* when we lived in our bodies, whether it was good or bad."
> —JB Phillips

> "....in the day of wrath and revelation of the *righteous judgment of God,* who WILL RENDER TO EACH ONE ACCORDING TO HIS DEEDS."
>
> —Romans 2:5-6

"Render" in the Greek is *"apodidomi"* meaning "to payoff," "discharge what is due," "to requite, recompense." Here is a word of encouragement, be not discouraged when recognition is not given, at a time when it was unjustly withheld from you. Here also is a truth to hold on to:

> "....when God's *righteous judgment* (just doom) will be revealed.... He will render to every *man according to his works* — justly, as his deeds deserve."
>
> —Romans 2:5-6 Amplified

> And if *you* address as Father the One who impartially *judges according to each one's work,* conduct yourselves in fear during the time of your stay upon earth;
>
> —1 Peter 1:17

> "And the dead were *judged according to their works* by the things which were written in the books."
>
> —Revelation 20:12

Please read Revelation 20 verses eleven to fifteen.

H. Divine impartiality

> And if *you* address as Father the One who *impartially judges* according to each man's work, conduct yourselves in fear during the time of your stay upon earth;
>
> —1 Peter 1:17

> *"....judges each one impartially...."*
>
> —1 Peter 1:17 Amplified

For Believers who experience a negative repeated pattern in their life of "damned if I do and damned if I don't," or for those who feel continually overlooked, no matter how much good they do, it is wonderful to know there is no favoritism here. Yahweh is an impartial judge and *you* can walk in the victory of believing this truth. We are encouraged by the Apostle Paul to "put on the mind of Christ and press on to the mark of the high calling in Christ Jesus".

I. Christ's brethren are favored

> 40 "Truly I say to you, Inasmuch as you did it to one of the least of these *my brethren, you* did it to Me."

Eternal Judgment I

> 46 "And these will go away into eternal punishment, but the <u>righteous</u> into eternal life."
>
> —Matthew 25:31-46

We are called to righteousness and the following is my simple definition. Righteousness is being **right** with God and with man. And evidence of **righteousness** is when someone makes the **right** decision (moral and ethical) at the **right** time for the **right** purpose. And with no excuse, there is a **right** way of acting in every situation. Although the Word of God is the intelligence of the Holy Spirit, in baptism we receive power — not intelligence. (Also read the 18th chapter of Ezekiel).

> "For whoever does the will of My Father in heaven is My brother and sister and mother."
>
> —Matthew 12:50

> "Which is manifest evidence of the *righteous judgment of God,* that *you* may be counted worthy of the kingdom of God, for which you also suffer; since it is a righteous thing with God to *repay with tribulation those who trouble you.*"
>
> —2 Thessalonians 1:5-6 NKJ

There is a subtle ministry going on here on our behalf. In Psalm 35:1, David cries out, "Contend, O Lord, with those who contend with me; Fight against those who fight against me," In Paul's second letter to the saints in Thessalonians chapter 1 verses 6-7, he writes, " For after all it is only just for God to repay with affliction those who afflict you and to give relief to you who are afflicted and to us as well when the Lord Jesus shall be revealed from heaven with His mighty angels in flaming fire,...." And again, in Romans 1:18, "For the wrath of God is revealed from heaven against all ungodliness and unrighteousness of men...."

Another translation reads in the present tense. "For the wrath of God is *ever being* revealed from heaven...."

> "These qualities show how justly *the judgment of God* works out in your case. Without doubt He intends to use your suffering to make you worthy of His kingdom; yet His justice will one day *repay trouble to those who have troubled you....*"
>
> —2 Thessalonians 1:5-6 Amplified

J. The Law

> "....and as many as have sinned in the law will *be judged by the law.*"
>
> —Romans 2:12

Truth is the *written Word*. There are three standards of truth here:

The first source is found in Psalms 119-142b, "....and thy law is truth" and in verse 151, "....all thy commandments are truth." Jesus' prayer recorded in John 17:17 says, "...sanctify them in the truth; thy word is truth...."

The second source of truth is found in the Good News as written by John in the first chapter, verse 14, "And the word became flesh, and dwelt among us, and we beheld His glory, glory as of the only begotten from the Father, full of grace and truth." And in verse 17, "For the law was given through Moses; grace and truth were realized through Jesus Christ." And in the fourteenth chapter verse 6, he wrote, "I am the way, and the truth, and the life." Paul said, "....if indeed you have heard Him and have been taught in Him, just as truth is in Jesus...." (Ephesians 4:21)

The third source of truth is found in John 14:16-17, "And I will ask the Father, and He will give you another Helper, that He may be with you forever, that is the Spirit of Truth...."

    K. Righteousness

> "*He shall judge the world in righteousness,* and He shall administer judgment for the people in uprightness."
>
> —Psalm 9:8

> "....He shall *judge the world with righteousness,* and the peoples with His Truth."
>
> —Psalm 96:13

> "....He has appointed a day on which He will *judge the world in righteousness....*"
>
> —Acts 17:31

> "....*the righteous judgment of God.*"
>
> —Romans 2:5

> "Finally, there is laid up for me the crown of righteousness, which the Lord, *the righteous judge,* will give to me on that day...."
>
> —2 Timothy 4:8

> "Henceforth there is laid up for me the (victor's) crown of righteousness—for being right with God and doing right—which the Lord, *the righteous judge,* will award to me and recompense me on that (great) day...."
>
> —2 Timothy 4:8 Amplified

> "Now I saw heaven opened, and behold, a white horse. And He who sat on him was called Faithful and True, and in *righteousness He judges* and makes war."
>
> —Revelation 19:11

Eternal Judgment I

> "After that I saw heaven opened, and behold, a white horse (appeared)! The One Who was riding it is called Faithful (trustworthy, loyal, incorruptible, steady) and True, and He *passes judgment and wages war in righteousness* — holiness, justice and uprightness."
>
> —Revelation 19:11 Amplified

    L. Motives and thought life

> "Therefore *judge* nothing before the time, until the Lord comes, who will both bring to light the hidden things of darkness and reveal the *counsels of the hearts*. Then each one's praise will come from God."
>
> —1 Corinthians 4:5

> "So do not make any hasty or *premature judgments* before the time when the Lord comes (again), for He will both bring to light the secret things that are (now hidden) in darkness, and disclose and expose the (*secret*) aims (*motives and purpose*) of hearts. Then every man will receive his (due) commendation from God."
>
> —1 Corinthians 4:5 Amplified

> "….in the day when God will *judge the secrets of men* by Jesus Christ, according to my gospel."
>
> —Romans 2:16 AKJV

> "On that day when, as my Gospel proclaims, God by Jesus Christ will *judge men in regard to the things which they conceal in their hidden thoughts.*"
>
> —Romans 2:16 Amplified

    M. The Gospel

> "….In flaming fire taking vengeance on those who do not know God, and on those who *do not obey the Gospel of our Lord Jesus Christ.*
>
> —2 Thessalonians 1:8

Additional Notes:

The above Scriptures are sober quotations. Perhaps we would do well to quote the following Scriptures every morning:

> "Finally, whatever is true, whatever is honorable, whatever is right, whatever is pure, whatever is lovely, whatever is of good repute, if there is any excellence and if anything worthy of praise, let your mind dwell on these things."
>
> —Philippians 4:8

> "And my God shall supply all your needs according to His riches in glory in Christ Jesus."
>
> —Philippians 4:19

> "And we know that God causes all things to work together for good to those who love God, to those who are called according to His purpose."
>
> —Romans 8:28

We do ourselves a disservice if we discriminate in our Bible reading. Remember—*there is a difference between memorizing the Scriptures and letting them live in you*! The Psalmist's prayer said, "Thy word I have treasured in my heart, that I may not sin against Thee." Ps 119:11

The New Testament in Modern English Revised Edition by J.B. Phillips translated from the latest and best Greek text published by the United Bible Societies in 1966 recognized by scholars of all denominations as the best source available.

Eternal Judgment I
Lesson Study Review 16

1. In what two ways is the word "judgment" used in the Old Testament?

   1. _____

   2. _____

2. What is the dictionary meaning of the word "judge"?

   _____

   _____

   _____

   _____

   _____

3. Why is judgment necessary?

   A. Rom. 2:12 _____

   B. 2 Pet. 3-7 _____

   C. 2 Pet 2:9 _____

   D. Jude 6 _____

   E. John 3:18 _____

   F. Rom. 5:18 _____

   G. John 3:19 _____

4. Who will do the judging at the time of judgment?

   A. Heb. 12:23 _____

   B. John 5:22, 27 _____

   C. 1 Cor. 6:2-3 _____

Eternal Life Principles & Beyond

5. What principles will govern judgment at that time?

   A. Matt. 10:14-15 _____
   B. John 8:15-16 _____
   C. Rev. 20:12, 15 _____
   D. Malachi 3:16 _____
   E. John 12:48-49 _____
   F. Rom. 14:10,12 _____
   G. 2 Cor. 5:10 _____
   H. 1 Peter 1:17 _____
   I. Matt. 12:50 _____
   J. Rom. 2:12 _____
   K. Ps. 9:8 _____
   L. 1 Cor. 4:5 _____
   M. 2 Thess. 1:8 _____

6. In what sense has judgment already taken place?

   A. John 16:11 _____
   B. John 12:31 _____
   C. John 3:18 _____

7. Is there a judgment proceeding at all times? _____ (Yes or No)

   A. Rom. 1:18 _____
   B. 1 Cor. 11:31 _____

8. Name the three standards of Truth by which we shall be judged.

   1. _____
   2. _____
   3. _____

My Inspirations, Challenges & Revelations:

Pivotal Judgments

Heretofore, we have discussed other judgments such as the judgments on Israel, the judgment of sin on the cross and the judgment of the nations at our Lord's second coming. However, the next two prophetic lessons are pivotal judgments.

These two outstanding judgments are The Judgment Seat of Christ and the judgment at the Great White Throne. The first has to do with Believers and occurs after meeting the Lord in the air and the second is concerned only with all unbelievers, believers who were born during the Millennial reign of Christ, and those beheaded because of their testimony of Jesus and came to life and reigned with Him. This second judgment occurs after the Millennial reign of Christ. (See Revelation 20:4).

The following is an overview of some contrasting facts respecting these two central judgments of the future.

As To	Judgment Seat of Christ	Great White Throne
Time:	Before the Millennium	After the Millennium
Place:	In the Heavens	At the Great White Throne
Subjects:	Only the Saints	Millennium Believers/Unbelievers
Basis:	Their works & faithfulness	The sins of the unbeliever
Result:	Rewarded or Suffer Loss	Rewards/Condemned
Destiny:	Eternal Life	Eternal Life/Eternal Death

To the Believer the Lord will say, "Enter into the joy of the Lord" and to the unbeliever He will say, "Depart, you cursed into everlasting fire, prepared for the devil and his angels.... I never knew you." The judgment is according to the justice and righteousness of Yahweh, and is, therefore, final.

My Inspirations, Challenges & Revelations:

Eternal Judgment II

> "For we must all appear before the judgment seat of Christ, that each one may be recompensed for his deeds in the body, according to what he has done, whether good or bad."
>
> —2 Corinthians 5:10

> "For we shall all stand before the judgment seat of God."
>
> —Romans 14:10

What Is The Judgment Seat Of Christ?

This particular lesson will examine only those Scriptures referring to the Judgment Seat of Christ.

It is the place where every Believer will stand alone and be judged by the Words of Christ, and where every nation in this world will be separated from Him and each other. Standing alone before the Judgment Seat of Christ, our true character will be manifested before God, not only to ourselves, but to the assembled intelligent universe. At this judgment, each Believer will be assigned their everlasting portion. Each Believer will receive His reward of Grace proportioned to *"the things done."* This is a searching judgment which shall sever the bad from the good, according to their respective deeds. *Faith and love to God* are the *sole motives that will be recognized by God* as spoken by Jesus in Matthew 12:36-37; 25:35-45, as sound and good.

What Will Happen Just Before This Day?

A. The catching up

> 16 "For the Lord Himself will descend from heaven with a shout, with the voice of the archangel, and with the trumpet of God; and the dead in Christ shall rise first.
> 17 Then we who are alive and remain shall be caught up together with them in the clouds to meet the Lord in the air, and thus we shall always be with the Lord."
>
> —1 Thessalonians 4

> 51 "Behold, I tell you a mystery; we shall not all sleep, but we shall all be changed.
> 52 In a moment, in the twinkling of an eye, at the last trumpet; for the trumpet will sound, and the dead will be raised imperishable, and we shall be changed."
>
> —1 Corinthians 15

Eternal Judgment II

A most unusual and astounding thing is taking place with those Believers who are being raised from their sleep. As the bodies of the righteous and faithful dead are released from their graves, whether in the dirt, water or scattered ashes their molecules, cells, living tissues, muscles and bones are wonderfully reunited unto themselves and raised an imperishable spiritual body. Who can explain the glorious wonder of it all?

    B. The promise

From the lips of the Good Shepherd He promised,

> "In My Father's house are many dwelling places; I go to prepare a place for you. And if I go and prepare a place for you, I will come again, and receive you unto Myself."
>
> —John 14:2-3

It is the blessed hope of Yahweh's Called for almost two thousand years. The personal return of Our Lord to receive His Bride up into their mansion/abode of glory and to receive us unto Himself and truly abide in Him and He in us for....

> "....when He shall appear, we shall be like Him, because we shall see Him just as He is."
>
> —1 John 3:2

The word "*Meno*" translated "dwelling places" (or "mansion" in another translation) in vs 2 of John 14 is the same word translated "abide" in John 15:1-3. The word abide is used 10 times in verses 1-11 and in no other place in the New Testament.

Where Shall This Judgment Take Place?

    A. The Throne of His glory

> 31 "When the Son of Man comes in His glory, and all the holy angels with Him, then He will sit on the throne of His glory."
>
> —Matthew 25:31-46

This Throne is the glory of His judicial authority. He is *coming* in the brightness of His Father's glory. Paul wrote to the church in Corinth, "Therefore *judge nothing* before the time, until the Lord comes...." (1 Corinthians 4:5). We are on trial and probation while dwelling on planet earth. Those who question the purpose of their life here on earth may find solace in the following:

What Are The First Things Christ Will Do?

    A. Believers as individuals are judged at the Judgment Seat of Christ

> 10 "For we shall all stand before the judgment seat of Christ."
>
> 12 " So then each one of us shall give account of himself to God."
>
> —Romans 14

10 "For we must all appear before the judgment seat of Christ...."

—2 Corinthians 5

The word "appear" means "be manifested" and "in our true character." Christ is the absolute Master of all Believers, who will rule their judgments and feelings toward each other while living. We shall not be obliged to account for the conduct of another, nor are they accountable for us. Responsibility necessitates accountability (Romans 14:10-12). This is a searching judgment and *shall sever* the bad from the good according to everyone's respective deeds. It is not the mere external act, but the motive of the deed, as well. Faith and love to Yahweh are the sole motives recognized by Yahweh as spoken by Jesus, is recorded in Matthew 12:36-37; 25:35-45 as sound and good. The sole motive expressed by Jesus, then, is to "do it unto Him," — meaning all that we do and say is done with reverence toward Jesus.

The following is an excerpt from a writing by the late Dr. James McKeever entitled *The Future Revealed,* used by permission:

> "At this judgment the saints will not be wrapped in anything and will have to answer to Christ for their good deeds and bad deeds. Jesus states in Matthew 16:27 "For the Son of Man is going to come in the glory of His Father with His angels; and *will then recompense every man according to his deeds* (doing)." This verse clearly states that we will be recompensed (paid back) for what we have done in our body. Each Believer's work will be tested by fire. If it is good work, it will remain and that person will receive a reward. If it is not good work, it will be burned up and we will "suffer loss." The Scriptures do not tell us what it means to "suffer loss," but I don't want any of it. Verse 15 tells us that we will be saved, but it will be like going through fire. This does not sound like a wonderful way to be saved after we have already been saved! Paul was not the only one who wrote about this. Jesus had something to say about it also: I do not want to be presumptive, for no one can know the specific questions that Christ will ask each of us at the Judgment Seat of Christ. However, from my gleaning of Scriptures, there appear to be five basic areas for which Christ is going to ask each of us to give an account: (1) Every word that we have spoken (2) Our thoughts (3) Our heart attitude (4) Our material/financial resources (5) Deeds done."

Since the above writing by the late Dr. McKeever, this author has discovered five more criteria all of which are listed.

    B. Some things on which we must give account

Jesus has not left us wondering on what He will judge us. He is very clear when He says, "....the word I spoke is what will judge him at the last day." (John 12:48). The following are ten warnings he specifically mentions.

Eternal Judgment II

1. Our words

    A. Verbosity

> 36 "And I say to you, that every careless word that men shall speak, they shall render account for it in the day of judgment."
> 37 "For by your words you shall be justified, and by your words you shall be condemned."
>
> —Matthew 12

Christ did not say that we will not only give an account for every bad word that we have spoken, but we will have to give an account for every careless/idle word we have spoken! He plainly tells us the rules of His Kingdom. He is even more explicit when he warns us about keeping our word to others.

> 37 "But let your statement be, 'yes, yes' or 'no, no'; and anything beyond these is of evil."
>
> —Matthew 5

McKeever paraphrases it this way. "Jesus said your yes better really mean 'yes' and your no better really mean 'no' and if it does not, it is evil and from the evil one."

    B. Swearing to our own hurt

> 1 "O LORD, who may abide in thy tent?
> Who may dwell on thy holy hill?
> 2 He who walks with integrity,
> and works righteousness,
> And speaks truth in his heart.
> 3 He does not slander with his tongue,
> Nor does evil to his neighbor.
> Nor takes up a reproach against his friend;
> 4 In whose eyes a reprobate is despised,
> But who honors those who fear the Lord;
> He swears to his own hurt, and does not change;
>
> —Psalm 15

Most of this Psalm deals either with works or words. Verse 4 says the righteous, who are going to dwell close to Jesus during the millennium, are those who *"swear to their own hurt and do not change."*

From the time I was a young girl, I have known that one of the most important tenets of honor in business deals with family members or neighbors was a person's word and a handshake. There were few formal contracts and law suits not of great concern, since a good name and reputation in the community were of great value. This was representative of what was true in the early days of America.

Eternal Life Principles & Beyond

There are at least two recordings in the Old Testament and one in the Gospels of men in a leadership position who swore to their "own hurt." Read the ninth chapter of Joshua and also read the story of Judge Jephthah's tragic vow, as recorded in the book of Judges 11:29-40. Also read Mark 6:26 regarding King Herod's sorrowful words.

It is not good to tell a person what they want to hear because, sooner or later, it will become evident that your word is worthless and that these words are idle words, at best, and lies, at worst. For Jesus said, "For by your words you shall be justified, and by your words you shall be condemned." (Matthew 12:37). He has forewarned us and such is to the shame of the body of Christ. At the Judgment Seat of Christ, Jesus will be pleased that you kept your word and that you had integrity.

    2. Our thoughts

> 19 "For out of the heart come evil thoughts, murders, adulteries, fornications, thefts, false witness, slanders.
> 20 These are the things which defile the man;...."
>
> —Matthew 15

> 20 And He was saying, "That which proceeds out of the man, that is what defiles the man.
> 21 For from within, out of the heart of men, proceed the evil thoughts fornication, thefts, murders, adulteries,
> 22 deeds of coveting and wickedness, as well as deceit, sensuality, envy, slander, pride and foolishness.
> 23 All these evil things proceed from within and defile the man."
>
> —Mark 7

> 51[b] "He (God) has scattered those who were proud in the *thoughts* of their heart."
>
> —Luke 1

> 34 "And Simeon blessed them, and said to Mary His mother, "Behold, this Child is appointed for the fall and rise of many in Israel, and for a sign to be opposed —
> 35 "and a sword will pierce even your own soul — to the end that *thoughts* from many hearts may be revealed."
>
> —Luke 2

> 5 "We are destroying speculations and every lofty thing raised up against the knowledge of God, and we are taking every *thought* captive to the obedience of Christ."
>
> —2 Corinthians 10

3. Our heart attitude

> "But the things that proceed out of the mouth *come from the heart*, and those defile the man."
>
> —Matthew 15:18

> "....but wait until the Lord comes who will both bring to light the things hidden in the darkness and *disclose the motives of men's hearts*; and then each man's praise will come to him from God."
>
> —1 Corinthians 4:5

Jesus is saying the evil that is in the heart, that is allowed to stir there, to rise up in thought and affection, and to flow forth in voluntary action, is what really defiles a man. There is no sin in word or deed, which was not first in the heart. The meaning for "in the heart" is the "center of our being". It is man's nature to voice in words those things that are deep within us, those hidden things from the core of our being. It is our heart/feelings that determine our thoughts, and consequently our words. Read the complete explanation in Matthew 15:17-19. (Also read Hebrews 4:12 and Proverbs 23:7)

4. Our material resources

> 21 His master said to him, "Well done, good and faithful slave; you were faithful with a few things, I will put you in charge of many things; enter into the joy of your master."
>
> —Matthew 25

Yet in the receiving of their reward, the Lord speaks in warm and delighted commendation to both slaves and to both, the reward is precisely the same. They were given dominion over many things. First He commends them. Secondly He rewards them. Read verses 14-23 and observe the disproportion between the work and the reward. What charge we receive from Yahweh, what work we do for Yahweh in this world, is but very little compared with the joy set before us.

5. Believers are judged for their deeds and rewarded accordingly

> "For the Son of Man is going to come in the glory of His Father with His angels; and *will then recompense every man according to his deeds....*"
>
> —Matthew 16:27

> "For we must all appear before the judgment seat of Christ, *that each one may receive the things done in the body, according to what he has done, whether good or bad."*
>
> —2 Corinthians 5:10

Jesus Himself, in no uncertain terms, tells us on what basis He will judge us. He said that He is going to pay back (recompense) every man according to his deeds (Matthew 16:27). These deeds and actions are those given in the Scriptures and are not to be confused with the different denominational religious dogmas, regardless of sincerity of heart. We can't do anything about the past, but we can do something from today forward. We need to be highly concerned about our thoughts since they lead to our actions. Would your neighbors classify you as a man or woman of good deeds and actions?

On the Day of Judgment, we will not be able to say someone else made us do it or "the devil made me do it," etc. We are responsible for ourselves and to The Truth, who is sitting before us on His Throne, who burns with the truth. When we blame someone else, it is a sign we are in rebellion, among having other character flaws. One of the fruit of the Holy Spirit is "self-control." With Christ's help, He can give us control over our emotions. He gave us the range of emotional octave. He gave us the power of choice. We should respond to the guidance of the Holy Spirit at every moment here on earth.

6. Believers are judged for their works and rewarded accordingly

12 "Now if anyone builds on this foundation with gold, silver, precious stones, wood, hay, straw,

13 each one's work *will become clear; for the day will declare it, because it will be revealed by fire;* and *the fire will test each one's work,* of what sort it is.

14 If anyone's work which he has built on it endures, *he will receive a reward.*

15 If anyone's work is burned, *he will suffer loss;* but he himself will be saved, yet so as through fire."

—1 Corinthians 3

"But if anyone builds upon the Foundation, whether it be with gold, silver, precious stones. wood, hay straw, the work of each (one) will become (plainly, openly) known — *shown for what it is; for the day (of Christ) will disclose and declare it, because it will be revealed with fire, and the fire will test and critically appraise the character and worth of the work each person has done.* If the work which any person has built on this Foundation — any product of his efforts whatever — survives (this test), *he will get his reward.* But if any person's work is burned up (under the test), *he will suffer the loss* (of it all, losing his reward), though he himself will be saved, but only as (one who has passed) through fire."

—1 Corinthians 3:12-15 Amplified

Eternal Judgment II

Some build upon their foundation with gold, silver and precious stones, namely, those people who speak nothing but the truth as it is in Jesus and preach nothing else. This is building well upon a good foundation. Those who build upon a wood, hay and/or stubble foundation depart from the mind of Christ in many particulars and will not pass the test when the day of trial shall come.

7. Our Actions

> "Boast no more so very proudly,
> Do not let arrogance come out of your mouth;
> For the Lord is a God of knowledge,
> And with Him actions are weighed."
>
> —1 Samuel 2:3

Years ago, when unruly children threw a temper tantrum, especially when the child would defend themselves after being corrected, parents would say, I don't believe you because "actions speak louder than words." Indicating, the child was not expressing the fruit of self-control.

On the other hand, the opposite is also true. This Scripture refers to Hannah, the wife of Elkanah, who being barren many years, finally conceived and gave birth to a boy child, thereby saving her reputation. In her holy joy and adoration and thanksgiving to the Lord, Hannah lost some self-control; when with exuberance, she sang a beautiful song to God, giving Him a tribute of thanks for taking away her reproach and for the divine goodness of a child that could only come from Him in answer to her petition, and claiming God's unerring justice.

8. How we used our time

> "....Cretans are always liars, evil beasts, *lazy gluttons*."
>
> —Titus 1:12

> "But his master answered and said to him, 'You wicked, *lazy slave,*
> you knew that I reap where I did not sow, and gather where I scattered
> no seed.'"
>
> —Matthew 25:26

> "Therefore, be careful how you walk, not as unwise men, but as wise,
> *making the most of your time,* because the days are evil."
>
> —Ephesians 5:15-16

> And if you address as Father the One who impartially judges
> according to each man's work, conduct yourselves in fear *during the
> time of your stay upon earth*;
>
> —1 Peter 1:17

Eternal Life Principles & Beyond

In reference to young widows, the Apostle Paul exhorted Pastor Timothy by saying,

> "And at the same time they also learn to be idle, as they go around from house to house; and not merely idle, but also gossips and busybodies, talking about things not proper to mention. Therefore, I want younger widows to get married, bear children, keep house, and give the enemy no occasion for reproach;...."
>
> —1 Timothy 5:13-14

God's Minute

> I have only just a minute
> Only sixty seconds in it,
> Forced upon me, don't refuse it
> Didn't seek it, didn't choose it
> But it's up to me to use it
> I must suffer if I abuse it
> Just a tiny little minute
> But Eternity is in it.
>
> —Author unknown

Even the neutral things, such as wasting time and efforts, will be burned up and we will "suffer loss." But again, the Bible does not indicate what that means, but be assured that it is not advantageous.

9. What did we do with the money He gave us?

Both all the Old Testament (Strongs #3603) and all the New Testament (Strongs #5007) Scriptures define talents as money. The talent is described as round, a measure of weight, a balance, that which is weighed and that a talent's weight is one hundred pounds!

In Matthew 25:24-28 Jesus tells a parable of a master who had to go out of town on business. Before doing so, he gave to each servant talents according to their ability. The master knew the abilities of each of his servants and distributed the money according to their ability.

> 22 The one also who had received the two talents came up and said, "Master, you entrusted to me two talents; see, I have gained two more talents."
> 23 His master said to him, "Well done, good and faithful slave; you were faithful with a few things, I will put you in charge of many things; enter into the joy of your master."
>
> —Matthew 25

According to verse 15 both slaves were given money "according to their own ability."

Eternal Judgment II

We need to consider four things here:

1. It's the master who distributes the money.
2. The servant has nothing, deserves nothing, and has no claim on the master. Yet the master delivers to each servant his goods, not for their advantage, but for their comfort and salvation.
3. The master distributes the money diversely, giving one servant five, to another two and to another one. No one can complain that he has been forgotten by the master.
4. The master distributes the money with wisdom. He gave to each according to their ability because he knew the power each had to improve what was given him.

Two of the servants took a <u>risk</u> and traded as soon as the master was gone. They immediately applied themselves to their business. Both men doubled what they initially received. The third servant refused to take a risk and dug a hole in the ground and buried it for safe keeping.

Upon the master's return home, he commends the first two servants. Then he rewards them <u>equally</u> regardless of each servant's profits. There is a disproportion between the work and the reward, however, Christ brings both servants equally into His joy.

The third servant first remarks, I have not increased my money but neither have I lost it. Secondly he confesses to burying it, as if he were prudent in the matter of not risking loss. Thirdly he becomes defensive saying, "I know you are a hard man." And fourthly he admits being afraid, and that it would be impossible to please him. The master called him wicked, slothful and careless in the work he gave him to do and took the money from him.

The conclusion to this parable is we should improve on what we have been given, no matter how small the improvement is and enter the Kingdom of God as a person who has received most from His master.

10. Preachers and teachers will have a stricter accountability

> "But avoid worldly and empty chatter for it will lead to further ungodliness, ..."
>
> —2 Timothy 2:16

Preachers and teachers are to avoid error and accurately divide the Word. Those who are not agreeable to the doctrines of truth, as laid down by Paul, is seen by Yahweh as, "empty and profane babblings", which usually leads to increasing confusion and in ungodliness. The infecting of just one point of doctrine often proves to infect other simple gospel truths. These babblers pretend to give spiritual pasture to their disciples are in fact only feeding them spiritual cancer that will only cause gangrene and putrefaction. Paul mentions Hymeneus and Philetus who were advancing erroneous doctrines as guilty of this practice.

Eternal Life Principles & Beyond

In Matthew 18:6, Mark 9:42 and Luke 17:2 Jesus emphatically speaks against anyone who causes another to quarrel and weaken in their belief and trust in Christ and His Words. This sin is so heinous and so great, that to ruin another person's faith and conviction in Yahweh and in his Messiah, Yeshua, that Jesus guarantees us that they will meet with the most perfect punishment.

A Cleansing Of Fire

> 10 According to the grace of God which was given to me, as a wise master builder I laid a foundation, and another is building upon it. But let each man be careful how he builds upon it.
>
> 11 For no man can lay a foundation other than the one which is laid, which is Jesus Christ.
>
> 12 Now if any man builds upon the foundation with gold, silver, precious stones, wood, hay, straw,
>
> 13 each man's work will become evident; for the day will show it, because it is to be revealed with fire; and the fire itself will test the quality of each man's work.
>
> 14 If any man's work which he has built upon it remains, he shall receive a reward.
>
> 15 If any man's work is burned up, he shall *suffer loss*; but he himself shall be saved, yet so as through fire."
>
> —1 Corinthians 3

When we stand before the Judgment Seat of Christ, the Lord is going to apply fire to our "building," (the character of our soul and our works) that we have built on His foundation. The good things we have done, represented by gold and silver, will not be burned up, but will remain. Verse 14 tells us that we will receive a reward for those good things. It is important to note this is not a literal fire, but it connotes "to test or weigh" our life's thoughts, words, deeds and actions. Works and virtues are not tangible, but it's as if they were.

However, the bad things that we have done will also be burned up and cause us to "suffer loss." In verse 15 we see that if the work that a man has built upon is not built on the foundation of Christ, it is totally burned up, but he will be saved "yet so as through fire." In other words, he will be saved, but it will be equivalent to him as going through the fire of judgment. It will be a difficult trial!

One example might be similar to a man who designs and labors daily and diligently to build his own house over a year's time and somehow inadvertently misses a step in the wiring process. After a month of great satisfaction and enjoying the fruits of his labor, he's suddenly awakened late one night only to discover his house engulfed in flames. The warning comes just in time for him to escape with his life. He has narrowly saved his life but lost his house, his goods, his comfort and satisfaction in his joy of labor.

Eternal Judgment II

Another example would be like that of a shipwrecked merchant in a severe thunder storm. Having spent years establishing and building his business of expensive goods and exotic spices, he suddenly finds himself in a category five hurricane. Though he loses his ship and his merchandise, he struggles for days to make it to shore on a piece of driftwood. Thoroughly exhausted and dehydrated from days of battling the fierce winds and waves, he finally makes it to land.

The Bride Has Made Herself Ready

> 7 "Let us rejoice and be glad and give the glory to Him, for the marriage of the Lamb has come and His bride has made herself ready.
> 8 And it was given to her to clothe herself in fine linen, bright and clean; for the fine linen is the righteous acts of the saints."
> —Revelation 19

The Believer is in a more glorious state of Christlikeness than ever before. The fine linen was purchased by her righteous acts and after the cleansing of suffering loss by fire at the judgment. The tremendous event of this heavenly marriage has now taken place. The Great Bridegroom receives the Bride and at this moment invites the Bride to the marriage supper of the Lamb. The time has come for the blessed event of the return of Our Lord and His Overcomers; the marriage - the marriage feast of the Lamb. Hallelujah!

Believers Will Be Rewarded

> "....but wait until the Lord comes who will both bring to light the things hidden in the darkness and disclose the motives of men's hearts; and then each man's praise will come to him from God."
> —1 Corinthians 4:5

The Lord is the sole Decider or Adjudicator. He has the prerogative of final judgment and praise.

> "See, I come quickly! I carry my reward with me, and repay every man according to his deeds."
> —Revelation 22:12

Jesus is saying, "I am coming to establish My cause and render comfort and support to each of My followers and punish the wicked." It will be Christ's rule of judgment on this great day, that He, the author and Finisher of our faith, will dispense rewards and punishments to men according to their works, as they agree with the Word of God.

This final word from Jesus in Revelation 22:12, "Behold, I am coming quickly, and My reward is with Me, to render to every man according to what he has done...." Should not these exacting words be our outlook for holy "ambition?" Ask Yahweh to help you

Eternal Life Principles & Beyond

emphasize good works, holiness and righteousness in your personal life. (Read also Hebrews 6:10; 2 John 8 and 2 Corinthians 9:6-9). The rewards are promises out of Yahweh's benevolence and are a trophy of a race well run, or a work well done.

The Rewards

The Lord now plaudits His Bride, those who have been obedient to His will, and says,

> "Well done, good and faithful slave, you were faithful with a few things, I will put you in charge of many things, enter into the joy of your master."
> —Matthew 25:21

The following list of rewards for the Believer is given according to their faithfulness and service for the Lord (See Ephesians 6:2).

1. The reward of the prophet and the righteous man - Matthew 10:41-42
2. The reward of faithfulness – Matthew 25:21-23
3. The reward of the incorruptible crown – 1 Corinthians 9:25-27, 1 John 2:28
4. The reward of the crown of rejoicing – 1 Thessalonians 2:19-20
5. The reward of the crown of righteousness - 2 Timothy 4:8
6. The reward of the crown of life – James 1:12, Revelation 2:10
7. The reward of the crown of glory – 1 Peter 5:2-4, Hebrews 2:9
8. The reward to Saints and Servants – Revelation 11:18
9. The Crown of God – Revelation 3:11; 4:4

The Bible, Our Absolute Guideline For Rewards

> 21 "Therefore, if a man cleanses himself from these things, he will be a vessel for honor, sanctified, useful to the Master, prepared for every good work."
> —2 Timothy 2

> 16 "All Scripture is inspired by God and profitable for teaching, for reproof, for correction, for training in righteousness;
> 17 that the man of God may be adequate, equipped for every good work."
> —2 Timothy 3

The Priceless Truth clearly tells us that Yahweh's Word is adequate to equip every man for every good work. One mentioned good work, (in Hebrews 10:23-24), is stimulating one another to love and the doing of good deeds.

Paul spent much time encouraging Timothy to "suffer hardship as a good soldier of Christ Jesus," (2 Timothy 2:3). He frequently reminded Timothy that he must see to it that in carrying on spiritual warfare he went by all the rules of spiritual warfare and that

Eternal Judgment II

he be careful to observe the laws of war (vs 5). In doing that which is good we must take care that we do it in a right manner with integrity and that our good may not be spoken as evil.

Paul exhorted to "cleanse ourselves and to be a vessel of honor for some purpose." "Therefore, if a man cleanses himself from these things, he will be a vessel for honor, sanctified, useful to the Master, prepared for every good work." (2 Timothy 2:21) For a list of things Paul wrote to cleanse the soul also read verses 19-25.

Summary:

This lesson is a convicting source of truth of what separates those who are on fire for Christ and those who are just lukewarm, or profess to be godly, but aren't.

During the hard times, encourage yourself to keep your integrity and hold fast to Christ. In a time of persecution, be fit for the Master's use by being a vessel of honor. Be prepared for every good work and word. Depart from all iniquity and walk uprightly with your God. Live as though Christ died yesterday, arose this morning, and is coming back tomorrow. For the way of error is downhill.

Additional Notes:

Some may question Christ's refusal to intervene in the matter according to (Luke 12).

> 13 And someone in the crowd said to Him, "Teacher, tell my brother to divide the family inheritance with me."
> 14 But He said to him. "Man, who appointed Me a judge or arbiter over you?"

The Greek word *"krites"* in verse 14 means *"judge,"* nothing more, nothing less. Christ would not assume either a legislative power, or a judicial power while on earth. His is a spiritual kingdom not of this world.

Matthew Henry explains the Lord's spiritual kingdom in this verse as follows:

1. It does not interfere with civil powers.
2. It does not intermeddle with civil rights: it obliges all to do justly according to the settled rules of equity.
3. It does not encourage our expectations of worldly advantages by our religion.
4. It does not encourage our contests with our brethren, and our being rigorous and high in our demands.

He further adds:

11. Keep an eye on your heart.
12. Take heed of covetousness.
13. Life does not consist in the abundance of things to possess.

Eternal Life Principles & Beyond

Adam Clarke puts it this way — "A minister of Christ ought not to concern himself with secular affairs any further than charity and the order of discipline require it. Better to leave all these things to the civil magistrate...."

In light of this lesson, it is important to again, address the seemingly contradicting statement by Jesus as recorded by John in chapter 12 of his gospel —

> 47 "And if anyone hears My sayings, and does not keep them, I do not judge him; for I did not come to judge the world, but to save the world.
> 48 "He who rejects Me, and does not receive My sayings, has one who judges him; the word I spoke is what will judge him at the last day."

Jesus' birth and the Will of the Father at that time, while He walked on earth, were to disclose His role as Savior to the people. This did not demand He draw upon His deity to judge. The Greek *"krino"* in these verses is a primary verb meaning to judge, act as judge, pass judgment, go to law, trial, decide, condemn. This He will do on the last day.

The gospels written by Matthew and Mark do not record any statement by Jesus as to His judging. Luke records only two and John records about ten. All Scriptures recorded by John use the Greek *"krino"*.

Also worthy of mention, the translation in (Romans 14:10) "judgment seat of God" is found in all the most ancient and best manuscripts. It seems to be joined to 2 Corinthians 5:10 because of the 11th and 12th verses.

> 11 For it is written, "As I live, says the Lord, every knee shall bow to Me, and every tongue shall give praise to God."
> 12 So then each one of us shall give account of himself to God.

To illustrate the sameness in the two Scriptures, Paul quotes the 11th and 12th passage out of the Old Testament which speaks of Christ's universal sovereignty and dominion, and that established with an oath. As I live (saith the Lord KJV) every knee shall bow to me. Here is proof that Christ is part of the Godhead.

Eternal Judgment II
Lesson Study Review 17

1. Describe in your own words what is taking place at the Judgment Seat of Christ.

   _____

   _____

   _____

   _____

   _____

   _____

   _____

   _____

   _____

2. Name at least five things we will be judged on.

   1. _____

   2. _____

   3. _____

   4. _____

   5. _____

3. Is there a judgment that is reserved for a particular time in the future? _____ (Yes or No)

   A. Matt. 25:31 _____

   B. Heb. 9:27 _____

4. How does the Bible describe the place where the judgment shall take place?

   Rom. 14:10 _____

5. After Jesus' water baptism, His ministry to the Jews was to heal, deliver, judge and reveal the love of the Father. _____ (True or False)

6. The Lord's love for us contains no wrath. _____ (True or False)

7. The Lord's love for us contains no chastisement. _____ (True or False)

8. The Lord's love for us contains no discipline. _____ (True or False)

9. Watching Christian TV Programming is not wasting time. _____ (True or False)

   Explain your answer:

   _____

   _____

   _____

   _____

   _____

   _____

   _____

   _____

   _____

   _____

My Inspirations, Challenges & Revelations:

Eternal Judgment III

> 11 "And I saw a great white throne and Him who sat upon it, from whose presence earth and heaven fled away, and no place was found for them.
>
> 12 And I saw the dead, the great and the small, standing before the throne, and books were opened; and another book was opened, which is the book of life; and the dead were judged from the things which were written in the books, according to their deeds.
>
> 13 And the sea gave up the dead which were in it, and death and Hades gave up the dead which were in them; and they were judged, every one of them according to their deeds.
>
> 14 And death and Hades were thrown into the lake of fire.
>
> 15 This is the second death, the lake of fire. And if anyone's name was not found written in the book of life, he was thrown into the lake of fire."
>
> —Revelation 20

What Is The Great White Throne Judgment?

This judgment is before the Throne of His Majesty, the Almighty, Holy and Everlasting God the Father, which occurs after the millennium (Revelation 20:7) and after the earth is destroyed/renovated by fire (2 Peter 3:10 and Revelation 20:11). At this judgment, the "overcomer" saints, now in part, "the Bride of Christ" and "ruler over many," and in their "imperishable bodies," will be wrapped in their white linen robes of the righteousness of Christ, and God will look at us as though we are perfect, for now we are "like Him." The Overcomers now take their place to judge myriads and myriads of angels, the nations and the unsaved who were born during the millennium.

What Will Happen On This Day?

> "And I saw the dead (alive), the great and the small, standing before the throne, and books were opened; and another book was opened, which is *the book of life*; and the dead were judged from the things which were written in the books, according to their deeds."
>
> —Revelation 20:12

Eternal Judgment III

This will be a "great day," the one and only day, also known as "that day." We shall behold the Throne, the *Great White Throne*, notably and exceptionally "fuller" glistening translucent white and very most glorious Throne. We shall behold the Judge, perfectly just and righteous, and the LORD of Hosts, Jesus the Christ, triumphantly sitting as King of kings, LORD of lords, King of lords and LORD of Kings (Daniel 2:47). Hallelujah!!

On an enormous table lay many very large thick books. It would not be unrealistic and unreasonable to say each book is as large as an ordinary kitchen tabletop. These large books are opened. They are the Book of Life, the Book of Remembrance, the Book of Deeds (good and evil), and the Scriptures, which are the statute books of heaven, the rule of life.

Again, in a moment, the sound of a *great* trumpet blast is heard throughout the world, which is known as Yahweh's trumpet in Thessalonians and not one of the seven listed in the Book of Revelation chapters 8, 9 & 11. He will send forth His angels to gather together His Believers from the four winds, from one end of the sky to the other (Matthew 24:31), and the sea and the earth, to give up all the bodies (1 Corinthians 15:52). As the bodies of the dead in Christ are released from their temporary holding place, their molecules, cells, living tissues, muscles and the bones of everyone's spirit, soul and body are reunited unto themselves and raised as an imperishable spiritual body.

Immediately following, Hades (the grave, the place of separated spirits) (Revelation 20:13) of the unbelievers gives up the dead it has held for thousands of years. Gravity can no longer contain them in this holding place. This is the second part of the first resurrection. It is now the receiving of the unbelievers who were in their graves and who were not taken up in the first gathering to Christ, and all those born during Christ's millennial Kingdom. All of this happens in the blinking of the eye. (If I, the author, believe this, then eternal damnation is everlasting. Nowhere does the Scripture say their bodies will not be an imperishable spiritual body. A different distinction is not made on this basis; therefore, we can conclude eternal damnation is forever and everlasting regarding this group also. This is not to contradict my comments in the lesson on Hell. This we will understand when we see Him. Please read my comments in the lesson on Hell.)

Where Does This Judgment Take Place?

> Thus says the LORD, "Heaven is My throne, and the earth is My footstool...."
>
> —Isaiah 66:1

If Yahweh has so bright a throne as described above, and so large a footstool, where then can we build a house for this God? If His residence is so full of glory, where else can He rest? He has a heaven and earth of His own making, but He looks with favor to His Called, His Chosen, the Believers and Overcomers, to those who are poor of spirit, to those who are humble, to those who are self-denying and whose heart is contrite toward sin, and eager to repent. Such a heart is a living temple for Yahweh to dwell in. It is the place of His rest. However, He will not find a penitent heart among those standing before Him on this day.

When Does This Happen?

> 5 The rest of the dead did not come to life and until the thousand years were completed. This is the first resurrection.
> 6 Blessed and holy is the one who has a part in the first resurrection; over these the second death has no power, but they will be priests of God and of Christ and will reign with Him for a thousand years.
>
> —Revelation 20

Notice this verse says, "the rest of the dead." Most denominations believe in the resurrection. However, the first and only resurrection is not a general resurrection. The time of the first resurrection for each group of individuals is separated by 1,000 years, as clearly stated in Revelation 20. There will be two first resurrections, the living and the dead, but every person is resurrected only once depending on which group they are in. It is known as "the resurrection of the just," and "the resurrection of the unjust" and also "the resurrection of life" and "the resurrection of damnation." (See John 5:28-29; Luke 14:13-14; 1 Corinthians 15:22-23 and Philippians 3:11). The Believers are resurrected to attend the Judgment Seat of Christ and the unbelievers, along with those born during the Millennium (Believers and unbelievers) are resurrected to attend the Great White Throne Judgment. The Believer to judge and the unbeliever to be judged. This is the second part of the first and only resurrection. To miss it here will only cause confusion.

What Does The Throne Room Look Like?

> 3 And He who was sitting was like a jasper stone and a sardis in appearance; and there was a rainbow around the throne, like an emerald in appearance.
> 4 And around the throne were twenty-four thrones; and upon the thrones I saw twenty-four elders sitting, clothed in white garments, and golden crowns on their heads.
> 5 And from the throne proceed flashes of lightning and sounds and peals of thunder. And there were seven lamps of fire burning before the throne, which are the seven Spirits of God;
> 6 and before the throne there was, as it were, a sea of glass like crystal; and in the center and around the throne, four living creatures full of eyes in front and behind.
>
> —Revelation 4

Eternal Judgment III

The rainbow could be a reference back to the promise to Noah. The Greek word "iris" could mean "halo." John could have seen an emerald colored, (or play of colors) rainbow. This rainbow of varied colored translucent and iridescent lights casts a glimmering halo affect around the Throne.

Daniel was given an indescribable glimpse of "that day" and in return, he gives us a spectacular and breath-taking account of his vision.

> 9 "I kept looking
> Until thrones were set up,
> And the Ancient of Days took His seat;
> His vesture was like white snow,
> And the hair of His head like pure wool.
> His throne was ablaze with flames,
> Its wheels were burning fire.
> 10 A river of fire was flowing
> And coming out from before Him;
> Thousands upon thousands were attending Him,
> And myriads upon myriads were standing before Him;
> The court sat,
> And the books were opened."
> 11 Then I kept looking because of the sound of the boastful words which the horn was speaking; I kept looking until the beast was slain, and its body was destroyed and given to the burning fire.
> 12 As for the rest of the beasts, their dominion was taken away, but an extension of life was granted to them for an appointed period of time.
> 13 I kept looking in the night visions,
> And behold, with the clouds of heaven
> One like a Son of Man was coming,
> And He came up to the Ancient of Days
> And was presented before Him.
> 14 And to Him was given dominion,
> Glory and a kingdom,
> That all the peoples, nations, and men
> of every language might serve Him.
> His dominion is an everlasting dominion
> which will not pass away;
> And His kingdom is one
> which will not be destroyed."
> —Daniel 7

This great day is fully orchestrated in wondrous harmony and power by the Holy Spirit. It is a day of cataclysmic events! The scene opens with the sound of long, shiny, golden trumpets as they herald the presence of the Almighty King of the universe. How solemn and impressive to watch the Ancient of Days as He slowly takes His seat. It is impossible to describe the Occupant of that Throne. Suddenly, simultaneous spectacular breathtaking events are occurring in harmonious unity, one split second after the other! Very long silver trumpets are sounding their well-ordered distinct tones announcing each event. Mighty and powerful angels are obediently and gloriously gathering His elect from the four corners of the earth. As Yahweh sits between the cherubim they are gloriously and joyously and lovingly crying out, "Holy, Holy, Holy, is the Lord God of Hosts." The four Living Beings, full of eyes, with one wheel inside another are radiantly sparkling and moving straight forward like bolts of lightning without turning saying, "Holy, Holy, Holy, is the Lord God the Almighty, who was and who is and who is to come." The cherubim are standing on the right side of the temple with their wings sounding like the voice of God Almighty when He speaks. And when the Cherubim move the Living Beings follow. The Seraphim are calling out to one another "Holy, Holy, Holy is the Lord of hosts. The whole earth is full of His glory" The four living creatures, each holding a harp and golden bowls full of incense, which are the prayers of the saints, are joyously singing a new song. The "twelve apostles of the Lamb" are standing by in awe and proudly, yet humbly, watching the wonder of it all. The 24 elders are majestically sitting upon 24 great thrones clothed in electrifying white garments with sparkling golden crowns on their heads. With an attitude of reverence and glory they will fall down and bow before Him who sits on the Throne. They honor Him by casting their crowns at His feet. And just above God's throne proceed flashes of lightning and sounds and peals of thunder. (See Ezekiel Chapters 1 and 10:16-17; Revelation 4:4 and Chapter 11, and 21:14).

No earthly movie production ever produced could begin to compare to these awesome events. Nor could this scene ever be captured and reduced to earthly imagination.

    A. Judgment will occur as Christ sits once again on His Throne of glory

> "Therefore *judge nothing* before the time, *until the Lord comes."*
> —1 Corinthians 4:5

> "For the mystery of lawlessness is already at work; only He who now restrains will do so until He is taken out of the way. And then the lawless one will be revealed whom the Lord will consume with the breath of His mouth and destroy with the brightness of His coming. The coming of the lawless one is according to the working of Satan, with all power, signs and lying wonders, and with all unrighteous deception among those who perish, because they did not receive the love of the truth, that they might be saved."
> —2 Thessalonians 2:7-10 NKJV

Jesus came the first time as our Savior. Now He returns as Judge with ten thousands upon thousands of His Overcomers to judge the nations and wage war (See Revelation 19:11-16). In verse 41 of Matthew 25 the words "everlasting fire, prepared for the devil and his angels" points out they were "first in transgression;" therefore, their sentence is executed first and cast out in the sight of the righteous.

Eternal Judgment III

> *"....when the Lord Jesus shall be revealed from heaven with His mighty angels,* in flaming fire taking vengeance on them that know not God, and that obey not the gospel of Our Lord Jesus Christ, who shall be punished with everlasting destruction from the presence of the Lord, and from the glory of his power; when He shall come to be glorified in His saints, and to be admired in all them that believe....in *that day."*
>
> —2 Thessalonians 1:7-10 AKJV

> "I charge you therefore, before God and the Lord Jesus Christ, who will *judge the living and the dead at His appearing and His kingdom."*
>
> —2 Timothy 4:1

> "Behold, *the Lord comes* with ten thousands of His saints, to *execute judgment on all...."*
>
> —Jude 14-15

What Will Happen At This Judgment?

Psalms 93:2 & 97:2b gives us an absolute that we can bank on. Yahweh's divine energy established His Throne on the foundation of Righteousness and Judgment before the beginning of time and creation of the world. "The Hebrew "tsedek" translated "righteousness" means - gives all due and holds all things in even balance. The Hebrew "mishpat" translated "judgment" means - determines everything according to truth and justice.

The Lord Jesus went one step further as recorded by John in 12:46-50. Verse 48 states "The words that I have spoken, the same shall judge him." Another translation reads, "The words that I have spoken, the same shall judge the unbelievers in the last day." The unbelievers will convict themselves of their crimes as His Words condemn them. His Words rule their doom.

The following is a list of happenings that are not necessarily in sequential order. They are simply a brief list of what will happen.

   A. Judge the nations

Immediately after the Judgment Seat of Christ the Lord Jesus is going to judge the nations. The "Overcomer" Believers in Christ, will be in attendance at this time and will also be sitting on the Judge's panel. For anyone who thinks we will be harsh, must know our emotions will not be involved in the judging process. We will be judging according to the Truth we've learned by rightly dividing His Word.

> 31 "But when the Son of man comes in His glory, and all the angels with Him, then He will sit on His glorious throne.
> 32 "And all the nations will be gathered before Him; and He will separate them from one another, as the shepherd separates the sheep from the goats;

Eternal Life Principles & Beyond

> 33 and He will put the sheep on his right, and the goats on the left.
> 34 "Then the King will say to those on His right, 'Come, you who are blessed of My Father, inherit the kingdom prepared for you from the foundation of the world....'"
>
> —Matthew 25

All nations of men, that are made of one blood, are summoned before Christ's tribunal. The distinction will then be made for *He shall separate* the nations *one from another* and He shall separate His followers from those who have rejected Him.

Jesus forewarned the cities in which most of His miracles were done that in the Day of Judgment it shall be more tolerable for the land of Sodom than for them because of their unrepentant hearts. Christ charged them for their shameful and ungrateful attitudes that He might lead them to repentance, but they repented not. (See Matthew 11:20-24.)

    1. A corporate inheritance is given

> 34 "Then the King will say to those on His right, 'Come, you who are blessed of My Father, inherit the kingdom prepared for you from the foundation of the world....'"
>
> —Matthew 25

Jesus words, *"you who are blessed of My Father"* is the glory conferred upon those on His right. When King Jesus exercises His power and pronounces them blessed, His authority confirms it. The Saints are reproached and cursed by the world, but blessed of God. *Inherit the kingdom prepared for you!*

    B. The saints have a role in the judging

> 2 "Or do you not know that the saints will judge the world? And if the world is judged by you, are you not competent to constitute the smallest law courts?
> 3 Do you not know that we shall judge angels?"
>
> —1 Corinthians 6

The saints of the Most High will be in their glorified bodies and they will execute judgment on the world and be given the kingdom of the earth that is promised to them.

    C. Judgment of the sinner to death and judgment of the Believers to the reward of Eternal Life.

> "The nations were angry, and Your wrath has come, and the *time of the dead, that they shall be judged,* and that You should reward Your servants the prophets and the saints, and those who fear Your name, small and great, and *should destroy those who destroy the earth."*
>
> —Revelation 11:18

Eternal Judgment III

> "And these (the unrighteous) will go away *into everlasting punishment,* but the righteous into eternal life."
>
> —Matthew 25:46

In this, the last phase of judgment and of the time Christ spoke of when He said, "There will be weeping and gnashing of teeth there when you see Abraham and Isaac and Jacob and all the prophets in the kingdom of God but yourselves being cast out" (Luke 13:28). It appears the wicked are sentenced first in the sight of the righteous — whose glory will not be beheld by the wicked — while their descent into "their own place" will be witnessed by the righteous.

    D. Rewards for the Saint

        1. Possession of the kingdom forever

One reward for the Believer is listed in the Book of Daniel 7:18.

> "But the saints of the Highest One will receive the kingdom and possess the kingdom forever for all ages to come."

(Read also verses 22 and 27).

        2. Crown of righteousness

In Paul's last letter to Timothy he informs him that the time of his departure has come. He says in chapter 4,

> 7 I have fought the good fight, I have finished the course, I have kept the faith;
> 8 in the future there is laid up for me the crown of righteousness, which the Lord, the righteous Judge, will award to me on that day; and not only to me, but also to all who have loved His appearing.

Paul preached the "whole purpose of God" never betraying any of the great doctrines. How important it is for the Believer to look with a heart of love for the second coming of our Lord and Savior Jesus Christ, that he/she may receive the "crown of righteousness." The "crown of righteousness" is a reward to be earned by the saved overcomer.

        3. Overcomer rewards

            a. Overcomers will eat of the tree of life, which is in the Paradise of God (Rev. 2:7).

            b. Overcomers will receive the crown of life and not be hurt by the second death (Rev. 2:10-11).

Eternal Life Principles & Beyond

    c. Overcomers will eat hidden manna and receive a white stone with a new name written on the stone which no one knows but he who receives it (Rev. 2-17b).

    d. Overcomers will be given authority over the nations (Rev. 2:26).

    e. Overcomers will be given the Morning Star (Rev. 2:28).

    f. Overcomers will be clothed in white garments, their name will not be erased from the book of life, and Jesus will confess their name before His Father and before His angels (Rev. 3:5).

    g. Overcomers will be a pillar in the temple of God and they will not go out from it anymore, and Jesus will write upon them the name of His God and the name of the city of His God, which is The New Jerusalem, which comes down out of heaven from His God and His new name (Rev. 3:12).

    h. Overcomers will be granted the privilege to sit down with Him on His throne (Rev. 3:21).

Note: Revelation 2:17b contains two rewards
          Revelation 3:5 contains three rewards
          Revelation 3:12 contains two rewards

These rewards are conditional and are based on two requirements — hearing and doing.

To quote the late Dr. James McKeever from page 10, in his book *You Can Overcome*:

> "Most Christians tend to think of all Christians as being equal for all eternity. Unfortunately the Bible does not teach this.... the Bible teaches that there is a subset of Christians called the overcomers. These overcomers are promised special positions and special privileges throughout eternity, yet the average born-again Christians know little, if anything, about the overcomers."

    E. Sinners judged for sin and consigned to punishment

King Solomon's very last written words published in Ecclesiastes states:

> "For God will bring every act to judgment, everything which is hidden, whether it is good or evil."
>
> —Ecclesiastes 12:14

> "....in flaming fire *taking vengeance* on those who do not know God, and on those who do not obey the gospel of our Lord Jesus Christ. *These shall be punished with everlasting destruction from the presence of the Lord and from the glory of his His power....*"
>
> —2 Thessalonians 1:8-9

Eternal Judgment III

> "And anyone not found written in the Book of Life *was cast into the lake of fire.*"
>
> —Revelation 20:15

All those who have made a covenant with death, and an agreement with hell/the lake of fire, shall then be condemned with their infernal confederates, and be cast with them into the Lake of Fire. If God did not bring man up for judgment, then His own justice would be violated, His righteous and holy law insulted. The character and deeds of the ungodly, which so often escape judgment in time, demand that Yahweh bring every work to judgment, and this He will do at the Great White Throne Judgment. There will be no appeal from that verdict by the Supreme Court of the Universe. The judgment is according to the justice and righteousness of God and is, therefore, final.

> "The nations were angry, and Your wrath has come, and the time of the dead, that they should be judged, and that You should reward Your servants, the prophets and the saints and those who fear Your name, small and great...."
>
> —Revelation 11:18

> "And these (the unrighteous) will go away into everlasting punishment, but the righteous into eternal life."
>
> —Matthew 25:46

> "So then each of us shall give account of himself to God." —Romans 14:12

As the tares and wheat are separated at the harvest, as the good fish and the bad fish are separated at the shore, and as the corn and chaff are separated on the threshing floor, they cannot separate themselves one from another in this world, nor can anyone else separate them. (Matthew 13:24-30, 36-43, 47-50). *But the Lord knows them that are His,* and His angels can separate them.

It is important to understand parables. Jesus used parables related to their daily lives and the events of His day. The hearers understood what He meant.

Tares were sown by an enemy landowner as a revenge tactic, as part of the battle between two families. A man wishing to do his enemy an injury watches for the time when his neighbor shall have finished plowing his field. Then in the middle of the night, this nocturnal villain goes into the field and scatters weed seeds. These weed seeds are usually of rapid growth and therefore, spring up before the good seeds sprout. After the weed seeds mature and ripen they scatter themselves before the wheat can be yielded, burdening the poor owner of the field for years, as he diligently and systematically works at ridding the soil of the roots of the troublesome weeds.

> "Therefore judge nothing before the time, until the Lord comes, who will both bring to light the hidden things of darkness and reveal the counsels of the hearts. Then each one's praise will come from God."
>
> —1 Corinthians 4:5

To judge in these cases, is to assume the seat of God. How bold it is for a sinner to be so forward. It is ill-timed and arrogant. But there is One who will judge the censurer and those he censures. There is a time coming that will convey men's secret sins into the open day and discover the secrets of their hearts. The Lord Jesus Christ has the knowledge of the judgments in our hearts or He could not make them manifest. We should be very careful how we judge others when we have to stand before a judge from whom we cannot conceal ourselves.

F. The sinner has judged himself.

> And Paul and Barnabas spoke out boldly and said, "it was necessary that the word of God should be spoken to *you* first; since *you* repudiate it, and judge yourselves unworthy *of* eternal life, *behold,* we are turning to the Gentiles."
>
> —Acts 13:46

Eternal destinies are settled here and at this time. The listeners have passed sentence upon themselves by rejecting the Good News given them according to the direction of Our Lord when He said, "....and that repentance for forgiveness of sins should be proclaimed in His name to all the nations, beginning from Jerusalem" (Luke 24:47). Paul and Barnabas, having great liberty of speech, showed the boldness of the lion as they did the harmlessness of the dove in preaching the good news. They knew in whom they trusted to shield them. They went to the Jews first, as they were entitled to the first offer of eternal truth. When the Jews refused the Word, the apostles charged them with the refusal of it. If man, woman or child, Jew or Gentile, regardless of race, color or creed, rejected the gospel of salvation, Yahweh justly takes it from them. Herein, out of their mouths they judge themselves unworthy of everlasting life.

G. Rewards of the unbelievers

Peter and Paul record that the Lord will reward the wicked according to their works.

> 13 "....suffering wrong is the wages of doing wrong. They count it a pleasure to revel in the daytime. They are stains and blemishes, reveling in their deceptions, as they carouse with you,
> 14 having eyes full of adultery and that never cease from sin, enticing unstable souls, having a heart trained in greed, accursed children;
> 15 forsaking the right way they have gone astray, having followed the way of Balaam, the son of Beor, who loved the wages of unrighteousness...."
>
> —2 Peter 2

> "Now this man acquired a field with the price of his wickedness; and falling headlong, he burst open in the middle and all his bowels gushed out."
>
> —Acts 1:18

Judas received "the reward of iniquity."

Eternal JUDGMENT III

The Books

> "And I saw the dead, the great and the small standing before the throne, and books were opened, and another book was opened, which is the book of life; and the dead were judged from the things which were written in the books according to their deeds."
>
> —Revelation 20:12

Although the Bible speaks of many different kinds of books, the books mentioned in the opening and throughout this lesson, are located on the shelves in Heaven's library and are large, very large books. They are the "Book of Life," the "Book of Remembrance," the "Book of Wars," "a Book," the "Book of Tears," and a possible "obituary." Listed below are their references:

The Book of Life – Exodus 32:32-33, Ps 69:28, Philippians 4:3, Revelation 3:5; 13:8; 20:12-13; 15; 21:27, & etc.

The Book of Remembrance – Psalm 56:8; 139:16; Malachi 3:16

The Book of Wars – Numbers 21:14

There is a book written "from the foundation of the world" (Revelation 13:8 and 17:8) that may be the book Isaiah refers to in chapter 4 verse 3 of "everyone who is recorded for life in Jerusalem."

The Book of Tears – Ps 56:8 (I doubt these are tears of self-pity but are tears for the lost and the sins of the saints)

Ps 139:16 The Lord has a book of everyone from before their existence. Even before we became an embryo, He wrote down our name and beside it He wrote how many days we will live. Actually, this resembles an obituary. God has a list of the days ordained for us. He knows how long we will live before we were ever conceived. He knows our last days.

Also on Heaven's library shelf is The Book with its seven seals – Revelation 5:1-2, 5.

New Heaven And New Earth

It is at this time the Lord renovates the existing heavens and earth.

> 7 But the present heavens and earth, by His Word, are being reserved for fire, kept for the day of judgment and destruction of ungodly men.
>
> 10 But the day of the Lord will come like a thief, in which the heavens will pass away with a roar and the elements will be destroyed with intense heat, and the earth and its works will be burned up (discovered).
>
> —2 Peter 3

Eternal Life Principles & Beyond

Peter says that these judgments shall be accompanied "with a great noise." It will be a terrible blast that shall be heard by every living soul. The force shall shake the earth with a mighty tremor. The deep-toned thunder of the Almighty shall roll out with such a deafening sound that the entire world will know what is taking place. Since *every* person ever born, saint and sinner, is standing at the Great White Throne at this very moment, it is possible the intense heat from the terrible blast is also (part of) the Lake Of Fire.

Additional Notes:

Quoting Dr. James Mckeever:

> "Many think that everyone will spend eternity in either heaven or hell/the Lake of Fire. Unfortunately that is not the truth. If you want to spend eternity in heaven, you are going to be very lonesome. God will create a new heaven and a new earth. (See 2 Peter 3:10-13). However, the new heaven is evidently going to be unoccupied because all of the Believers, Father God and Jesus Christ are going to be on the new earth in the New Jerusalem, ruling and reigning (See Revelation 21). Certain Believers will be appointed officials to serve the King of kings, as the government will then rest upon His shoulders (See Isaiah 9:6). It is the one form of government that will bring about ideal political, social and morale conditions. It is called a Theocracy — a government in which God Himself shall rule."

He shall rule from the city — New Jerusalem — His Bride. He is married to the Land.

In the Scriptures, a desolate land is represented under the notion of a widow; and as an inhabited land. Chapter 62 of Isaiah explains, it is Yahweh's Zion and His Jerusalem and it is, therefore, dear to Him. As the owner and builder He reverences the land as a husband. The word "Beulah" in verse 4 means "Thou are married" implying not only ownership of the land, but protection on His part. Vs 3 says this land will be a crown of beauty in His hands and a royal turban (diadem) in His hand (held as His glory) for it is pure beauty to Him. He shall call her (Jerusalem) His spouse (vss 4-5). New Jerusalem is also the church's righteousness and salvation that will go forth as brightness, and as a lamp that burns, "in that day".

Even though all Believers and Christians are going to spend eternity on the new earth, some of them will spend it living in one of the nations and some will spend it residing in the New Jerusalem, as part of the bride (overcomers) of Christ (See Revelation 21:9-10).

It is also important to note that John the Revelator wrote his revelations and visions after his release from the Isle of Patmos and return to Ephesus. (Halley's Bible Handbook p. 683-684). His writings may be sequential; however, the order of "the

Eternal Judgment III

Revelation of Jesus Christ, which God gave Him to show to His bond-servants" (Revelation 1:1) may not necessarily be sequential. It's important that a teacher not be dogmatic and make categorical statements and I can only share what the Spirit of God has shown me up to this point in time.

Eternal Judgment III

Lesson Study Review 18

1. Is there a judgment that is reserved for a particular time in the future? _____ (Yes or No)

    A. Heb. 9:27

    B. John 12:48

    C. Matt. 10:15

2. How does the Bible describe the place that this judgment shall take place?

    Rev. 20:11-15

3. Does it tell us what will happen at this time?

    A. Rev. 11:18 }
       Matt. 25:46 }

    B. 2 Thess. 1:8-9 }
       Rev. 20:15 }

    C. Daniel 7

    D. Ezekiel 1

    E. Ezekiel 10

Final Summary Review

1. Water baptism relates to cleansing of the soul. According to the doctrinal aspects of water baptism, describe our position from the following Scriptures:

    A. Acts. 22:16 In Water Baptism _____ washes away our sins.

    B. John 15:3 In Water Baptism we are _____ cleansed by the words Jesus spoke to us.

    C. Rev. 1:5b Water Baptism _____ releases us from our sins by His Blood.

    D. Luke 24:47 _____ our sins are wiped away through Repentance, Believing and Water Baptism.

2. Repentance, Faith and Baptism can be taught separately. They were in the beginning; therefore, it was no problem for Paul to refer to baptism as a base important teaching applicable to all Believers. _____ (True or False)

3. Where in the record of the acts of the Holy Spirit through the Apostles were hands laid on for healing and by whom? Name at least four.

    A. _____   C. _____

    B. _____   D. _____

4. What is the difference between Baptism and Washings? And is Baptism always in water?

    _____
    _____
    _____
    _____
    _____

5. At the end of this course, we will leave these principles and go on to _____!

6. If these six elementary principles, which we have learned during this course, is the foundation to a Believer's life, then is this what is meant by receiving the fullness of Christ?

    _____ (True or False)

Eternal Life Principles & Beyond

7. The Apostles, Paul and Jesus preached Repentance. When a pastor or evangelist preaches salvation by accepting Christ into your heart, is it the same thing? Tell why or why not.

_____

_____

_____

_____

_____

8. God chose and ordained what physical means to introduce His Son Jesus to Israel?

_____

9. Before Pentecost, Peter was an emotional weakling. After Pentecost, he spent all of his time strengthening his brethren. Peter experienced the process of

_____

10. Receiving Christ just for what He is, as represented in His Gospels, with an unqualified surrender of the will, and obtaining salvation of our whole being through Him, this process is called:

_____

11. Jesus commanded we go and baptize in the Name of the Father and of the Son and of the Holy Spirit; yet the Apostles seem to contradict the Great Commission. According to Acts 2:33, and verse 41 and other Scriptures, they baptized only in the Name of Jesus. Was this heresy or were they just being disobedient and rebellious? Support your answer?

_____

_____

_____

_____

_____

12. When we are Water Baptized, it is an outward expression of our _____

and we are telling the world we have _____ in Christ and have been

_____ with Him.

Final Summary Review

13. The Laying-On-Of-Hands is a meaningful act. In the New Testament it signifies we are conveying a message. What are the four messages communicated?

    _____   _____

    _____   _____

14. In terms of foundation principles; the Laying-On-Of-Hands, when signifying the reception of the Holy Spirit, releases

    _____

15. There are six special purposes for Laying-On-Of-Hands. Name three.

    1. _____
    2. _____
    3. _____

16. Explain the three Resurrections of the Believer after receiving salvation. Give a complete answer.

    A. _____
    B. _____
    C. _____

17. Was Jesus resurrected body the same as that which was crucified? Explain your answer.

    _____

    _____

    _____

    _____

    _____

18. The Believer must examine himself daily, and especially before receiving communion. He must keep himself pure before God. On what seven things will the Believer be judged at the Judgment Seat of Christ?

1. _____
2. _____
3. _____
4. _____
5. _____
6. _____
7. _____

19. We must build our work on the foundation of Jesus Christ. On the Day of Judgment our work will become manifest and will be revealed by _____

20. Explain why judgment is necessary.

My Inspirations, Challenges & Revelations:

INDEX

HELL – Historical Study

    What Do These Words Really Mean?...256

    Two Different Hells In The New Testament...258

    A Lake Of Fire...258

    What Will The Lake Of Fire Be Like?..260

    Is There A Sentencing Of Various Degrees?...261

    The Fire..262

    The Second Death...262

    Other Questionable Verses To Be Considered..263

My Inspirations, Challenges & Revelations:

Hell -
Historical Study

The following is not an elaborate nor complete and faultless compilation of information on this doctrine, by any means, because it is not part of the six elementary principles of Hebrews 6:1-2. It is, however, an extension of the Great White Throne Judgment. The author simply desires to whet your appetite and suggests further research on your part.

Scripture reveals two sides of God: The first is His loving, compassionate, caring side. He is the God who created us and all life, and made the supreme sacrifice to offer us eternal life. Then there is the God of Holiness, the God of wrath, the God who judges sin during His judicial administration. The Hebrew word *"Nakam"* describes the Lord's vengeance as retribution and justice, not as retaliation. It is not an evil passion, but rather the righteous and unerring vindication of His people, and of His own course of action to those who set themselves in opposition to Him. He will mete out this justice on such a day, or at such a time, as seems fitting to Him. (See Isaiah 34:8; 61:2; 63:4, Jeremiah 46:10; 51:6, Luke 18:7-8; 21:22, 1 Thessalonians 4:6, 2 Thessalonians 1:8, Revelation 6:10; 19:2). Many churches today have lost the balance between these two sides to God's nature.

Luke records the following in chapter 12:1 that, as thousands of the multitude gathered together, they were actually stepping on one another as they rushed toward the great Rabbi of Israel, as He taught –

> "But I will warn you whom to fear: fear the One who after He has killed has authority to cast into hell (Gehenna): yes, I tell you, fear Him!"
> —Luke 12:5

and

> "But I say that everyone who is angry with his brother shall be guilty before the court; and whoever shall say to his brother, 'Raca' shall be guilty before the supreme court; and whoever shall say, 'You fool,' shall be guilty enough to go into the fiery hell (Gehenna)".
> —Matthew 5:22

Hell is an English word. Keep in mind the Old Testament was written in Hebrew and the Gospels were written in Chaldee/Aramaic and the New Testament in Greek.

Quoting from *A Dictionary of the Bible,* edited by James Hastings, which says "The translators of the Authorized Version of 1611 unfortunately used the word "hell" as the rendering of three distinct words with different ideas [or meanings]." How shocking this news will be to some readers.

The English word "hell" represents (1) the "sheol" of the Hebrew Old Testament and the *"hades"* of .... the New Testament.... The 1611 English revisers, therefore have substituted *"hades"* [going back to the original Greek word] for "hell" in the New Testament.... In the American Revision the word "hell" is entirely discarded in this connection....

The English word "hell" also represents (2) the Greek word *"tartaros"* in 2 Peter 2:4 and (3) the Greek word *"gehenna"* in all other New Testament Scriptures. The words *"tartaros"* and *"gehenna"* are not equivalent meanings to each other, as we will soon see, nor is it equivalent to *"hades"* or *"sheol."*

The word "hell" is an entirely misleading rendering of the Hebrew and Greek, especially in the New Testament passages. The 1611 translators have attempted to make the one English word "hell" cover the definitions of all three words. No wonder millions have been confused about this subject! Enough said.

Nowhere in the Old Testament is the abode of the dead regarded as a place of torment or punishment. The concept of an infernal "hell" developed in Israel during the Hellenistic period. The same distinction is preserved in the New Testament especially Revelation 20:13-14. Only in the gospel of Luke 16:23 is the rich man of the parable depicted as being tormented in *"hades."* There are two distinct concepts — the abode of the dead and the place of torment, and they are clearly differentiated.

What Do These Words Really Mean?

There is no listing of the word "hell" in the Old Testament of the *New American Standard Bible* and its corresponding exhaustive concordance. There are, however, 31 listings in the *Strong's Exhaustive Concordance* of the word "hell" in the Old Testament. (*Strong's Exhaustive Concordance* corresponds with the Authorized and Revised Versions of the *King James Bible*.)

    A. Sheol and Hades

The Old Testament Hebrew word "sheol", in Strong's #7585, means "The world of the dead — a subterranean retreat including its accessories and inmates — grave, hell, pit." Its locality is down as contrasted to up. This abode of the dead is sometimes described as an insatiable demon in Proverbs 1:12; Isaiah 5:14; and Habakkuk 2:5. It is a dark and silent hiding place. However, nowhere in the Old Testament is the abode of the dead regarded as a place of torment or punishment. It is also known as the "nether world."

There is no doubt that what the grave or pit is to the body that *"sheol"* is to the soul (Nephesh) in Psalm 16 & Acts 2:27. *"Nephesh"* is also translated "dead body."

"Sheol" of the Old Testament and *"hades"* of the New Testament mean the same thing. These words have been correctly translated as "grave" in many places in the Bible. Kenneth Wuest's meaning for *"hades"* is "The Unseen." Wuest goes on to say, ".... It

is the temporary place of confinement until the Great White Throne Judgment in the case of the wicked dead, and until the resurrection of Christ, in the case of the righteous dead...." (Philippians 1:23) p. 45.

Strong's Exhaustive Concordance, #86 for "hades" means the place of departed souls — grave, hell. However, both these words have been translated into the English word "hell."

The people of England commonly talked of "putting their potatoes in hell for the winter" — a good way of preserving potatoes — for the word then meant merely a hole in the ground, below the freeze line, that was covered up — a dark and silent place — a grave. Early American settlers dug "root cellars" in the basement of their homes for the same purpose. Hades does not refer to fire at all, but to a grave, a hole in the ground.

In Matthew 16:18 it is of this place, (hades), that Jesus referred when He spoke of the church of Christ, that the gates of hades shall not prevail against it.

This New Testament word, "hades," the abode of the dead, is found in Matthew 11:23; 16; 18, Luke 10:15; 16:23, Acts 2:27; 31 and Revelation 1:18; 20:13-14 and nothing is added to the Old Testament description of it except Luke in Chapter 16:23, he calls it a place of torment.

Jesus was buried in a tomb *"Kever"* (hades/hell/grave/sepulcher), the local habitation of His physical frame, for three full days and three full nights.

There is a Biblical conception of hades being divided into two parts, the one called paradise Luke 23:43 for the righteous dead, (but not 2 Corinthians 12:4 and Revelation 2:7) or, as in the story of Abraham's bosom, there is a place that exists for the unrighteous as seen in the condition of the rich man in Luke 16:22. This subject is further discussed.

    B. Gehenna

The second New Testament Greek word is *"gehenna"*, representative of the Hebrew *"Ge-Hinnom."* (Before the time of Josiah, idolatrous Jews sacrificed their children to the god Molech in this valley). *Strong's Exhaustive Concordance* #1067 lists Gehenna used 10 times and means "Valley of Hinnom, a valley of Jerus." Strong's also refers this word to the Greek word *"eirenikos"*, meaning undisturbed and #2011 *"epitrope"*, meaning commissioned authority. It is a name for the place or state of everlasting punishment. This Greek word is derived from the name of the narrow, rocky Valley of Hinnom, which lies just outside and to the south of Jerusalem. It is associated with fire (Mark 9:3-48). It was the place where refuse was completely burned. Trash, filth, the dead bodies of animals and despised criminals were thrown into the fires of Gehenna, or on the Valley of Ge-Hinnom. Ordinarily, everything thrown into this valley was destroyed by fire — completely burned up or annihilated. However, the fire never went out, due to the continuous dumping of refuse on a daily basis.

Hell - Historical Study

In Luke 12:5, Jesus said, "But I will warn you whom to fear; fear the One who after He has killed has authority to cast into hell (Gehenna); yes, I tell you, fear Him!" Christ used Gehenna to picture the fate of unrepentant sinners.

    C. Tartaros

The third New Testament Greek word is *"tartaros"* and occurs as a verb form. In *Strong's Exhaustive Concordance* #5020, it means "the deepest abyss of Hades – to incarcerate in eternal torment." It is also a symbolic name for the final place of punishment of the ungodly." It is found only in 2 Peter 2:4, where it has been translated into the English expression "cast down to hell." Tartaros does not refer to humans in this verse, but to the restrained condition of fallen angels (or demons) that sinned at the time of the flood (Genesis 6:1-4). Its meaning translated into English is, "darkness of the material universe," "dark abyss" or "prison." It denotes the dispatch of the rebel angels to the fire of punishment.

Two Different Hells In The New Testament

In many passages of the New Testament where we see the Word "hell", the word is either "hades" which does not refer to fire at all, but to a grave — a hole in the ground or "gehenna" — the place where refuse and dead bodies were thrown and destroyed by fire. Luke 12:5 is "Gehenna" and Acts 2:31 is "Hades." We must keep in mind these two vastly different meanings and carefully determine by the context whether it refers to destruction by fire, or the grave where the dead lie buried and are asleep. When in doubt about the intended meaning of the word "hell", look it up in an exhaustive concordance. Seek the Greek word from which it was translated, study its true meaning, and carefully determine by the context whether it refers to destruction by fire or the grave where the dead lie buried.

A Lake Of Fire

> 14 "And death and Hades were thrown into the lake of fire. This is the second death, the lake of fire.
> 15 And if anyone's name was not found written in the book of life, he was thrown into the lake of fire."
>
> —Revelation 20

Also read Revelation 19:20; 20:10; 13-15 and 21:8.

It is obvious from the above verses that death is not annihilation the first time. The Lake of Fire is spoken of five times in the book of Revelation. It is also called the second death. In the *Gospel* of Matthew 5:22 the phrase "….the hell of fire….," refers to the final abode of the wicked dead which is thrown into the "lake of fire burning with brimstone" in Revelation 19:20.

The following is a direct quote. "This lake of fire is in existence now for the word "prepared" in the Greek of Matthew 25:41 is in the perfect tense which refers to a past completed action having present results. Hell had been already prepared and was in existence when Jesus spoke these words. There is no one there now. The first occupants of that dreadful place will be the Beast and the False Prophet, with Satan following them 1000 years afterward. Then, at the Great White Throne Judgment, which occurs at the close of the Millennium, all lost human beings, the fallen angels, and the demons will also be sent there for eternity. Our word "hell" is the correct rendering of the word "Gehenna," and should be so translated in the following passages, Matthew 5:22; 29; 30; 10:28; 18:9; 23:15; 33, Mark 9:43; 45; 47, Luke 12:5, James 3:6." By Kenneth S. Wuest, *Word Studies in the Greek New Testament,* Volume 111, page 44.

It is also associated with Peter's words in 2 Peter 3:10 "....the elements will be destroyed with intense heat." The King James translation reads "....the elements shall melt with fervent heat."

The terror of the Lake of Fire to many is the most hated truth in the world today because the world, not understanding God's wrath against sin, blindly continue on their course. The Lake of Fire is also no longer a doctrine frequently preached in evangelism. Some churches even deny there is a Lake of Fire, teaching instead that a God of love would not banish anyone from His presence. But the Lake of Fire is not compatible with the love of Jesus Christ, His Lordship and His Kingship. God is patient, but He is not tolerant. God is not ashamed to disclose the truth of it and boldly declares it in His Word. God is a wrathful God against sin, *ALL SIN*. God is not hiding His wrath, but openly proclaims His standards for us to meet in the here and now. (Read the entire 22nd chapter of Ezekiel and take note of verses 20-22.)

The Lake of Fire will be like a raging sea and the wicked will be searching for rest, but will find none. Hell is the absence of mercy, love, joy, peace and serenity. For only Jesus can give rest to the soul. It will not be like land where they can rest their feet. They shall seek death, but will not find it and no place is found for them.

The fire and brimstone thrown down on Sodom and Gomorrah is an example of His treatment toward cities of sin. (See Genesis 19:1-29).

The Lake of Fire is a place created and prepared by Yahweh as the eternal abode for Satan, as well as his demons, the fallen angels who left their first estate (Jude 1:6-7), the prince of darkness, the dragon, the dictator beast, the false prophet-ruler, the antichrists (plural), for populations of cities and goat nations, i.e., Sodom and Gomorrah, all evil and all transgressors (Revelation 20:10). It is the same fate against those who reject Him and His Only Begotten Son. Unbelievers who heard the good news of salvation through Jesus Christ and denied His work on the cross, thereby rejecting their salvation, will be judged eternally guilty. During the Great Tribulation, Yahweh will pour out continuous heart-stopping spectacular performances of the elements in an extravaganza of all sights ever to behold. The warning regarding this global disaster is posted in the Book of Revelation. It will just be a foretaste to the Lake of Fire.

"And I saw another sign in heaven, great and marvelous, seven angels who had seven plagues, which are the last, because in them the wrath of God is finished" (Revelation 15:1d). This chapter goes on to say that the bondslaves of God will sing and declare, "For Thy righteous acts have been revealed." (Revelation 15:4d)

What Will The Lake Of Fire Be Like?

Our Lord gave a fearful description of the Lake of Fire in Luke's Gospel chapter 16. Chapter 16 is not a parable, but a narrative of something which actually happened and the true names of the men are given. The rich man said he was being tormented in this flame and there was no comfort. The awful facts stand out that people there are alive, conscious and possessing all their faculties. They can reason, remember, and know why they are there. They can suffer remorse; they can endure physical and mental torment. They can see and look up into Heaven and recognize people in glory and can know of their bliss.

They can plead for help, but know it is utterly hopeless. They thirst with no relief. They suffer the memories of all the missed opportunities to salvation. Abraham replied to this man and said, "Son, remember…."

Jesus said, "There shall be wailing and gnashing of teeth." There is no way to describe the Lake of Fire. Nothing on earth can compare to it. *It is the full expression of God's hatred toward sin.* It is not the Lord's Will that anyone end up there. After the judging at the Great White Throne Judgment, death and Hades will be thrown into the everlasting Lake of Fire. Pastor and author David Wilkerson wrote that he thinks, "hell is a planet God casts into outer darkness" still others believe it is in the center of our earth.

The Lake of Fire will never reach bottom and moves further and further away from God. Those there will not find an exit. It offers a furnace of fire, a prison, eternal bondage and eternal slavery to the person's lusts. It is a place where a person's lusts will burn and are never satisfied. Death will only intensify their lusts. There is no repentance, only anger, agony, foul odors, slime, putrid and rotting stench, blaspheming, rage, agonizing and deafening screams, agony of this kind and agony of another, moaning, suffering, abandonment, loneliness, hatred toward Yahweh, scorching with fire, punishment, terrorizing demons, vengeance and confusion because they will believe lies. It is ungodly, tormenting, suffocating, deep deep darkness, gloom and horror. They will experience extreme exhaustion never to be relieved. They will have "no hope" and their expectations never stop perishing. It will be so incredibly severe that those cast into the outer black dense darkness shall be weeping and gnashing their teeth and gnaw their tongues for pain. It will be unrelenting pain of body and mind, their own conscience tormenting them. In light of lesson III on Eternal Judgment, I believe the most horrifying part of the torment will be having stood at the Great White Throne, and having attended the spectacular and stunning events taking place there, shall then be banished from it all. The memory of it, the longing for it, the self-condemnation of not believing will be just too much for the mind. It's a measure of pain that cannot be measured.

The Lake of Fire was created by Yahweh as a place of total natural and spiritual darkness for the damned. It is more than being forsaken by Yahweh; it is complete separation from Yahweh who is unconditional love, everlasting peace and unspeakable joy, full of glory and light. It is the punishment of an angry God in flaming fire taking "vengeance" on sin. There will be a Lake of Fire as long as Yahweh hates sin. It is a fearful thing to fall into the hands of the living Lord at the Great White Throne Judgment. Yahweh is going to use the glory of His power to punish; it will be at this time that these horrible aspects of hell will then be thrown into the Lake of Fire.

Is There A Sentencing Of Various Degrees?

In Ezekiel 33:11 there is a profound word from the Lord about how great His love is for all peoples. "As I live!" declares the Lord God, "I take no pleasure in the death of the wicked, but rather that the wicked turn from his way and live. Turn back, turn back from your evil ways!" However, He cannot go against His own Laws and as Judge, He will execute a sentence of various degrees.

> "Truly I say to you, it will be more tolerable for the land of Sodom and Gomorrah in the day of judgment, than for that city."
> —Matthew 10:15

> "Woe to you, scribes and Pharisees, hypocrites, because you devour widows' houses, even while for a pretense you make long prayers; therefore you shall receive a greater condemnation"
> —Matthew 23:14

> 50 ....the master of that slave will come on a day when he does not expect him and at an hour which he does not know,
> 51 and shall cut him in pieces and assign him a place with the hypocrites; weeping shall be there and the gnashing of teeth.
> —Matthew 24

> 45 But if that slave says in his heart, "My master will be a long time in coming," and begins to beat the slaves, both men and women, and to eat and drink and get drunk;
> 46 the master of that slave will come on a day when he does not expect him, and at an hour he does not know, and will cut him in pieces, and assign him a place with the unbelievers.
> —Luke 12

Hell - Historical Study

The Fire

The "fire" of Revelation 21:8 as found in the NASEC and Strong's #4442, *"pur"* means fiery, burning fire and #4447 *"purinos"* a fiery fire.

Earth's natural fire has light. However this extraordinary fire of hell and the Lake of Fire is spiritual and has no light because Jesus who is light (for there is no darkness in Him), will not be Reigning there. The intensity of this fire is correlated to the fiery surface of the sun with its solar flares or as a refiner's white-hot molten metal fire pouring from an open-hearth furnace.

Hebrews 12:29 says "God is a consuming fire." The Greek word for consuming is *"katanalisko"* meaning "to use up." Truly our God is to be feared. He is love; however, there is another side of His character; Yahweh has wrath against sin. Adam Clarke writes, "Although we are not under the law but under the gospel of grace, sin continues to be an abomination in Yahweh's sight: and that man who does not labor to serve God with the principle *(of reverence)*, and in the way already prescribed *(in His Word)*, will find that the fire will consume him which would otherwise have consumed his sin." Pg 1338 *The Bethany Parallel Commentary*. (Italics mine)

The author of the book of Hebrews in chapter 10 warns:

> 26 "For if we go on sinning willfully after receiving the knowledge of the truth, there no longer remains a sacrifice for sins,
> 27 but a certain terrifying expectation of judgment, and the fury of a fire which will consume (esthio) the adversaries."

The Greek word *"esthio"* means to "eat up". The fire will "eat up" and devour what is thrown into it at the time of the Great White Throne Judgment.

The Second Death

> "But for the cowardly and unbelieving and abominable and murderers and immoral persons and sorcerers and idolaters and all liars, their part will be in the lake that burns with fire and brimstone, which is the second death (thanatos)."
>
> —Revelation 21:8

The Greek word *"thanatos"*, #2288 described in the *New American Standard Exhaustive Concordance*, translates this word as "danger of death," "death," "fatal" and "pestilence". It refers to #2348, *"thnesko"* meaning "to die, dead and died."

Now many questions remain, does it mean annihilation, eternal oblivion, eternal life in torment in and by fire or - will the unrepentant be devoured by it? Does it mean punishment or punishing or some of the many other thoughts on the subject? Is combustible material that is put into a fire only tormented or is it completely burned?

Jesus said "I tell *you*, but, unless *you* repent, *you* will all likewise perish." The word "perish" in Luke 13:3 means "cease existing." It does not mean to continue living.

Death, as we know it, is the opposite of life. The final wages the incorrigible will receive is the complete cessation of life.

The Believer's *"thanatopsis"* is that they shall absolutely not ever see death. It even goes one step further. When a Believer is dying, he will not look at "death" with interest; he will be an indifferent spectator of "death" for he will have his eyes fixed on Jesus. The terrors of death are not experienced by the one who puts his faith in the Lord Jesus. His attention will not focus on death, nor will he feel its bitterness.

The warnings of Jesus in Matthew 7:15-19 and 23:33 of being cast into the fire of hell (Gehenna) is a type of final fate indicated as complete destruction in fire. In other words, it means annihilation.

Other Questionable Verses To Be Considered

A. The worm that dieth not

> 44 [where THEIR WORM DOES NOT DIE AND THE FIRE IS NOT QUENCHED.]
> 45 "And if your foot causes you to stumble, cut it off; it is better for you to enter life lame, than having your two feet, to be cast into hell (Gehenna).
> 46 [where THEIR WORM DOES NOT DIE AND THE FIRE IS NOT QUENCHED.]
> 47 And if your eye causes you to stumble, cast it out; it is better for you to enter the kingdom of God with one eye, than having two eyes, to be cast into hell (Gehenna)
> 48 where THEIR WORM DOES NOT DIE AND THE FIRE IS NOT QUENCHED.

Some may ask about Mark 9:44-48. Did Christ speak of a worm that "dieth not?" (AKJ) Let's take a closer look at this verse. In verses 44 and 47 the word "fire" is "Gehenna;" therefore, it is a consuming fire. Verses 44, 46 and 48 reveals it is not "a worm," but "their worm." The Greek word *"skolex,"* translated "worm," is a "grub or maggot" in the Greek and Hebrew.

The *Authorized King James Version* translators of 1611 added verses 44 and 46. However, the scribes of the *New American Standard Bible*, the *Catholic Confraternity Bible*, the *Revised Standard Version*, the *New King James Version* and *The New Testament From 26 Translations* bracket or footnote verses 44 and 46 stating these verses are not found in the best ancient manuscripts and are now recognized as not adequately supported by original manuscripts.

Hell - Historical Study

Now, what about verse 48? Jesus has referenced Isaiah 66:24, which reads, ".... for their worm shall not die and their fire shall not be quenched:...." Our blessed Savior is expressing the everlasting punishment of the wicked in Gehenna. It shall not be inconsistent with true love for the godly to look with satisfaction on Yahweh's vengeance on the wicked (Revelation 14:10).

B. Fire never quenched

Matthew 3:12 and Luke 3:17 reads as follows:

> "And His winnowing fork is in His hand, and He will thoroughly clear His threshing floor; and He will gather His wheat into His barn, but He will burn up the chaff with unquenchable fire."

It has been carelessly assumed the "fire that never shall be quenched" in these verses and in Mark 9:43-48 that has been in existence for centuries will continue to exist for eternity. 2500 years ago God warned the inhabitants of Jerusalem, through Jeremiah 17:27, He would kindle a fire in Jerusalem's gates that would not be quenched. This fire occurred a few years later and it destroyed all the houses of Jerusalem (Jeremiah 52:13). Since it is not burning today, it obviously went out by itself after devouring all combustible material. The same is true of Sodom and Gomorrah as is referenced in Genesis 19:24, Luke 17:29 and Jude 7. The expression "eternal fire" in Jude 7 means a fire whose results are permanent or everlasting—obviously not a fire that burns forever. The fires that burned these wicked cities simply died out after consuming all combustible material. The fires were never quenched or put out prematurely by anyone. The flames merely died out when they had nothing more to consume. So it will be with the final Lake of Fire. It will consume the wicked. It will not be quenched. It will finally burn itself out when there is nothing more to consume. How long will this take? Only the Administrating Judge will determine the punishment to fit the sins.

C. Annihilation or rendered useless

> "I have decided to deliver such a one to Satan for the destruction of his flesh, that his spirit may be saved in the day of the Lord Jesus."

Let's look at these words "destruction of the flesh" as spoken of by the Apostle Paul in 1 Corinthians 5:5. Here reference is made to the special temporal chastisement that is inflicted so that the salvation of the spirit is made whole for the day of Christ.

However, the destruction, *"apoleia"*, of those on the broad path (Matthew 7:13) and those who set themselves against the Gospel (Philippians 1:28), those who live a carnal life (Philippians 3:19), those who yield to lusts and covetousness (1 Timothy 6:9), etc., are synchronous with the Day of Judgment and the burning of the heavens and earth (2 Peter 3:7). In these cases it is not annihilation, but such injury as makes the object practically useless for its original purpose.

Eternal Life Principles & Beyond

In Matthew 10:28 Jesus said, "....fear Him who is able to destroy both soul and body in Gehenna." The destruction of the body is compared to the disintegration of the seed which falls into the ground and dies. It is dismemberment and dissolution and renders the body useless, but it is not annihilation. It is simply the blotting out of existence in the body.

Lastly, Marvin Rosenthal, whose teachings I admire greatly, in his September-October issue Volume 21 No 5 of Zion's Fire states: "There is no such thing as "total annihilation"" and quotes from John's gospel chapter 5:28-29 "Marvel not at this: for the hour is coming, in the which all that are in the graves shall hear his voice, And shall come forth; they that have done good, unto resurrection of life; and they that have done evil, unto the resurrection of damnation (*condemnation*)." Italics mine".

At the time of this writing, their appeared to be no mention of the disposition of the spiritman of the unrighteous concerning the Lake of Fire. Can the spirit of man be annihilated? Please refer back to my personal comments on the previous page.

Additional Notes:

It is important to tell you I fasted frequently, prayed and researched this topic for almost ten weeks regarding the conclusions of the words eternal, eternal fire, eternal death and punishment vs punishing. The most respected Greek scholars are silent or at the most, vague when it comes to the afterlife. One aspect they all have agreed upon is - Yahweh is everlasting and forever and that the Saints who reign with Him will also live forever and ever, which is eternal life. The vagueness is with the terms "eternal death" and "eternal fire." Is it annihilation by fire to ashes? Is it ongoing punishing? Or how long does the punishment last? The theological arguments on both sides are strong and convincing and the Holy Spirit did not give me any further revelation on the matter. I have done my best to not tread where angels fear to go. I recognize the contradictions and choose to leave them as such.

Comments:

I end on this note. Rev. Mike Pici gives an excellent reason for this vagueness and has given permission to quote him. "The Bible tells us very little about the afterlife; that is not its purpose. The Bible is to help us live in the here and now. Once we leave this life, we will not need the Written Word because we will be walking and talking with the Living Word."

My Inspirations, Challenges & Revelations:

INDEX

SIN – Historical Study

What Are The Meanings Of The Words To Describe
The Condition From Which We Must Repent?...270

What Is The Origin Of Sin?...273

What Sins Do The Scriptures Specifically List?..274

My Inspirations, Challenges & Revelations:

Sin -
Historical Study

If we are to fully appreciate the meaning of repentance and move on into maturity, we must know that from which we are to repent.

The lesson entitled Repentance from Dead Works is the first of the "elementary principles" listed for us in Hebrews 6:1-2. To go wrong here is to endanger the whole foundation.

"Dead works" are the deeds and actions of a life that is a lived apart from the "living God." The ultimate sin, which is the cardinal sin, is rejecting Yahweh Himself and His only Begotten Son, Jesus, the Christ. These "dead works" may be religious works, gross deeds, or the hypocritical actions and attitudes of the self-righteous moralist. All acts of a man in himself, separated from Yahweh, are "dead works." This book is specifically written for the Believer and not the unsaved, therefore, the following list of the manifestations of the ultimate sin of "missing the mark" is directed categorically toward the repentance process.

These acts are variously referred to in the Bible. "Sin" is the word most often used. However, there are other words to describe the different aspects of man's sinful condition.

The essential principle of sin is selfishness. It is the love of self as opposed to the love of Yahweh. This love of self may express itself in many ways, but each of these ways is "our own way," not His way. It is evident that there is something wrong in the universe, with both the earth and its inhabitants. The source of all chaos, disharmony and strife in the world can be traced back to the existence of sin.

> "All we like sheep have gone astray; we have turned every one, to his own way; and the Lord has laid on Him the iniquity of us all."
> —Isaiah 53:6

> "... and He died for all, that those who live should live no longer for themselves, but for Him who died for them and rose again."
> —2 Corinthians 5:15

In writing to the Believer's in Rome, Paul admonished:

> 9 What then? Are we better than they? Not at all;
> for we have already charged that both Jews and Greeks
> are all under sin;
> 10 as it is written,
>
> > "THERE IS NONE RIGHTEOUS, NOT EVEN ONE;
> > THERE IS NONE WHO UNDERSTANDS,
> > THERE IS NONE WHO SEEKS FOR GOD;

Sin: Historical Study

> 12 ALL HAVE TURNED ASIDE, TOGETHER
> THEY HAVE BECOME USELESS;
> THERE IS NONE WHO DOES GOOD,
> THERE IS NOT EVEN ONE."
> 13 "THEIR THROAT IS AN OPEN GRAVE,
> WITH THEIR TONGUES THEY KEEP DECEIVING,"
> THE POISON OF ASPS IS UNDER THEIR LIPS";
> 14 "WHOSE MOUTH IS FULL OF CURSING AND BITTERNESS";
> 15 "THEIR FEET ARE SWIFT TO SHED BLOOD,"
> 16 "DESTRUCTION AND MISERY ARE IN THEIR PATHS"
> 17 "AND THE PATH OF PEACE HAVE THEY NOT KNOWN."
> 18 "THERE IS NO FEAR OF GOD BEFORE THEIR EYES."
> 19 Now we know that whatever the Law says,
> it speaks to those who are under the Law,
> that every mouth may be closed, and all
> the world may become accountable to God;
> 20 because by the works of the Law no flesh will be justified
> in His sight; for through the Law comes the knowledge of sin.
>
> —Romans 3

What Are The Meanings Of The Words Used In The Bible To Describe The Condition From Which We Must Repent?

A. SIN (*hamartia*) – To miss a mark; to be in error.

> "And she will bring forth a Son, and you shall call His name Jesus, for He will save His people from their SINS."
>
> —Matthew 1:21

The Doctrine of Sin is called *"Hamartiology,"* which comes from two Greek words. *"Hamartiology"* is the Biblical teaching concerning sin, its origin, its definition, its expression and is final. This is the common, yet rarely used, word for sin in the New Testament. It was not originally an ethical word at all. It was, in fact, a word used in marksmanship; and it meant a missing of the target. Sin is failing to hit the target. It is failing to be what we should be; it's falling short of God's glorious desire for us.

> "for all have sinned and fall SHORT of the glory of God...."
>
> —Romans 3:23

The sinner is one who has missed or come short of the glory of God. Total disregard of Yahweh is the ultimate sin and what is known as, "missing the mark." All other sins that are listed here are what Yahweh sees as sin after we have hit the target. An important definition of sin is given by James, "to him that knoweth to do good, and doeth it not, to him it is sin." (4:17 KJ). Absolute ignorance is excusable, even though it is a missing of the mark, but negligence is not (see Hebrews 2:3). These sins that seek to entrap the souls of men are as follows:

Eternal Life Principles & Beyond

1. EVIL (Kakos) – Bad, of a bad quality or disposition, worthless, corrupt, depraved, wicked, criminal, morally bad.

> 21 "For from within, out of the heart of men, proceed EVIL thoughts, adulteries, fornication, murders,
> 22 thefts, covetousness, wickedness, deceit, licentiousness, an evil eye, blasphemy, pride, foolishness.
> 23 All these EVIL things come from within and defile a man."
> —Mark 7

In the parable of the servants (Matthew 24:42-51), "the evil servant" (vs 48) is contrasted with the "faithful and wise servant" (vs 45).

2. WICKEDNESS (Poneria) – Evil disposition of mind, mischief, malignity.

> "So it will be at the end of the age. The angels will come forth, separate the *wicked* from among the just...."
> —Matthew 13:49

This indicates a "mental disregard for justice, righteousness, truth, honor, virtue as opposed to evil in thought and life, depravity, sinfulness, criminality."

> 15 On one occasion the Pharisees, "took counsel how they might entangle Him in His talk."

And then they proceeded to present to Him a loaded question.

> 18 But Jesus perceived their WICKEDNESS, and said, "Why do you test Me, you hypocrites?"
> —Matthew 22

3. TRANSGRESSION (Parabasis) – A stepping by the side, deviation, violation of law."

> "What purpose then does the law serve? It was added because of TRANSGRESSIONS, till the Seed should come to whom the promise was made...."
> —Galatians 3:19

This word literally means "a stepping across." The picture is of a man stepping across a line, across which he has no right to step, a man invading forbidden territory, and crossing the bounds of that which is right. This is the sin of deliberately crossing over the boundary between right and wrong.

4. UNRIGHTEOUSNESS (Adikia) – injustice, wrong, iniquity, falsehood, deceitfulness.

> "ALL UNRIGHTEOUSNESS (adikia) is SIN (hamartia)...."
> —1 John 5:17

Sin: Historical Study

Unrighteousness is the failure to give to God and to man what is their due. The unrighteous man fails to give God his love and obedience and fails to give man his charity and his service.

> 5. UNGODLINESS (Asebeia) Impiety, improbity (dishonesty), wickedness.
>
>> "For the wrath of God is revealed from heaven against all *ungodliness* and unrighteousness of men, who suppress the truth in unrighteousness."
>>
>> —Romans 1:18

This sin is substituting some god, or gods, for the real God in total disregard of Yahweh; it is treating Yahweh as if He did not exist. It is not atheism, for atheism does not believe there is a God. A Godless person knows there is a god but totally disregards the true God who is Yahweh. Godliness is following a god of some kind or another. Some men are their own gods saying, "I am the master of my universe." Everyone has some kind of a god. It could be fame, money, or another person, (especially their children). This sin is following the wrong god.

> 6. INIQUITY (Anomia) – Without law, not subject to law, violating law, lawless.
>
>> "And then I will declare to them, "I never knew you, depart from Me, you who practice *lawlessness!*"
>>
>> —Matthew 7:23

"Nomos" means law; and the sinner is the man who disobeys Yahweh's law. This word stresses the deliberation of sin; it describes the man who knows the right, and who yet does the wrong.

> 7. DISOBEDIENCE (Parakoe) – An erroneous or imperfect hearing, disobedience; a deviation from obedience.
>
>> "For as by one man's *disobedience* many were made sinners, so also by one Man's obedience many will be made righteous."
>>
>> —Romans 5:19

The verb form of this word originally meant "to mishear or to fail to hear." It could be used of the man who did not catch something that someone else said, because it was indistinctly spoken, or because he himself was deaf. Then it came to mean *deliberately not to hear,* as it were, "to close the ears to." This sin means "closing the ears to Yahweh in order to listen to one's self." It is also known as selective hearing.

> 8. TRESPASS (Paraptoma) – A falling aside, deviation from the right path.
>
>> "And you He made alive who were dead in trespasses (paraptoma) and sins (hamartia)...."
>>
>> —Ephesians 2:1

Eternal Life Principles & Beyond

This word describes the "slip" which a man may make when he is off guard, when he is not looking where he is going, when he takes his eyes off the goal. It is the failure in concentration, the failure in self-control, though which a man is swept or slips into sin.

What Is The Origin Of Sin?

A. Historically

> "Therefore, just as through one man entered the world, and death through sin, and thus death spread to all men, because all sinned.
> —Roman 5:12

This one man was Adam the first man. Before Adam partook of the tree of the knowledge of Good and evil, there was no sin in the world. The Apostle Paul affirms that death passed upon all men by the first Adam's one transgression. There was neither sin nor death before the offense. We all are born as partakers of the consequences of Adam's sin.

B. Individually

> 14 But each one (or every man KJV) is tempted when he is drawn away by his own desires and enticed.
> 15 Then, when desire has conceived, it gives birth to sin, and when it is full-grown, brings forth death.
> —James 1

1. How many are sinners?

   a. "....for all have sinned and fall short of the glory of God...."
   —Romans 3:23

   b. "For we have previously charged both Jews and Greeks that they are all under sin."
   —Romans 3:9

   c. "As it is written: There is *none* righteous, no not one."
   —Romans 3:10

   d. "They have *all* gone out of the way; they have together become unprofitable; There is *none* who does good, no not one."
   —Romans 3:12

   e. "Now we know that whatever the law says, it says to those who are under the law, that every mouth may be stopped, and *all the world* may become guilty before God."
   —Romans 3:19

Sin: Historical Study

    f. "Therefore, just as through one man sin entered the world and death through sin, and thus death spread to all men, because *all sinned.*"

—Romans 5:12

    g. "But the Scripture has confined <u>*all*</u> under sin, that the promise by faith in Jesus Christ might be given to those who believe."

—Galatians 3:22

What Sins Do The Scriptures Specifically List?

A. Seven which come from the natural heart and defile

18 "But those things which proceed out of the mouth come from the heart, and they defile a man.
19 For out of the heart proceed evil thoughts, murders, adulteries, fornications, thefts, false witness *and* blasphemies.
20 These are the things which defile a man...."

—Matthew 15

B. Thirteen which come from the natural heart and defile

21 "For from within, out of the heart of men, proceed evil thoughts, adulteries, fornications, murders,
22 thefts, covetousness, wickedness, deceit, licentiousness, an evil eye, blasphemy, pride, and foolishness.
23 All things come from within and defile a man."

—Mark 7

C. Twenty-three which bring the judgment of God

28 "And even as they did not like to retain God in their knowledge, God gave them over to a debased mind, to do those things which are not fitting;
29 being filled with all unrighteousness, sexual immorality, wickedness, covetousness, maliciousness, full of envy, murder, strife, deceit, evil-mindedness, they are whisperers,
30 backbiters, haters of God, violent, proud, boasters, inventors of evil things, disobedient to parents,
31 undiscerning, untrustworthy, unloving, unforgiving, unmerciful;
32 who, knowing the righteous judgment of God, that those who practice such things are worthy of death, not only do the same but also approve of those who practice them."

—Roman 1

Eternal Life Principles & Beyond

D. Seven which Believers must not do

> 12 "Therefore let us cast off the works of darkness, and let us put on the armor of light.
> 13 Let us walk properly, as in the day, not in revelry and drunkenness, not in licentiousness and lewdness, not in strife and envy.
> 14 But put on the Lord Jesus Christ, and make no provision for the flesh, to fulfill its lusts."
> —Romans 13

E. Six with which Believers must not associate

> 9 "I wrote to you in my epistle not to keep company with sexually immoral people.
> 10 Yet I certainly did not mean with the sexually immoral people of this world, or with the covetous, or extortioners, or idolators, since then you would need to go out of the world.
> 11 But now I have written to you not to keep company with anyone named a brother, who is a fornicator, or covetous, or an idolater, or a reviler, or a drunkard, or an extortioner — not even to eat with such a person."
> —1 Corinthians 5

F. Ten which bar Believers from the kingdom of God

> 9 "Do you not know that the unrighteous will not inherit the kingdom of God? Do not be deceived. Neither fornicators, nor idolaters, nor adulterers, nor homosexuals, nor sodomites,
> 10 nor thieves, nor covetous, nor drunkards, nor revilers, nor extortioners will inherit the kingdom of God."
> —1 Corinthians 6

G. Eleven from which Saints must turn away

> 20 "For I fear lest, when I come, I shall not find you such as I wish, and that I shall be found by you such as you do not wish; lest there be contentions, jealousies, outbursts of wrath, selfish ambitions, backbitings, whisperings, conceits, tumults;
> 21 and lest, when I come again, my God will humble me among you, and I shall mourn for the many who have sinned before and have not repented of the uncleanness, fornication and licentiousness which they have practiced."
> —2 Corinthians 12

H. Seventeen which bar The Called from the kingdom of God

> 19 "Now the works of the flesh are evident, which are: adultery, fornication, uncleanness, licentiousness,

20 idolatry, sorcery, hatred, contentious, jealousies, outbursts, outbursts of wrath, selfish ambitions, dissensions, heresies."

—Galatians 5

I. Nine in which the unsaved live and in which the saved must not live

17 "This I say, therefore, and testify in the Lord, that you should no longer walk as the rest of the Gentiles walk, in the futility of their mind,
18 having their understanding darkened, being alienated from the life of God, because of the ignorance that is in them, because of the hardening of their heart;
19 who, being past feeling, have given themselves over to licentiousness, to work all uncleanness with greediness."

—Ephesians 4

J. Nine which The Beloved of God must put away

25 Therefore, putting away lying, each one speak truth with his neighbor, for we are members of one another.

28 Let him who stole steal no longer, but rather let him labor, working with his hands what is good, that he may have something to give him who has need.
29 Let no corrupt communication proceed out of your mouth, but what is good for necessary edification, that it may impart grace to the hearers.

31 Let all bitterness, wrath, anger, clamor, and evil speaking be put away from you, with all malice."

—Ephesians 4

K. Six which must not be named as existing among Believers

3 "But fornication and all uncleanness or covetousness, let it not even be named among you, as is fitting for all saints;
4 neither filthiness, nor foolish talking, nor coarse jesting, which are not fitting, but rather giving of thanks."

—Ephesians 5

L. Four which bar from the kingdom of God and of Christ and which bring the wrath of God

5 "For this you know, that no fornicator, unclean person, nor covetous man, who is an idolater, has any inheritance in the kingdom of Christ and God.
6 Let no one deceive you with empty words, for because of these things the wrath of God comes upon the sons of disobedience."

—Ephesians 5

Eternal Life Principles & Beyond

M. Six which Believers must mortify, and which bring the wrath of God.

5 "Therefore put to death your members which are on the earth; fornication, uncleanness, passion, evil desire, and covetousness, which is idolatry.
6 Because of these things the wrath of God is coming upon the sons of disobedience."

—Colossians 3

N. Six which the Saints must put off

8 "But now you must also put off all these; anger, wrath, malice, blasphemy, filthy language out of your mouth.
9 Do not lie to one another, since you have put off the old man with his deeds, …."

—Colossians 3

O. Fourteen for which the law was given

9 "….the law is not made for a righteous person, but for the lawless and insubordinate, for the ungodly and for sinners, for the unholy and profane, for murderers of fathers and murderers of mothers, for manslayers,
10 for fornicators, for sodomites, for kidnappers, for liars, for perjurers, and if there is any other thing that is contrary to sound doctrine, …."

—1 Timothy 1

P. Nineteen from which the Saint must turn away

1 "But know this, that in the last days perilous times will come;
2 For men will be lovers of themselves, lovers of money, boasters, proud, blasphemers, disobedient to parents, unthankful, unholy,
3 unloving, unforgiving, slanderers, without self-control, brutal, despisers of good,
4 traitors, headstrong, haughty, lovers of pleasure rather than lovers of God,
5 having a form of godliness but denying its power. And from such people TURN AWAY!"

—2 Timothy 3

Q. Nine from which Saints are saved

3 "For we ourselves were also once foolish, disobedient, deceived, serving various lusts and pleasures, living in malice and envy, hateful and hating one another."

—Titus 3

Sin: Historical Study

    R. Five which His Peculiar People must lay aside

      1 "Therefore, laying aside all malice, all guile, hypocrisy, envy, and all evil speaking."

—1 Peter 2

    S. Seven sins of the flesh in which Believers used to live

      3 "For we have spent enough of our past lifetime in doing the will of the Gentiles – when we walked in licentiousness, lusts, drunkenness, revelries, drinking parties, and abominable idolatries."

—1 Peter 4

    T. Eight which condemn the unsaved to the Lake of Fire

      8 "But the cowardly, unbelieving, abominable, murderers, sexually immoral, sorcerers, idolaters, and all liars shall have their part in the lake which burns with fire and brimstone, which is the second death."

—Revelation 21

    U. Six which bar from the Tree of Life and the Holy City

      14 "Blessed are those who do His commandments, that they may have the right to the tree of life, and may enter through the gates into the city.
      15 But outside are dogs and sorcerers and sexually immoral and murderers and idolaters, and whoever loves and practices a lie."

—Revelation 22

These 21 lists constitute a total of 202 sins. Some are found in more than one verse, so there are at least 103 sins mentioned here. There are probably more, but according to the list, *you* have a general idea of how to guide your conscience.

Addendum:

The spirit of man can sin: Psalm 32:1-3; 11, and Job 19:1-29.

Also, it might surprise you to learn the drudgery and wearisomeness of sin is not dwelt upon in the New Testament. The words which imply "to sin" are usually found in a noble sense. They are in connection with labor for Christ, particularly 1 Corinthians 3:8. "Now he who plants and he who waters are one; but each will receive his own reward according to his own labor." A few verses down explains that we will not be rewarded by the results produced, but by the amount of labor expended. It is not the outward show or bulk, but the real value of the work done. The labor and value are what shall be the test of a man's faithfulness at "the Great Day."

Sin

Lesson Study Review 19

1. What is the essential principle of sin?

   _____

   _____

2. What is the most common word for sin in the New Testament?

   _____

   _____

3. List four other words used for sin in the New Testament.

   _____   _____

   _____   _____

4. According to the Bible, what is the historical origin of sin?

   _____

5. How does the Bible describe the individual act of sin?

   _____

   _____

   _____

6. How many of the human race are sinners?

   A. _____

   B. _____

Lesson Study Review 19

7. How many sins are listed in the New Testament?

   A. _____

   B. _____

   C. _____

Note: Although sin starts in the heart, a thought is not sin. When a thought becomes a lustful thought, it is sin. A lustful thought put into action is death.

8. The following is a practical application of this lesson. Arrange for a time when you can be alone with Yahweh for at least an hour. As you sit humbly before the King of the universe, completely exposed before His radiant Holiness and love for you, with His arms outstretched waiting to pour His forgiveness and healing power upon you, allow the Holy Spirit to do His cleansing in your soul setting you free of all that weighs you down.

   Starting with number 1 on page 271 and continuing to number 8 on page 272, confess all the sins listed. Again, do not skip any sin listed assuming *you* did not commit that sin, but let Yahweh be the judge. Confess each sin listed in the 21 lists even if they are duplicated, because each Greek word has a different expression. Again, do not skip any sin, just confess it and move on. After completing this time with Yahweh, try to keep yourself isolated from others and retire for the evening. Trust Yahweh to heal you as you rest in His forgiveness and love as you fall asleep.

   Then the day after *you* have completed this act of humility with grace write below how *you* feel. Do not write about your sins; just record the results of your act of obedience. May Yahweh pour out an experience you will never forget.

   _____
   _____
   _____
   _____
   _____
   _____
   _____
   _____

Answer Section

At this time, please review the Welcome Dear Reader letter at the beginning of this book entitled A Word From The Author. Your answers depend upon the instructions in that letter. Be blessed.

Answers - Lesson Study Review 1

Foundation

Lesson Study Review 1

1. What did the Lord indicate constitutes a sound life for His Called Ones?

   Luke 6:47   HE THAT COMETH TO HIM, HEARS HIS WORDS, AND DOES THEM

2. How important is a foundation to a building?

   EXTREMELY IMPORTANT. THE FOUNDATION MUST BE SOLID ENOUGH TO HOLD THE DESIGN OF THE BUILDING

3. Is it possible to erect a building without a proper foundation?   YES

   Explain Your Answer: BUT A HOUSE BUILT ON EARTH WILL CRUMBLE IN THE STORMS OF LIFE

   A. List the four storms found in Colossians 2:8.

TRADITIONS OF MEN	PRINCIPLES OF THE WORLD
VAIN DECEIT	PHILOSOPHY

   B. List five storms that face families today that are not mentioned in the lesson.

DIVORCE	IMPRISONED LOVED ONES
TERMINAL DISEASE	UNEXPECTED FAMILY DEATH
FINANCIAL REVERSAL	JOB LOSS
KIDS ON DRUGS	UNWED PREGNANCY
OUR CHILD LIES TO US	ELDERLY LIVING ALONE

4. In the Lord's parable, what is inevitable in the lives of all human beings?

   STRONG WINDS; DRIVING RAINS; FLOODS; STORMS OF LIFE

Eternal Life Principles & Beyond

5. According to the parable of the two houses what does the Lord consider to be the process to lay a good foundation?

Luke 6:48 DIGGING DEEP AND LAYING A FOUNDATION ON THE ROCK WHO IS JESUS, THE CHRIST

   A. What is some of the dirt (iniquities) that many have to face in their primary relationships that can negatively impact their relationship with Jesus? (Draw from your personal experience.)

TRADITIONS OF MEN	PRINCIPLES OF THE WORLD
TRADITIONS	UNBRIDLED TONGUE
LYING-STEALING	RELIGIOSITY
UNRESOLVED CONFLICT	FALSE INDOCTRINATIONS
LEGALISM	SINS OF THE SPIRIT, FLESH, SOUL AND BODY

(Flesh is the inclination of our nature to self-satisfying or gratifying behavior.)

6. Describe the steps to secure a good foundation for this life.

   REMOVING ALL THE DIRT (FLESH & SINS) BETWEEN US AND THE ROCK

7. God expects us to build a good foundation when we have received information on how to do it.   **TRUE**   (True or False)

   Justify your answer: GOD WOULD NOT HAVE US IGNORANT OF HIS WAYS.

   (This was discussed in the *Introduction*) GOD IS WANTING HIS PEOPLE TO BE

   OVERCOMERS AND CHALLENGERS

Answers - Lesson Study Review 1

8. According to Hebrews 6:1-2, what constitutes the foundation of a Believer's life?

    A. REPENTANCE FROM DEAD WORKS

    B. FAITH TOWARD GOD

    C. DOCTRINES OF BAPTISMS/WASHINGS

    D. LAYING-ON-OF-HANDS

    E. RESURRECTION OF THE DEAD

    F. ETERNAL JUDGMENT

9. List some New Testament principles that enable us to progress on to spiritual maturity.

    A. MASTERING THESE DOCTRINES & MOVING ON TO PERFECTION

    B. GETTING OFF THE MILK OF THE WORD AND EATING SOLID FOOD

    C. DYING TO THE SELF-LIFE   (I am crucified with Christ)

    D. HEBREWS 5:12

    E. WALKING IN THE FRUIT OF THE HOLY SPIRIT

    F. MOVING IN SPIRITUAL WARFARE

    G. MEETING THE NEEDS OF OTHERS, ETC.

    H.

Eternal Life Principles & Beyond

Foundation

Addendum:

Lesson Study Review 2

Read 2 Timothy 2:1-7. In Paul's second letter to Timothy, he draws three illustrations. Write out the key words that exemplify the believers' character that are to be part of the foundation of their house.

vs 1	BE STRONG in the Lord	
vs 2	BE FAITHFUL to the Lord, family, employer and employees, etc.	
vs 3	SUFFER HARDSHIPS/ENDURING	
vs 4	DOES NOT ENTANGLE HIMSELF IN THE AFFAIRS OF EVERYDAY LIFE	
vs 5	COMPETES ACCORDING TO THE RULES	
vs 6	HARD WORKING	

In vs 2 did Paul mention eloquent men? Did he speak of good-looking men? Did he declare educated men? NO

Name two attributes noted in vss 1-6 that Paul listed for Believers:

HARDWORKING   and   RELIABLE

Our heavenly Father is a God of love; therefore, He has given us the power of choice. In making decisions, we can choose the direction, but we cannot choose the results. In the following verses what virtues were Paul and Jesus exalting?

1 Timothy 1:12	FAITHFULNESS	
1 Corinthians 4:1	SERVANT/STEWARD	
1 Corinthians 4:2	TRUSTWORTHYNESS (NAS) –	This steward is recognized as the manager of a house, not as being brilliant. NKJV reads - faithful
1 Corinthians 4:17	FAITHFULNESS	
Luke 16:10-12	FAITHFULNESS	

Answers - Lesson Study Review 2

Read the following Scriptures for character building virtues and circle the ones that can be added to the above list.

    1 Corinthians 10:13   2 Corinthians 1:18   2 Thessalonians 3:3

    (Hebrews 3:5)   (10:23)   (11:6)   1 Thessalonians 5:24   (1 Peter 4:19)

Two final illustrations:

Read Matthew 24:45-51 and write down what vs 48 reveals as the opposite of "faithful".

    __EVIL__   Notice it is not "unfaithful".

In Matthew 25:14-21 Jesus spoke on the parable of the talents.

    In vs 21 He calls this slave __FAITHFUL__

    In vs 23 He calls this slave __FAITHFUL__

    But in vs 26 Jesus calls this slave __WICKED__ and __LAZY__ (or __SLOTHFUL__)

    Is this the opposite of faithful? __YES__

A most neglected virtue is not showing appreciation at the time of receiving a generous gift of sorts.

Answers - Lesson Study Review 3

Repentance From Dead Works
Lesson Study Review 3

1. Define the word REPENTANCE:

   (OT) Nacham   TO LAMENT OR GRIEVE

   A.   REFERS TO THE AROUSED EMOTIONS OF GOD OR MAN WHEN UNDERTAKING A DIFFERENT COURSE OF ACTION.

   B.   TO ADMIT GOD IS HOLY RIGHT AND I AM WHOLLY WRONG

   C.   A RADICAL CHANGE IN ONE'S ATTITUDE FROM SIN TO GOD'S MIND

   (OT) Shuwb   TO WITHDRAW, IMPLIES A CONSCIOUS MORAL SEPARATION AND EXPRESSES GENUINE REPENTANCE

   (NT) Metamellomai   TO HAVE A FEELING, CARE, CONCERN OR REGRET

   (NT) Metanoeo TO HAVE ANOTHER MIND; A 180° TURN; A DEEP RADICAL CHANGE

2. Give Charles G. Finney's definition of "repentance"

   AN INTELLECTUAL AND HEARTY GIVING-UP OF ALL CONTROVERSY WITH GOD ON ALL AND EVERY POINT. A THOROUGH ABANDONMENT OF ALL EXCUSES AND APOLOGIES FOR SIN.

3. What is the summary definition of "repentance"?

   A.   TO REFORM AND CHANGE THE MIND

   B.   TO STIR AND DIRECT THE EMOTIONS TO THE REQUIRED CHANGE

   C.   TO COMMAND THE WILL AND THE WHOLE MAN FROM SIN TO GOD

4. Describe the difference between dead works and fruitful (living works).

DEAD WORKS SERVE SELF - LIVING WORKS SERVE GOD

DEAD WORKS WILL CAUSE US TO "SUFFER LOSS BY FIRE"

GOOD WORKS WILL GAIN US ETERNAL REWARDS

LIVING WORKS IS THE DIVINE NATURE OF GOD MANIFESTING "THROUGH" YOU.

IT'S THE DIFFERENCE BETWEEN PLEASING GOD OR PLEASING MAN

IT'S RIGHTEOUS DEEDS; BEARING FRUIT UNTO HOLINESS; BEING FRUITFUL IN EVERY GOOD WORK

5. Is repentance to be preached in all the world?

Luke 24: 47   YES

Why?   WE ARE COMMANDED TO PREACH REPENTANCE FOR FORGIVENESS OF SINS AND PROCLAIM IT IN HIS NAME TO ALL NATIONS BEGINNING FROM JERUSALEM

6. Why is it necessary?

A. Luke 5:32   REPENTANCE IS ONE REASON FOR CHRIST'S COMING INTO THE WORLD

B. Luke 13:3   REPENTANCE IS NECESSARY TO AVOID DESTRUCTION

C. Acts 11:18   REPENTANCE IS NECESSARY TO ETERNAL LIFE

D. Acts 2:38   REPENTANCE IS NECESSARY FOR FORGIVENESS

E. 2 Peter 3:9   REPENTANCE IS GOD'S DESIRE FOR ALL

F. Matthew 4:17   BECAUSE JESUS PREACHED REPENTANCE FREQUENTLY AND IT WAS HIS FIRST MESSAGE WHEN STARTING HIS MINISTRY

Answers - Lesson Study Review 3

John the Baptist – Matthew 3:2   REPENTANCE BECAUSE THE KINGDOM OF GOD IS AT HAND

Jesus – Luke 24:47   "REPENTANCE FOR FORGIVENESS OF SINS SHOULD BE PROCLAIMED IN HIS NAME TO ALL NATIONS, BEGINNING FROM JERUSALEM"

Apostles - Mark 6:12   AND THEY WENT OUT AND PREACHED THAT MEN SHOULD REPENT

Paul – Acts 20:21   WAS SOLEMNLY TESTIFYING TO BOTH JEWS AND GREEKS OF REPENTANCE TOWARD GOD

Note: Jesus preached Repentance throughout His three-year ministry, as indicated in all four Gospels.

7. Is repentance required of all?   YES   Give Scriptural support for your answer:

   Acts 17:30   IT IS A DIRECT COMMAND FROM GOD

8. What brings man to repentance?

   A. Romans 2:4   THE GOODNESS/KINDNESS OF GOD

   B. Matthew 9:13   CHRIST'S CALL

   C. Matthew 12:41   GOOD PREACHING

   D. Luke 17:13   REBUKE (CONFRONTED HIM)

   E. 2 Corinthians 7:9   GODLY SORROW or WILL OF GOD

         vs 10   WILL OF GOD or GODLY SORROW

   F. Acts 11:15   HEARING THE HOLY SPIRIT FELL UPON THE GENTILES

         vs 18   THE GIFT (granted) OF GOD (the Holy Spirit) CAUSED THEM TO QUIET DOWN

   Acts 5:31   GOD GRANTED IT (repentance to Israel)

   2 Timothy 2:25   GENTLE CORRECTION

9. What are some evidences that one has truly repented?

   A. Mark 1:15 & Acts 20:21   FAITH IS ASSOCIATED WITH REPENTANCE

   B. Acts 2:38   WATER BAPTISM IS AN ACCOMPANIMENT OF REPENTANCE

   C. Acts 2:38   THE GIFT OF THE HOLY SPIRIT IS AN ACCOMPANIMENT OF REPENTANCE

   D. Acts 3:19   CONVERSION IS ASSOCIATED WITH REPENTANCE

   Explain in your own words: THERE IS NO SUCH THING AS A REPENTANCE THAT DOES NOT RESULT IN A TURNING AROUND. WE MUST STOP WALKING IN SIN AND, BY THE GRACE OF GOD, WALK IN RIGHTEOUSNESS

   E. Acts 26:20   WORKS/DEEDS ARE ASSOCIATED WITH REPENTANCE

   F. Matt 3:8   GOOD FRUITS ARE ASSOCIATED WITH REPENTANCE

   G. Rev. 2:21   JEZEBELLE WILLED NOT TO REPENT (see #2 above)

10. Give five Biblical instances where whole body of Believers needed to repent.

    2 Corinthians 7:9   THE CHURCH IN CORINTH WAS CALLED TO REPENTANCE

    2 Corinthians 12:20-21   THE CHURCH IN CORINTH WAS CALLED TO REPENTANCE FOR THE THIRD TIME

    Revelation 2:16   THE CHURCH IN PERGAMUM WAS CALLED TO REPENTANCE

    Revelation 3:2-3   THE CHURCH IN SARDIS WAS CALLED TO REPENTANCE

    Revelation 3:19   THE CHURCH IN LAODICEA WAS CALLED TO REPENTANCE

Answers - Lesson Study Review 3

The following is a commentary from The Bible Knowledge Commentary, New Testament Edition, Walvoord & Zuck, Vol 2, pg 793. Victor books, regarding Hebrews 6:1-2:

> "**Acts that lead to death**": dead works, an expression occurring again in a context where it seems to refer to the Levitical ritual (9:14). Here it would be appropriate in the same sense since many of the readers had been converted to Christianity from Judaism. The rituals they had left behind were lifeless ones, incapable of imparting the experiences of life they had found in Christ. The author implied that they should not return to these dead works in any form since to do so would be to lay again a basis for repenting from them —though such repentance would not be easily reached, however appropriate it might be."

The following is a commentary from the John MacArthur Study Bible, pg 1874:

> "Repentance from dead works: This OT from of repentance is the turning away from evil deeds that bring death (cf. Ezekiel 18:4; Romans 6:23) and turning to God. Too often the Jew only turned to God in a superficial fashion—fulfilling the letter of the law as evidence of his repentance. The inner man was still dead (Matthew 23:25-28); Romans 2:28-29). Such repentance was not the kind which brought salvation (Hebrews 6:6, 12:17; cf. Acts 11:18; 2 Corinthians 7:10). Under the New Covenant, however, "repentance...toward God" is coupled with "faith in our Lord Jesus Christ" (Acts 20:21). Christ's atoning sacrifice saves from "dead works" (9:14; cf. John 14:6)."

The following is a comment from Dr. Douglas J. Wingate, President and Founder of Life Christian University after he read this book which was a dissertation toward my doctorate:

> "The entire Book of Hebrews is originally addressed to Hebrew Believers in Christ, and much of the author's emphasis in the whole book is the superiority of Christ over the Law of Moses. The dead works originally addressed for these Jews would be the futile work of adherence to the keeping of the Law of Moses in order to obtain salvation. Though there was much to be gained by the keeping of the Law by the Jew, if it was mixed with faith, eternal life in the presence of God was not one of them. That is only available through faith in the completed redemptive work of Christ alone.

Of course, your point is well taken, that today the Word of God is primarily addressing the entire body of Christ, irrespective of their background. To most, repentance from the dead works of keeping the law would be quite foreign to them, but the historical setting of the book might bring some additional enlightenment to the reader."

Answers - Lesson Study Review 4

Repentance From Dead Works
Lesson Study Review 4

Addendum:

Now that we want to move on to good works, we need to establish what good works are.

A person who walks in the fruit of self-control is in possession of good works by righteous decisions. Works do not save us, but after salvation, that coin flips 180° and works indicate the attitude of our heart and faith toward God. Our Lord's (half) brother speaks of the profit in possessing faith in doing good works. Read James 2:14-26 and list the four good works mentioned.

1. vs. 15-16 FEEDING AND CLOTHING THOSE IN NEED

2 a. vs 21 ABRAHAM OFFERING ISAAC ON THE ALTAR

  b. therefore, vs 23 TELLS US THAT BELIEVING GOD IS CONSIDERED GOOD WORKS AS SEEN BY GOD

3. vs 25 RAHAB WAS JUSTIFIED BEFORE MEN BECAUSE SHE WAS TRYING TO PLEASE GOD AND NOT MAN. WHEN SHE SENT THE MESSENGERS OUT BY ANOTHER WAY, SHE WAS PRESERVING THE LIFE OF GOD'S PEOPLE. SHE WAS HONORING GOD. OBVIOUSLY, GOD HAD REVEALED HIMSELF TO HER

Joshua 2:1-14 Rahab lied to the enemies of God when she sheltered two sons of Israel who were sent secretly to Jericho to spy out the land. Her lie was for a greater cause.

Write out the key verse:

vs 26 "FOR JUST AS THE BODY WITHOUT THE SPIRIT IS DEAD, SO ALSO FAITH WITHOUT WORKS IS DEAD"

Eternal Life Principles & Beyond

4. Based on other New Testament Scripture verses revealing what good works truly are, write a fifty word essay about three or more other disciples mentioned that performed good works, and tell exactly what function they carried out.

PAUL PREACHED REPENTANCE

DORCAS ABOUNDED WITH DEEDS OF KINDNESS AND CHARITY IN HER

COMMUNITY   (Acts 9:36 & 39)

STEPHEN AND SIX OTHER MEN WERE CHARGED WITH OVERLOOKING

THE DAILY SERVING OF FOOD TO HELLENISTIC WIDOWS   (Acts 6:1-3)

ANANIAS WAS DIRECTED TO ARISE AND THEN GO LAY HANDS ON PAUL

(Acts 9:11-12)

THE BOOK OF ACTS IS FULL OF GOOD WORKS

THE GOOD SAMARITAN SHOWED MERCY   (Luke 10:37)

Note: An in-depth examination on good deeds will be studied in the lesson, Faith Toward God.

Answers - Lesson Study Review 5

Conversion
Lesson Study Review 5

1. What is the meaning of the word "conversion"?

   TO TURN FROM THE WRONG WAY TO THE RIGHT WAY

2. Is conversion essential to salvation?   YES

   Why? (Acts 3:19)

   A.   TO BLOT OUT SINS

   B.   TO SAVE US FROM DEATH

   C.   SO WE MIGHT ENTER INTO THE KINGDOM OF HEAVEN

3. Can one be in the Kingdom of God without being converted?   NO   (Yes or No)

   Explain why or why not?   Romans 14:17 and 1 Corinthians 4:20

   BECAUSE: (1) ROMANS 14:17 "For the kingdom of God is not eating and drinking, but righteousness and peace and joy in the Holy Spirit" AND

   (2) 1 COR 4:20 "For the kingdom of God does not consist in words, but in power" AND

   (3) JESUS HAS TO BE LORD OF OUR LIVES TO QUALIFY

4. According to Paul, what happens when one is converted?

   WE TURN FROM THE POWERS OF SATAN UNTO THE POWER OF GOD.

   WE TURN FROM VANITIES AND IDOLS

5. Describe the effects of conversion of the Apostle Peter according to Luke 22:32.

   BEFORE PENTECOST PETER WAS AN EMOTIONAL WEAKLING. AFTER HIS

   CONVERSION, HE SPENT ALL HIS TIME STRENGTHENING HIS BRETHREN

6. Describe repentance and conversion using the story of the prodigal son. Explain the necessary conclusions.

Steps Toward Repentance:

HE "*LOOKED*" AT THE GARBAGE AND SAID, "THE SERVANTS IN MY FATHER'S HOUSE EAT BETTER THAN THIS. HE "*TURNED*" FROM HIS EVIL WAYS AND "*WENT*" HOME

Steps Toward Conversion:

1. HE *INFORMED* HIS MIND
2. HE *STIRRED* HIS EMOTIONS
3. HE *COMMANDED* HIS WILL

What is the conclusion of the story?

THESE THREE STEPS ARE NECESSARY DECISIONS FOR REPENTANCE TO HIS GOING HOME - WHICH IS CONVERSION

Answers - Lesson Study Review 6

Faith Toward God
Lesson Study Review 6

1. Can a Believer have a genuine saving faith in Christ without repentance?   NO

   Acts 20:21   FAITH AND REPENTANCE ARE INSEPARABLE. (The NAS Bible does not use a comma after the words "dead works."   Hebrews 6:1)

2. Describe the relationship of faith and repentance as expressed in the Thessalonians Epistle.

   1 Thess.1:9   THEY TURNED FROM IDOLS AND LIVED A NEW LIFE SERVING THE LORD WHILE WAITING FOR THE LORD TO RETURN FROM HEAVEN. FAITH AND REPENTANCE ARE A BALANCED MESSAGE

3. What are the definitions of the words "faith" and "believe"?

   Faith   PISTIS – FIRM CONVICTION, FIRM ASSURANCE, FIRM PERSUASION, HONESTY, INTEGRITY, FAITHFULNESS, TRUTHFULNESS

   Believe   PISTEUO – TO TRUST IN, TO CONFIDE IN, PUT FAITH IN, RELY ON A PERSON OR THING, TO HAVE A MENTAL PERSUASION, TO ENTRUST, COMMIT TO THE TRUST OR POWER OF

4. What is Charles G. Finney's definition of faith?

   IT IS RECEIVING OF CHRIST FOR JUST WHAT HE IS AS REPRESENTED IN HIS GOSPEL, AND AN UNQUALIFIED SURRENDER OF THE WILL, AND OF THE WHOLE BEING, TO HIM

Eternal Life Principles & Beyond

5. Write out your Bible's definition of faith

Heb. 11:1 "FAITH IS THE SUBSTANCE (ASSURANCE) OF THINGS HOPED FOR, THE EVIDENCE (CONVICTION) OF THINGS NOT SEEN." (KJV)
FAITH IS PERCEIVING AS REAL WHAT IS NOT REVEALED TO THE SENSES (AMPLIFIED)

6. One can be a born-again Believer without faith.   FALSE

Give Scriptural support for your answer:

EPHESIANS 2:8 "FOR BY GRACE YOU HAVE BEEN SAVED THROUGH FAITH." ALTHOUGH THIS SCRIPTURE DOES NOT MENTION REPENTANCE, REPENTANCE ALWAYS ACCOMPANIES FAITH (Acts 20:21)

7. Show from Scripture what part of man must be involved in the faith process.

A. THE MIND MUST BE INFORMED BY HEARING – WE THEN BELIEVE
John 12:30, Acts 4:4, Acts 8:12, Romans 10:17

B. THE EMOTIONS ARE STIRRED – WITH GODLY SORROW UNTO REPENTANCE   Matthew 13:20-21; Acts 8:5-8; Romans 15:18, Romans 16:25-26; 2 Corinthians 7:10; 1 Thessalonians 1:6; 1 Peter 1:8

C. COMMAND THE WILL – TO BE OBEDIENT TO THE WORD – THEN JOY FOLLOWS. ENCOURAGING US TO THE GOAL OF BRINGING OTHERS INTO OBEDIENCE

Answers - Lesson Study Review 6

8. Abraham was cited as an excellent example of faith. List the five reasons why this is so.

   A. Rom 4:13,21   HE HEARD THE WORD FROM GOD AND HE BELIEVED

   B. Rom. 4:18-19   HE DID NOT CONSIDER HIS HOPELESS CONDITION

   C. Rom. 4:18   HE EMBRACED THE HOPE EXPRESSED IN THE DIVINE PROMISE

   D. Rom. 4:20   HE DID NOT WAIVER IN HIS COMMITMENT

   E. Rom. 4:20   HE REJOICED IN THE "WORD" AS THE ACCOMPLISHED FACT

9. List each person/or personal pronouns of faith as recorded in Hebrews 11 and their unusual/unthought-of heroic deed that God considered a good work.

   A. vs 2, ELDERS/MEN OF OLD   Deed: BY FAITH GAVE A GOOD REPORT

   B. vs 3, US   Deed: UNDERSTANDS THAT THE WORLDS WERE PREPARED BY THE WORD OF GOD

   C. vs 4, ABEL   Deed: OFFERED GOD A BETTER SACRIFICE

   D. vs 5, ENOCH   Deed: PLEASED GOD

   E. vs 7a, NOAH   Deed: PREPARED AN ARK FOR THE SALVATION OF HIS HOUSEHOLD

   F. vs 8a, ABRAHAM   Deed: OBEYED BY GOING.

   vs 8b,   Deed: HE WENT OUT

   vs 8c,   Deed: NOT KNOWING WHERE HE WAS GOING

   vs 9a,   Deed: HE LIVED AS AN ALIEN IN THE LAND OF PROMISE

G. vs 11a, SARAH   Deed: RECEIVED THE GIFT TO CONCEIVE BEYOND THE PROPER TIME OF LIFE.

H vs 11b, SARAH   Deed: SHE JUDGED GOD FAITHFUL

I vs 17, ABRAHAM   Deed: OFFERED UP ISAAC **ISAAC WAS THE CHILD OF THE PROMISE

J vs 20, ISAAC   Deed: BLESSED JACOB AND ESAU REGARDING THINGS TO COME

K vs 21, JACOB   Deed: BLESSED EACH OF THE SONS OF JOSEPH AND THEN HE WORSHIPED

L vs 22, JOSEPH   Deed: GAVE ORDERS CONCERNING HIS BONES

M vs 23, MOSES' PARENTS   Deed: HID MOSES (BECAUSE THEY WERE NOT AFRAID OF THE KING'S EDICT)

N vs 24a, MOSES   Deed: REFUSED TO BE CALLED THE SON OF PHARAOH'S DAUGHTER THEREBY:

   (a) vs 24b, LOSING ALL INHERITANCE TO EGYPT

   (b) vs 25a, CHOOSING TO ENDURE ILL TREATMENT

   (c) vs 25b, GIVING UP ALL PLEASURE OF SIN

   (d) vs 26, CONSIDERING THE REPROACH OF CHRIST (the promised Deliverer) GREATER RICHES

   (e) vs 27, LEFT EGYPT NOT FEARING THE WRATH OF PHAROAH

   (f) vs 28, HE KEPT THE PASSOVER

   (g) vs 29, PASSED THROUGH THE RED SEA

Answers - Lesson Study Review 6

O. vs 30 , JOSHUA/ALL ISRAEL   Deed: MANY EXPLOITS

P. vs 31 , RAHAB   Deed: SHE LIED TO HER OWN PEOPLE AND WELCOMED ISRAELI SPIES INTO HER HOME

Q. vs 32 , ALL CHOSEN   Deed: OBEYED GOD'S CALL

10. Jesus spoke of various kinds of faith. Can you name four and give their reference?

   A.   GREAT FAITH (LONG TERM) Matthew 8:10

   B.   LITTLE FAITH (SHORT TERM, INTERMEDIATE) Matthew 6:30; 8:26; 16:8

   C.   MUSTARD SEED FAITH (SMALLEST OF ALL FAITH) Matthew 17:20

   D.   HEALING FAITH – Matthew 9:22

   E.   SAVING FAITH – Luke 7:50 & Mark 16:16

Note: The Scripture does not reveal the faith of the paralytic. It's assumed he had "no faith" but was healed on the faith of his friends. Otherwise known as welfare faith.

11. There are several places where we can misplace our faith.   What are they?

   Psalm 44:6   IN WEAPONS

   Luke 12:21   IN WEALTH

   Psalm 62:10 (A)   OPPRESSION

          (B)   EXTORTION

          (C)   INCREASED RICHES, (KEEP YOUR HEART DETACHED)

   Psalm 146:3 HUMAN GREATNESS (PRINCES – GOVERNMENTS – RULERS – MORTAL MAN – KINGS – PRIME MINISTERS – ETC.)

   Proverbs 28:26   IN ONE'S SELF - IN YOUR EMOTIONS

   Isaiah 42:17   IN IDOLS

   Jeremiah 7:4-8   DECEPTIVE WORDS

Eternal Life Principles & Beyond

12. here are organizations and cults which are contrary to the Word of God. Name at least six.

MASONS

POWER OF POSITIVE THINKING

CULTS

SPIRITISM

ECLECTIC RELIGIONS

SILVA MIND CONTROL

BUDDHA & ETC

Answers - Lesson Study Review 7

Baptism I

Lesson Study Review 7

1. Name four types of baptisms mentioned in this lesson? Give a short Scriptural illustration of each and document your answer.

   A. MATT 3:11   JOHN'S BAPTISM – REPENTANCE

   B. ACTS 2:38   THE BELIEVER'S BAPTISM – WATER

       (vs 41   GLADLY RECEIVED THE WORD AND WERE BAPTIZED)

   C. ACTS 11:16   BAPTISM OF THE HOLY SPIRIT

2. Define the word "baptize."

   TO PUT INTO OR UNDER WATER – TO FULLY IMMERSE AND SUBMERGE

   (DYED IN THE WOOL)

3. Where is water baptism first recorded in the New Testament?

   MATTHEW 3:11a

4. Who was John the Immerser?

   A. LUKE 1:5, 13 – SON OF ZACHARIAS AND ELIZABETH

   B. LUKE 7:28 – THE GREATEST OF PROPHETS

   C. JOHN 1:31
      MATT 3:3   } HE WAS SENT TO INTRODUCE JESUS TO ISRAEL
      LUKE 1:76-77

Eternal Life Principles & Beyond

5. Was water baptism John's own idea? __NO__

   Explain your answer:

   A. John 1:33   HE WAS DIVINELY SENT TO BAPTIZE

   B. Luke 16:16   HIS MINISTRY MARKED THE BEGINNING OF A NEW AGE

   C. Luke 3:2-3   HIS MINISTRY MARKED A NEW ORDER OF DIVINE
                   REQUIREMENT AND THAT REQUIREMENT INCLUDES
                   IMMERSION IN WATER.

   D. Luke 7:30   IT WAS THE "COUNSEL OF GOD" (PURPOSE OR WILL)

   E. Luke 7:29   THOSE WHO WERE BAPTIZED JUSTIFIED GOD

   F. Acts 19:4-5 JOHN'S BAPTISM OF REPENTANCE SUPERSEDED THE
                   BELIEVER'S BAPTISM

6. What did the lawyers and the Pharisees reject in refusing to be baptized with John's baptism?

   THEY REFUSED THE WILL OF GOD

7. What mandated the church's practice of the Believer's baptism?

   Matt. 28:19 & Mk. 16:16   THE GREAT COMMISSION

8. How did the practice of the apostles in administering water baptism seem to contradict the Great Commission as contained in Matt. 28:19

   Acts 2: 38, 41 ⎫
   Acts 8:16   ⎬   THEY WERE BAPTIZING ONLY IN THE NAME OF JESUS
   Acts 19:5   ⎭

Answers - Lesson Study Review 7

9. There are many passages of Scripture that describes "fully immersed" other than water. Try to recall at least eight incidences starting in the Book of Genesis.

1. GENESIS 5:22-24   ENOCH WHO WALKED WITH GOD AND WALKED STRAIGHT UP INTO HEAVEN

2. EXODUS. 3:2   THE BURNING BUSH – IT WAS NOT CONSUMED

3. 2 KINGS 2:11   ELIJAH WHO WAS TAKEN UP IN A WHIRLWIND ON A CHARIOT OF FIRE AND HORSES

4. ACTS 2:3-4   THE 120 DISCIPLES IN THE UPPER ROOM ON THE DAY OF PENTECOST WERE FULLY IMMERSED

5. ACTS 16:14   LYDIA – DYING CLOTH PURPLE.

6. GALATIONS 2:1-2b   PAUL WAS ALONE IN THE DESERT FOR FOURTEEN YEARS RECEVING MANY REVELATIONS FROM THE LORD WHICH HE RECORDED IN HIS EPISTLES

7. REV. Ch 1 to Ch 22   JOHN ON THE ISLE OF PATMOS. AT TIMES HE WAS CAUGHT UP IN THE SPIRIT AND AT TIMES FULLY IMMERSED

8. MARK 9:2-3   JESUS TRANSFIGURED IN THE GLORY OF GOD ON THE MOUNT OF OLIVES

9. JESUS' SUFFERING IN THE GARDEN OF GETHSEMANE - HE SWEAT DROPS OF BLOOD IT WAS SO AGONIZING.

10. JESUS SUFFERING ON THE CROSS – HE CRIED OUT TO HIS FATHER, "WHY HAVE YOU FORSAKEN ME?"

11. HIS HUMILIATION - EVERYTHING FROM THE GARDEN TO HIS DEATH ON THE CROSS

12. 2 CORINTHIANS 12:2   PAUL WAS CAUGHT UP TO THE THIRD HEAVEN.

Note: In reference to John's baptism unto repentance and the baptism by the Holy Spirit with fire were fulfilled prophecies from Joel 28-29 and Malachi 3:2-5.

Joel had given the promise of the outpouring of the Holy Spirit on Israel and an actual outpouring of the Spirit did occur in Acts 2 on the day of Pentecost, but experientially all of Israel did not enter into the benefits of that event. She will yet experience the benefits of this accomplished work when she turns in repentance at the Lord's second coming.

The baptism "with fire" referred to the judging and cleansing of those who would enter the kingdom of God as prophesied in Malachi 3. This symbolism was carried through by John the immerser, who spoke of the separation that occurs when a winnowing fork tosses up grain, and the wheat is gathered into the barn and the chaff is burned up.

Answers - Lesson Study Review 8

Instruction About Washings II
Lesson Study Review 8

1. Did Our Lord Jesus Christ impart all revelation before He returned to Heaven?

   __NO__ (Yes or No)   Justify your answer.

   John 16:12   JESUS TOLD HIS DISCIPLES "YOU CANNOT BEAR THEM NOW"

2. What did Christ promise His apostles concerning further revelation of truth?

   JOHN 14:26 & 16:13 HE PROMISED THERE WOULD BE MORE REVELATION AND NEW REVELATION GIVEN BY THE HOLY SPIRIT

3. What did God declare His Name to be in the Old Testament?

   YHWH – YAHWEH – YAH (Hebrew)   OR   JHVH – JEHOVAH (German)

4. Where does the Threeness of God reside bodily?

   Col. 2:9   "FOR IN HIM ALL THE FULLNESS OF DEITY DWELLS IN BODILY FORM."

5. What is the significance of baptism into the Name of the Lord Jesus Christ?

   Rom. 6:3   WE HAVE BEEN BAPTIZED INTO HIS DEATH

6. What are those things which qualify one for water baptism?

   A.   ACTS 2:41; 16:14-15; 19:5   HEARING AND HEEDING THE WORD

   B.   ACTS 2:37   CONVICTION

   C.   ACTS 2:38   REPENTANCE – HAVE A CHANGE OF MIND/HEART

   D.   MARK 16:16, ACTS 8:12; 36-37, ACTS 16:31, 33   FAITH TOWARD GOD

   E.   ACTS 9:6 & 18   OBEDIENCE

7. In the New Testament, how soon were repentant, believing sinners baptized?

   A. Acts 2:41   THE SAME DAY

   B. Acts 8:12; 37-38, 18:8   WHEN THEY BELIEVED

   C. Acts 16:31-33   THE SAME HOUR

Answers - Lesson Study Review 9

Instruction About Washings III
Lesson Study Review 9

1. Explain the Scripture that relates water baptism and sin.

   Acts 2:38 REPENT, AND LET EACH OF YOU BE BAPTIZED IN THE NAME OF JESUS CHRIST FOR THE FORGIVENESS OF YOUR SINS. (WE HAVE REMISSION OF SINS THROUGH WATER BAPTISM BECAUSE OF FORGIVENESS)

2. Does water baptism relate to cleansing? YES If so, how?

   A. Acts 22:16 (ACTUALLY) IT WASHES AWAY OUR SINS

   B. Rev. 1:5b (LEGALLY) (TO HIM WHO LOVES US), AND RELEASED US FROM OUR SINS BY HIS BLOOD

   C. John 15:3 (POSITIONALLY) CLEANSED BY THE WORDS JESUS SPOKE TO US (See Ps 119:9)

   D. Luke 24:47 (EXPERIENTIALLY) REPENT THAT YOUR SINS MAY BE WIPED AWAY (See Acts 2:38; 3:19)

3. According to Romans 6, what is spirit baptism (placed into the body of Christ) telling us?

   Romans 6:3-5 WE HAVE DIED WITH HIM

   WE WERE BURIED WITH HIM

   WE WERE RAISED WITH HIM

Note: Can we have newness of life without death to the self-life?

4. Should repentance, faith, and baptism be separated? NO Why or Why not?

   THEY WERE NOT SEPARATED IN THE BEGINNING

   Explain 1 Cor. 10:1-2 MOSES IS A TYPE OF OUR LORD JESUS

   VS 2 ALL WERE BAPTIZED INTO MOSES IN THE CLOUD AND IN THE SEA

   "BAPTIZED" IN THE SEA - WATER

   "BAPTIZED" IN THE CLOUD - SPIRIT

Comment: Acts 2:38 – It seems water baptism is a prerequisite to the gift of the Holy Spirit.

Answers - Lesson Study Review 10

Instruction About Washings IV
Lesson Study Review 10

1. What are the four things signifying the relationship between Old Testament circumcision and New Testament water baptism?

   (Col. 2:11-12)

   A. WE ARE BURIED

   B. SIGNIFYING DEATH TO THE SELF-LIFE

   C. CUTTING OFF OUR FLESH

   D. NOT WITH HUMAN HANDS BUT THROUGH THE OPERATION OF GOD WHO HAS RAISED HIM/US FROM THE DEAD

Comment: Water baptism is a sign of belonging to His covenant people when dedicating oneself to God. (See Genesis 17:10-11 and Romans 2:28-29)

2. Describe the relationship between Israel, Moses and water baptism.

   1 Cor. 10:1-2   MOSES WAS A TYPE OF JESUS. THE ISRAELITES WERE COMMITTED TO THE LEADERSHIP AND AUTHORITY OF MOSES. THE SEA AND THE CLOUD WERE A TYPE OF BAPTISM

The pillar of fire that moved by night and the cloud that moved by day means they were led of the Holy Spirit. The pillar of fire also kept them warm at night in the desert's bitter cold and the cloud that moved by day kept them from the scorching heat of the sun. As the Israelites passed through the sea, they saw the faces of the Egyptians no more. They closed the door to their past. Water baptism can close the door to your past.

3. Does water baptism have anything to do with the conscience?   YES

   Explain your answer: 1 Peter 3:20b-21   WATER BAPTISM IS THE ACT OF OBEDIENCE THAT DEMONSTRATES OUR REPENTANCE AND FAITH AND DESIRE TO HAVE A GOOD CONSCIENCE BEFORE GOD

Eternal Life Principles & Beyond

4. Research and write a 50-word essay giving reference to the responsibility of parents toward baby dedication in the New Testament and Old Testament.

ALMOST EVERY READER WILL TALK ABOUT "WATER BAPTISM" OR CIRCUMCISION AND TOTALLY MISS THE WORDS "BABY DEDICATION."

LUKE 1:58-60 NEIGHBORS AND RELATIVES WENT TO ZACHARIS' HOUSE TO DEDICATE JOHN.

LUKE 2:21-22 MARY AND JOSEPH WENT TO THE TEMPLE TO PRESENT JESUS TO THE LORD.

1 SAMUEL 1:11 – HANNA "GAVE HIM" (her son, Samuel) TO THE LORD

TODAY, IN MOST CHURCHES THE PASTOR, FAMILY AND CHURCH MEMBERS PUBLICLY PRAY A BLESSING OVER THE CHILD

Answers - Mid Summary Review

Mid-Study Review

1. __FAITH__ and __REPENTANCE__ toward God are inseparable in effecting a genuine conversion.

2. What is the summary definition of Repentance?

   A. __TO INFORM AND CHANGE THE MIND__

   B. __TO STIR THE EMOTIONS TO ACT UPON THE CHANGE OF MIND__

   C. __TO COMMAND THE WILL__

3. Scripture says, "We are __BAPTIZED__ into His Lordship."

4. Give the meaning of the word "Repentance" in 50 words or more and give a short description of a typical experience.

   (Your answer must contain having experienced the following.)

   __TO HAVE ANOTHER MIND__

   __TO TURN AWAY FROM SIN__

   __180° TURN AROUND AWAY FROM SIN__

5. Name the six foundation stones God has provided as a solid foundation before we go on to maturity.

   1. REPENTANCE FROM DEAD WORKS
   2. FAITH TOWARD GOD
   3. RESURRECTION OF DEAD
   4. BAPTISM/INSTRUCTION WASHINGS
   5. LAYING-ON-OF-HANDS
   6. ETERNAL JUDGMENT

6. Baptism had to do with cleansing, according to Acts 22:16, but the Word reveals we are not only cleansed by the water, but we are also cleansed by __REPENTANCE__ and by the __BLOOD OF JESUS__ and by the __WORD OF GOD__.

7. Describe John the Immerser's calling and why it was so significantly different than that of the Prophets of the OT, and that of the Apostles of the NT.

HE PREACHED THE KINGDOM OF GOD IS AT HAND

HE INTRODUCED THE MESSIAH TO ISRAEL

HIS CALLING WAS TO PREPARE THE WAY FOR JESUS, THE CHRIST

HE TAUGHT NEW DOCTRINE WHICH WOULD BECOME PART OF THE

NEW COVENANT AFTER PENTECOST

HE WAS FILLED WITH THE HOLY SPIRIT WHILE IN HIS MOTHER'S

WOMB

Describe the changes in custom and law he was bringing to the people.

NEW DIVINE REQUIREMENT NOW INCLUDES WOMEN (in their schools,

services and many other aspects of their lives)

WATER BAPTISM WASHES AWAY SINS POSITIONALLY

WATER BAPTISM WAS A SIGN THAT REPLACED THE COVENANT OF

CIRCUMCISION POSITIONALLY

WATER BAPTISM WAS A SIGN THAT REPLACED ANIMAL SACRIFICE

8. The foundation of a building determines the maximum height of the building. So, when the winds blow and the rains fall, peace is not freedom from the storm, but there is __SECURITY__ in the midst of the storm.

9. Do the elementary principles in Heb 6:1-2 give us what we need in a storm?

__YES__

In 25 words give support for your answer.

ALL SIX DOCTRINES ARE THE BASIS OF OUR FAITH, GROWTH AND

MATURITY

Answers - Lesson Study Review 11

Laying On Of Hands I
Lesson Study Review 11

1. Listed are the Old Testament occurrences of laying-on-of-hands. Tell what is actually taking place.

   Gen 48:14-16 — FIRST OCCURRENCE – IT SYMBOLIZED THE TRANSMISSION OF A SPIRITUAL BLESSING

   Lev. 1:4 & 3:2 — TRANSFERRED SIN AND GUILT TO THE ANIMAL

   Lev. 16:21 — DAY OF ATONEMENT – NATIONAL CONTRITION

   Nu. 8:9-11 — TRANSFERRING RESPONSIBILITY - FROM THE WHOLE CONGREGATION TO THE LEVITE

   Nu. 27:15-23 — TRANSFER OF HONOR, LEADERSHIP, RESPONSIBILITY, AND AUTHORITY FROM THE GREATER (LEADER) TO THE LESSER

   Deut. 34:9 — IMPARTING OF A SPIRITUAL ENABLEMENT

2. For what purpose did our Lord lay on hands during His earthly ministry?

   A. Mark 5:5 — TO HEAL A FEW SICK FOLK – (For the purpose of healing)

   Lk. 4:40 — TO HEAL EVERY ONE OF THEM

   Lk 13:13 — TO HEAL THE INDIVIDUAL – (She was made straight)

   B. Matt. 9:18,25 — TO RAISE THE DEAD

   C. Matt. 19:13, 15 — HE IMPARTED A BLESSING – (To the little children)

   D. Mk. 16:18 — HEALING – (Part of the Great Commission)

3. What does the act of laying-on-of-hands in the New Testament signify?

   (In The New Testament) – RECEPTION OF THE HOLY SPIRIT

   A. TRANSFERENCE – TO SHIFT FROM ONE PERSON TO ANOTHER

   B. TRANSMISSION – TO CONVEY FROM ONE PERSON TO ANOTHER

   C. IMPARTATION – TO BESTOW TO OR SHARE WITH ANOTHER

Eternal Life Principles & Beyond

D. IDENTIFICATION – WE IDENTIFY THE PROBLEM OR CAUSE AND WE ARE GOING TO TRANSFER A RESPONSE FROM GOD. A TRANSFER OF HIS ENERGY OR TRANSMIT HIS MESSAGE.

E. SPIRITUAL ENABLEMENT

Note: Mark 16:18 Jesus said, "….they will lay hands on the sick, and they will recover."

4. The following Scriptures are the fulfillment of the Great Commission. Write, by whom and what happened.

Acts 5:12	BY THE HANDS OF THE APOSTLES – SIGNS AND WONDERS.
Acts 9:17	BY ANANIAS – PAUL RECEIVED HIS SIGHT AND WAS FILLED WITH THE HOLY SPIRIT
Acts 14:3	BY PAUL AND BARNABAS – SIGNS AND WONDERS
Acts 19:11	BY PAUL – EXTRAORDINARY MIRACLES (i.e. Paul's apron & handkerchief)
Acts 28:8	BY PAUL – PUBLIUS' FATHER WAS HEALED OF FEVER AND DYSENTERY

Answers - Lesson Study Review 12

Laying On Of Hands II
Lesson Study Review 12

1. What is the significance of the laying-on-of-hands in terms of foundation principles? Tell what happened.

    A. Acts 8:12-17   THEY RECEIVED THE BAPTISM IN THE HOLY SPIRIT

    B. Acts 9:1-18   PAUL RECEIVED HIS SIGHT AND WAS ALSO BAPTIZED IN THE HOLY SPIRIT

    C. Acts 19:1-7   THEY WERE BAPTIZED IN THE HOLY SPIRIT

2. Why did the Apostles lay hands on the deacons?

    ACTS 6:1-6   TO APPOINT THEM FOR DAILY MINISTRATION

    (ALSO, MOSES AND THE 70)

3. What accompanied the laying-on-of-hands in the ordination of ministers?

    A. 1 Tim 4:14   GIFT GIVEN THROUGH PROPHECY

    B. 2 Tim 1:6   A GIFT WAS GIVEN

4. Are there special purposes for the laying-on-of-hands?

    Acts 13:2-3   SEPARATION TO A SPECIFIC MINISTRY

5. Should care be taken by the elders in the laying-on-of-hands for ordination?   YES   Why?

    1 Tim 5:22a   BECAUSE THE PERSON SHOULD HAVE BEEN TRIED AND TESTED IN GOD'S FURNACE OF PURIFICATION AND GIVE EVIDENCE HE/SHE IS SEASONED

6. Who is qualified to minister with the laying-on-of-hands?

    A. Mark 16:17-18   BELIEVERS

    B. Acts 8:18   APOSTLES AND DISCIPLES

    C. 1 Tim 4:14   PRESBYTERY/BOARD OF ELDERS

Eternal Life Principles & Beyond

7. Was the "laying-on-of-hands" to be practiced after Christ returned to heaven? Support your answer in 50 words or more.

YES, IT IS OBEDIENCE AND A FULFILLMENT OF THE GREAT

COMMISSION   (Matthew 28:19 and Mark 16:15-18)

Give a short example of your experience, if applicable

Answers - Resurrection of the Dead: Lesson Study Review 13

Resurrection Of The Dead I
Lesson Study Review 13

1. What are the three resurrections that relate to our salvation?

   1   JESUS – PAST

   2   OF THE BELIEVER IN JESUS – SPIRITUAL – PRESENT

   3   ALL THAT ARE IN THE GRAVES – FUTURE

2. What is the meaning of the word "resurrection"?

   A RAISING UP – TO CAUSE TO STAND UP; TO RAISE FROM SLEEP AND FROM THE DEAD

3. Did Jesus rise from the dead? __YES__

   Mathew 28:6   HE HAS RISEN

   Acts 2:24 & 4:10   WHOM GOD HAS RAISED UP

   1 Cor. 15:20   HAS BEEN RAISED FROM THE DEAD

4. Was Jesus Christ visible after His resurrection? __YES__

   A. Acts 1:3   FOR 40 DAYS

   B. 1 Cor. 15:5-8   CEPHAS; THE 12; 500 BRETHREN; JAMES; APOSTLES AND PAUL

   C. Matt. 28:16-17   THE ELEVEN DISCIPLES – (Judas is missing)

5. Was the body raised the same one which was crucified? (YES) NO (Circle Answer)

   A. Luke 23:55 to 24:3   HE WAS NOT A SPIRIT BUT

   B. Luke 24:36-40   HAD FLESH AND BONES

   C. John 20: 27-31   IT IS POSSIBLE HE HAD NO BLOOD

THE SCRIPTURES ARE VAGUE HERE, BUT OBVIOUSLY HIS COUNTENANCE DID NOT LOOK THE SAME

Eternal Life Principles & Beyond

6. What does the Old Testament say about the resurrection of Christ?

   Acts 2:30-31   GOD SWORE TO DAVID THAT OF THE FRUIT OF HIS LOINS, GOD WOULD SET THE CHRIST UPON HIS THRONE

7. Must one believe in the resurrection of Jesus Christ to be saved?   YES

   Rom. 10:9   IF YOU CONFESS WITH YOUR MOUTH THE LORD JESUS AND BELIEVE IN YOUR HEART THAT GOD HAS RAISED HIM FROM THE DEAD, YOU WILL BE SAVED

8. List the seven things insured by the resurrection of Jesus Christ

   1. Rom. 1:4   (AMP) JESUS CHRIST IS THE SON OF GOD
   2. Rom. 6:9   (JBP) DEATH IS DEFEATED
   3. Matt 28:18 & Eph 1:20-23   (JBP) JESUS IS SUPREME POWER OVER ALL CREATED BEINGS
   4. Heb 10:12   CHRIST IN HIS FLESH & BONES (The man Jesus) NOW SITTING AT THE RIGHT HAND OF GOD ON THE THRONE OF THE UNIVERSE
   5. Rom. 4:25   BELIEVERS ARE JUSTIFIED
   6. 1 Peter 1:3   THERE IS A NEW LIFE SOURCE FOR MAN
   7. Acts 17:31   (AMP) FUTURE JUDGMENT IS ASSURED

Resurrection Of The Dead II
Lesson Study Review 14

1. Is there a present resurrection for the Saints?

    A. Eph. 2:1, & 5-6 — WE WERE ONCE DEAD IN OUR SINS, BUT CHRIST QUICKENED US TO LIFE IN FELLOWSHIP WITH HIM

    B. Rom. 6:1-9 (vs 8) — WE DIED WITH CHRIST – WE SHALL ALSO LIVE WITH HIM

    C. Col 2:12-13 — BEING DEAD IN OUR SINS, HE RAISED US TOGETHER WITH HIM

    D. Gal. 2:19-20 — WE SHARED HIS CRUCIFIXION, WE LIVE IN HIM, HE LIVES IN US

    E. 2 Cor. 5:14-15, 17 — ALL HAVE DIED – WE ARE A NEW CREATION

2. What "Divine Ordinance" signifies the Believer's resurrection?

    Col 2:12 — WATER BAPTISM – INTO CHRIST'S DEATH

3. How do we relate to the resurrection?

    Rom. 6: 4-5 — A WHOLE NEW LIFESTYLE AND PATTTERN

4. What things in a Believer's life would indicate he has experienced spiritual resurrection?

    A. Rom. 6:11 — DEAD TO SIN – ATTITUDE OF FAITH – ALIVE TO GOD

    B. Rom. 6:4 — A NEWNESS OF LIFE IS MANIFESTED

    C. 2 Cor 5:15 — OBEYING A NEW MASTER

    D. Col 3:1-2 — WE EMBRACE A NEW PURPOSE FOR OUR LIVES

Note: We seek the eternal treasures that are above and not the temporal things this world offers.

Resurrection Of The Dead III
Lesson Study Review 15

1. When is the future resurrection to take place?

    John. 6:39, 44, 54 — AT THE LAST DAY

2. How many shall be resurrected at that time?   ALL

    John 5:28-29 — THOSE WHO HAVE DONE GOOD/THE RIGHTEOUS

    Acts 24:15 — THOSE WHO HAVE DONE EVIL/THE UNRIGHTEOUS

3. Who, according to the Scriptures, raises the dead?

    A. 1 Cor. 6:14 — GOD THE FATHER

    B. John 6:39-40; 44; 54 — GOD THE SON

4. Was the future resurrection a prominent feature of the apostolic preaching?   YES

    Acts 4:2 — PETER AND JOHN – PREACHED JESUS AND THE RESURRECTION

    Acts 17: 18, 32 — PAUL PREACHED JESUS AND THE RESURRECTION

5. How much information do we have about the kind of body that we will receive at the resurrection?   MUCH

    A. 1 Cor. 15:38 — A BODY ACCORDING TO THE WILL OF GOD

    B. 1 Cor. 15:43a — A GLORIOUS BODY

    C. 1 Cor. 15:43b — A POWERFUL BODY

    D. 1 Cor. 15:44 — A SPIRITUAL BODY – OUR SPIRIT WILL COMMUNICATE WITH HIS SPIRIT WITHOUT THE INFLUENCE OF OUR SOUL

    E. 1 Cor. 15:42; 50-53 — AN INCORRUPTIBLE AND IMMORTAL BODY

    F. 1 Cor. 15:49 — A BODY LIKE THAT OF OUR RISEN LORD

Eternal Life Principles & Beyond

6. Should the fact of the coming resurrection affect the conduct of The Called?   YES

    A. 1 Cor. 15:32-34   WE SHOULD KEEP FROM SINFUL INDULGENCES

    B. 1 Cor. 15:58   WE SHOULD BE COMMITTED TO INTELLIGENT SERVICE

Answers - Lesson Study Review 16

Eternal Judgment I
Lesson Study Review 16

1. In what two ways is the word "judgment" used in the Old Testament?

   1. REFERS TO STATUTES, TESTIMONIES AND THE LAWS OF GOD.
      (Notice all ordinances are in the plural)

   2. DEALING WITH GOD'S JUDGMENTS ON THE AFFAIRS OF MEN AND NATIONS – IN HISTORY AND AT THE END OF HISTORY. IT IS IN THIS SENSE THAT IT IS USED IN THE NEW TESTAMENT.

2. What is the dictionary meaning of the word "judge"?

TO SEPARATE; TO MAKE A DISTINCTION BETWEEN; TO EXERCISE JUDGMENT UPON; TO ESTIMATE; TO ASSUME A CENSORIAL POWER OVER; TO CALL TO ACCOUNT; TO BRING UNDER QUESTION; TO TRY AS A JUDGE; TO ADMINISTER GOVERNMENT OVER; TO GOVERN

3. Why is judgment necessary?

   A. Rom. 2:12   BECAUSE OF SIN AGAINST GOD'S LAW

   B. 2 Peter 3:7   BECAUSE OF UNGODLINESS

   C. 2 Peter 2:9   BECAUSE OF UNRIGHTEOUSNESS

   D. Jude 6   BECAUSE OF DISOBEDIENCE

   E. John 3:18   BECAUSE OF UNBELIEF

   F. Rom. 5:18   BECAUSE OF TRESPASSES

   G. John 3:19   BECAUSE OF EVIL DEEDS

4. Who will do the judging at the time of judgment?

   A. Heb. 12:23   GOD, THE JUDGE OF ALL

   B. John 5:22, 27   THE SON – GIVEN TO HIM BY GOD THE FATHER

   C. 1 Cor. 6:2-3   THE SAINTS

Eternal Life Principles & Beyond

5. What principles will govern judgment at that time?

   A. Matthew 10:14-15 — MEASURE OF LIGHT AND PRIVILEGE

   B. John 8:15-16 — DIVINE ALL KNOWLEDGE

   C. Rev. 20:12, 15 — THE BOOK OF LIFE

   D. Malachi 3:16 — THE BOOK OF REMEMBRANCE

   E. John 12:48-49 — THE WORD

   F. Rom. 14:10,12 — PERSONAL RESPONSIBILITY

   G. 2 Corinthians 5:10 — PERSONAL CONDUCT

   H. 1 Peter 1:17 — DIVINE IMPARTIALITY

   I. Matthew 12:50 — TREATMENT OF CHRIST'S BRETHREN

   J. Romans 2:12 — THE LAW

   K. Psalms 9:8 — IN RIGHTEOUSNESS, UPRIGHTNESS

   L. 1 Corinthians 4:5 — MOTIVES AND THOUGHT LIFE

   M. 2 Thessalonians 1:8 — THE GOSPEL

6. In what sense has judgment already taken place?

   A. John 16:11 — SATAN IS ALREADY JUDGED AND CONDEMNED

   B. John 12:31 — THE WORLD IS DOOMED IN CHRIST'S CROSS AND IT IS DECREED TO END IN FIRE

   C. John 3:18 — MAN – WHO BELIEVETH NOT

7. Is there a judgment proceeding at all times? YES

   A. Rom. 1:18 — FOR THE SINNER WHO HINDERS TRUTH

   B. 1 Cor. 11:31 — BELIEVERS MUST CONSTANTLY EXAMINE SELF

Answers - Lesson Study Review 16

8. Name the three standards of Truth by which we shall be judged.

1. THY LAW

2. JESUS, THE CHRIST

3. SPIRIT OF TRUTH

Answers - Lesson Study Review 17

Eternal Judgment II
Lesson Study Review 17

1. Describe in your own words what is taking place at the Judgment Seat of Christ.

   BELIEVERS ARE STANDING BEFORE CHRIST JESUS. WE ARE INDIVIDUALLY JUDGED AND HELD ACCOUNTABLE FOR ALL THINGS GOOD OR EVIL, OUR THOUGHTS, WORDS, DEEDS, ACTIONS AND SWEARING TO OUR OWN HURT. AND ALSO OUR MATERIAL AND FINANCIAL RESOURCES. BELIEVERS WILL RECEIVE REWARDS OR LOSS BY FIRE

2. Name at least five things we will be judged on.

    1. GOOD DEEDS AND EVIL DEEDS
    2. GOOD ACTIONS AND EVIL ACTIONS
    3. GOOD WORDS AND EVIL WORDS
    4. INTENTIONS OF THE HEART
    5. SWEARING TO OUR OWN HURT
    6. SPEAKING, TEACHING OR PREACHING DOCTRINAL ERROR

3. Is there a judgment that is reserved for a particular time in the future?   YES

    A. Matt. 25:31   AT CHRIST'S COMING

    B. Heb. 9:27   AFTER DEATH

4. How does the Bible describe the place where the judgment shall take place?

    Rom. 14:10   THE JUDGMENT SEAT OF CHRIST

5. After Jesus' water baptism, His ministry to the Jews was to heal, deliver, judge and reveal the love of the Father. FALSE

6. The Lord's love for Believers contains no wrath. TRUE

7. The Lord's love for Believers contains no chastisement. FALSE

8. The Lord's love for Believers contains no discipline. FALSE

Eternal Life Principles & Beyond

9. Watching Christian TV Programming is not wasting time. _____

   Explain your answer:

   THIS IS A SOUL SEARCHING QUESTION, THEREFORE, THE BELIEVER'S

   ANSWER WILL DETERMINE WHETHER THE QUESTION IS TRUE OR FALSE

Additional Note:

We find in Mark 6:26 a heathen by the name of King Herod who painfully kept his honor when he swore to his own hurt.

To celebrate his birthday, King Herod threw a banquet for his lords, military commanders and the leading men of Galilee. After his step-daughter danced for him he was so pleased that he jubilantly announced, in front of all his guests, that he would give her whatever she asked for; up to half of his kingdom. When she asked for the head of John the Baptist, he truly regretted his words and became exceedingly sorrowful for making such a hasty oath.

Eternal Judgment: Lesson Study Review 18

Eternal Judgment III
Lesson Study Review 18

1. Is there a judgment that is reserved for a particular time in the future?   YES

    A. Heb. 9:27   AFTER DEATH

    B. John 12:48   THE LAST DAY

    C. Matt. 10:15   AT CHRIST'S COMING

2. How does the Bible describe the place that this judgment shall take place?

    Rev. 20:11-15   A GREAT WHITE THRONE

3. Does it tell us what will happen at this time?

    A. Rev. 11:18   JUDGMENT OF THE SINNER TO EVERLASTING DEATH

    Matt. 25:46   JUDGMENT OF THE BELIEVER TO EVERLASTING LIFE AND REWARDS

    B. 2 Thess. 1:8-9 } SINNER IS JUDGED FOR HIS SIN

    Rev. 20:15 } AND CONSIGNED TO PUNISHMENT

    C. Daniel 7   THE ANCIENT OF DAYS WILL TAKE HIS SEAT; HIS THRONE WILL ABLAZE WITH FLAMES; A RIVER OF FIRE IS FLOWING BEFORE HIM; THE COURT MEMBERS ARE SITTING; MYRIADS ARE STANDING BEFORE HIM AND THE BOOKS ARE OPENED, AND ETC.

    D. Ezekiel 1   VISION OF THE THRONE

    E. Ezekiel 10   VISION OF THE THRONE

Answers - Final Summary Review

Final Summary Review

1. Water baptism relates to cleansing of the soul. According to the doctrinal aspects of water baptism, describe our position from the following Scriptures:

   A. Acts 22:16 In Water Baptism __ACTUALLY__ washes away our sins.

   B. John 15:3 In Water Baptism we are __POSITIONALLY__ cleansed by the words Jesus spoke to us.

   C. Rev. 1:5b Water Baptism __LEGALLY__ releases us from our sins by His Blood.

   D. Luke 24:47 __EXPERIENTIALLY__ our sins are wiped away through Repentance, Believing and Water Baptism.

2. Repentance, Faith and Baptism can be taught separately. They were in the beginning; therefore, it was no problem for Paul to refer to baptism as a base important teaching applicable to all Believers. __FALSE__

3. Where in the record of the Acts of the Holy Spirit through the Apostles were hands laid on for healing and by whom? Name at least four.

A.	ACTS 5:12 – APOSTLES	D.	ACTS 19:11 & 28:8 – PAUL
B.	ACTS 9:17 – ANANIAS	E.	ACTS 3:6-7 – PETER
C.	ACTS 14:3 – PAUL & BARNABAS	F.	ETC.

   * Ananias is named as a disciple; however, God called him and sent him to Paul. Barnabas is an apostle of the secondary group.

4. What is the difference between Baptism and Washings? And is Baptism always in water?

   BAPTISM MEANS SUBMERGED INTO WATER, SUFFERING, FIRE OR THE HOLY SPIRIT

   DYED IN THE WOOL / WASHINGS HAS TO DO WITH THE BELIEVER'S BAPTIZING INTO WATER.

   BAPTIZO YES, IF IT'S WATER BAPTISM. NO, IF IT'S THE BAPTISM OF SUFFERING OR BAPTISM OF FIRE.

Eternal Life Principles & Beyond

5. At the end of this course, we will leave these principles and go on to

<u>MATURITY/PERFECTION</u>

6. If these six elementary principles, which we have learned during this course, is the foundation to a Believer's life, then is this what is meant by receiving the fullness of Christ? <u>TRUE</u>

7. The Apostles, Paul and Jesus preached Repentance. When a pastor or evangelist preaches salvation by accepting Christ into your heart, is it the same thing? Tell why or why not.

<u>IT IS NOT THE SAME THING. IT IS NOT SCRIPTURAL. IT IS NOT THE PETER</u>

<u>PACKAGE, AND ETC.</u>

8. God chose and ordained what physical means to introduce His Son Jesus to Israel?

<u>WATER BAPTISM</u>

9. Before Pentecost, Peter was an emotional weakling. After Pentecost, he spent all of his time strengthening his brethren. Peter experienced the process of

<u>CONVERSION</u>

10. Receiving Christ just for what He is, as represented in His Gospels, with an unqualified surrender of the will, and obtaining salvation of our whole being through Him, this process is called

<u>SAVING FAITH</u>

11. Jesus commanded we go and baptize in the Name of the Father and of the Son and of the Holy Spirit; yet the Apostles seem to contradict the Great Commission. According to Acts 2:33, and verse 41 and other Scriptures, they baptized only in the Name of Jesus. Was this heresy or were they just being disobedient and rebellious? <u>NO</u>

Support your answer?

<u>COLOSSIANS 2:9   THE FULLNESS OF THE DEITY DWELT IN JESUS</u>

12. When we are Water Baptized, it is an outward expression of our <u>FAITH</u> and we are telling the world we have <u>DIED/BURIED</u> in Christ and have been <u>RAISED</u> with Him.

13. The Laying-On-Of-Hands is a meaningful act. In the New Testament it signifies we are conveying a message. What are the four messages communicated?

TRANSFERENCE	IMPARTATION
TRANSMISSION	IDENTIFICATION

Answers - Final Summary Review

14. In terms of foundation principles; the Laying-On-Of-Hands, when signifying the reception of the Holy Spirit, releases

    SPIRITUAL BENEFITS / SOMETHING GIVEN

15. There are six special purposes for Laying-On-Of-Hands. Name three.

    1. ORDINATION
    2. SEPARATION TO A SPECIFIC WORK
    3. FOR DAILY MINISTRATION
    4. TO STIR UP A GIFT
    5. TO GIVE A GIFT THROUGH PROPHECY
    6. RECEPTION OF HOLY SPIRIT

16. Explain the three Resurrections of the Believer after receiving salvation. Give a complete answer.

    A. PAST – BORN-AGAIN AND BAPTIZED IN WATER
    B. PRESENT – DYING TO SELF SO AS WE DECREASE CHRIST INCREASES
    C. FUTURE – RESURRECTION OF THE BODY INTO THE HEAVENLIES

17. Was Jesus resurrected body the same as that which was crucified?   NO

    Explain your answer.

    HE WAS NOT A SPIRIT. A SPIRIT DOES NOT HAVE FLESH AND BONES. HE HAS FLESH AND BONES. IT'S POSSIBLE HE HAD NO BLOOD. BLOOD GIVES COLOR TO THE COUNTENANCE. HE HAS A GLORIFIED BODY

Eternal Life Principles & Beyond

18. The Believer must examine himself daily, and especially before receiving communion. He must keep himself pure before God. On what seven things will the Believer be judged at the Judgment Seat of Christ?

   1. ROMANS 2:5-6   WE WILL BE JUDGED FOR OUR DEEDS AND WORKS

   2. CORINTHIANS 5:10   WE SHALL ALL STAND BEFORE THE JUDGMENT SEAT OF CHRIST JESUS ON WHAT DEEDS WE HAVE DONE GOOD OR BAD

   3. ROMANS 14:12   EACH SHALL GIVE A PERSONAL ACCOUNT OF HIMSELF TO GOD

   4. 1 CORINTHIANS 3:12-15   OUR WORKS WILL GO THROUGH A FIRE

   5. MATTHEW 12:36-37   EVERY CARELESS WORD

   6. PSALM 15   SWEARING TO OUR OWN HURT

   7. MATTHEW 15:19-20   THE THOUGHTS IN OUR HEARTS

   8. 1 CORINTHIANS 4:5   OUR HEART ATTITUDE

   9. MATTHEW 25: 21-23   OUR MATERIAL/FINANCIAL RESOURCES

   10. 1 PETER 1:17   HOW WE USED OUR TIME

   11. 1 SAMUEL 2:3   OUR ACTIONS

19. We must build our work on the foundation of Jesus Christ. On the Day of Judgment our work will become manifest and will be revealed by   FIRE .

20. Explain why judgment is necessary.

   1. ROMANS 2:12 - BECAUSE OF SIN AGAINST GOD'S LAW

   2. 2 PETER 3:7 – BECAUSE OF UNGODLINESS

   3. 2 PETER 2:9 - BECAUSE OF UNRIGHTEOUSNESS

   4. JUDE 6 – BECAUSE OF DISOBEDIENCE

   5. JOHN 3:18 – BECAUSE OF UNBELIEF

   6. ROMANS 5:18 – BECAUSE OF TRESPASS

   7. JOHN 3:19 – BECAUSE OF EVIL DEEDS

Answers - Lesson Study Review 19

Sin

Lesson Study Review 19

1. What is the essential principle of sin?   <u>SELFISHNESS</u>

   <u>IT IS THE LOVE OF SELF AS OPPOSED TO THE LOVE OF GOD</u>

2. What is the most common word for sin in the New Testament?

   <u>HARMARTIA – TO MISS THE MARK; TO BE IN CONTROVERSY WITH GOD</u>

3. List four other words used for sin in the New Testament.

DISOBEDIENCE	TRESPASS
TRANSGRESSION	EVIL
WICKEDNESS	UNRIGHTEOUSNESS
INIQUITY	UNGODLINESS & ETC.

4. According to the Bible, what is the historical origin of sin?

   <u>ADAM'S DISOBEDIENCE</u>

5. How does the Bible describe the individual act of sin?

   <u>FIRST A PERSON IS TEMPTED BY HIS OWN DESIRES; THEN ENTICED;</u>

   <u>THEN WHEN DESIRE IS CONCEIVED IT GIVES BIRTH TO SIN – JAMES 1:14-15</u>

6. How many of the human race are sinners?

   A.   <u>ROMANS 3:10 – THERE IS NONE RIGHTEOUS</u>

   B.   <u>ROMANS 5:12 – ALL HAVE SINNED</u>

7. How many sins are listed in the New Testament?

    A.   103 INDIVIDUAL SINS on

    B.   21 LISTS CONSTITUTING A TOTAL OF

    C.   202 SINS

Note: Although sin starts in the heart, a thought is not sin. When a thought becomes a lustful thought, it is sin. A lustful thought put into action is death.

8. The following is a practical application of this lesson. Arrange for a time when you can be alone with God for at least an hour. As you sit humbly before the King of the universe, completely exposed before His radiant Holiness and love for you, with His arms outstretched waiting to pour His forgiveness and healing power upon you, allow the Holy Spirit to do His cleansing in your soul setting you free of all that weighs you down.

Starting with number 1 on page 271, and continuing to number 8 on page 272, confess all the sins listed. Again, do not skip any sin listed assuming *you* did not commit that sin, but let God be the judge. Confess each sin listed in the 21 lists even if they are duplicated, because each Greek word has a different expression. Again, do not skip any sin, just confess it and move on. After completing this time with God, try to keep yourself isolated from others and retire for the evening. Trust God to heal you as you rest in His forgiveness and love as you fall asleep.

Then the day after *you* have completed this act of humility with grace write below how *you* feel. Do not write about your sins; just record the results of your act of obedience. May God pour out an experience you will never forget.

Rejoice and be exceedingly glad
for your name has been written
in the
Lamb's book of life.

You did not choose Me,
but I chose you,
and appointed you,
that you should go and bear fruit,
and that your fruit should remain,
That whatever you ask of the Father in My name,
He may give to you.

Sincerely,

Jesus

Congratulations

Congratulations! Upon the completion of learning the milk of the Word, which is the six New Testament doctrines.

According to 1 Peter 2:2 "you were like a newborn baby, longing for the pure milk of the word, that by it you may grow in respect to salvation, because you have tasted the kindness of the Lord."

You have completed a full study on the Elementary Principles of six doctrines that are foundational to your faith. You have been diligent and steadfast to apply yourself to this lengthy study on the doctrines of your faith. In your thorough study, on the historical studies, particularly the lesson on Sin, and its varieties and how they affect your "eternal life" is most assuring of your determination. You may not have thought these lessons were the milk of the Word, but really there is more meat than milk. And in taking this course you have matured in your faith and understanding of His truths. May you continue in your growth in Christ. Certainly this is not an exhaustive study but will move you into more of the "meat" of the Word. It is clarified that you are —

moving on to maturity.

My Comments

As I compiled the information for this work, seven aspects of Salvation become apparent. As I see it, the following Scriptures are equal in value and are foundational to salvation. No one Scripture should be considered more important than the other. Each Scripture is part of the whole doctrine as one foundation. The Bible does not record a "prayer of salvation" or a "sinner's prayer" nor "accepting Christ into your heart." I give the following Scriptures without commentary, as Hebrews 6:1-2 is for the maturing Believer and is not evangelistic doctrine.

BIBLICAL ASPECTS FOR SALVATION

1. Repentance

    Luke 24:47 – The Lord's commission

    "….and that repentance for forgiveness of sins should be proclaimed in His name to all the nations, beginning from Jerusalem."

    Acts 17:30 – God commands it

    "Therefore having overlooked the times of ignorance, God is now declaring to men that all everywhere should repent…."

In receiving this knowledge the "mind is informed."

2. Conversion

    Acts 3:19 – Peter's second sermon

    "Repent therefore and convert, that your sins may be wiped away, in order that times of refreshing may come from the presence of the Lord;…."

The "emotions are stirred" by action.

3. Jesus' blood releases us

    Revelation 1:5

    "….and from Jesus Christ, the faithful witness, the first-born of the dead, and the ruler of the kings of the earth. To Him who loves us, and released us from our sins by His blood, …."

4. Faith toward God

    Mark 16:16 – Jesus' words

    "He who has believed and has been baptized shall be saved; but he who has delivered shall be condemned."

Jesus also said, in Luke 8:12

> "And those beside the road are those who have heard; then the devil comes and takes away the word from their heart, so that they may not believe and be saved."

The will must be commanded. Read 1 Corinthians 1:1-21 and Ephesians 2:8.

5. Baptism in water

Acts 2:38 – Peter preached

> "….Repent, and let each of you be baptized in the name of Jesus Christ for the forgiveness of your sins; …."

Acts 22:16 – Ananias speaking to Paul

> "And now why do you delay? Arise, and be baptized [in water], and wash away your sins, calling on His name."

6. Confession

Romans 10:9-10 – Paul writing

> "….that if you confess with your mouth Jesus as Lord, and believe in your heart that God raised Him from the dead, you shall be saved; for with the heart man believes, resulting in righteousness, and with the mouth he confesses, resulting in salvation."

7. Ongoing salvation

John 15:3 – Jesus said

> "You are already clean because of the Word which I have spoken to you."

Philippians 2:12-13 – Paul writing

> "….work out your salvation with fear and trembling; for it is God who is at work in you, both to will and to work for His good pleasure."

Additional Notes:

Lest anyone write me asking why accepting Christ into your heart works or not, let me ask you a question. Why are most Believers not concerned with the holiness of God or why is their heart not on fire for God?

My Comments

To those who would think this is a negative statement, let me say, I am not an electrician, but this I know. In order for appliances to operate there must be power to that appliance. Power is produced by a negative wire and a positive wire. Amen!

Bibliography

Baxter, Ern, **Laying On Hands Lectures**, Morris Cerullo School of Ministry, San Diego, CA., 1979

Bethany Parallel Commentary, on the New Testament, Bethany House Publishers, Minneapolis, MN 55438

Bethany Parallel Commentary, on the Old Testament, Bethany House Publishers, Minneapolis, MN 55438

Bible Knowledge Commentary, The, pg 793, New Testament Edition, Walvoord & Zuck, Victor Books

Conner, Kevin J., B. Th., M. Div., Th. D. (Hon), **The Foundations of Christian Doctrine**, Chapter 12 "The Eternal States", Bible Temple Publishing, Portland, OR 97213

Crowley, Dale, D.D. **The Soon Coming of our Lord**, 1958, pgs. 115-124, Loizeaux Brothers, Neptune, NJ

Deen, Edith, **All of the Women of the Bible**, 1955, pgs 230-232; 348, Harper & Row Publishers, NY and Evanston

Fizer, Undrai & Bridget, Prophecy, **His Name is John**, Elijahlist@aol.com, January 8, 2003

Girdlestone, Rev. Robert Baker, M.A., **Synonyms of the Old Testament**, Wm. B. Eerdmans Publishing Company, Grand Rapids, MI

MacArthur Study Bible The, by John MacArthur, pg 1874, Division of Thomas Nelson Publishers, 2006

McKeever, James Dr., "Keeping Your Word" article, **End Times News Digest**, January 1995 issue; pgs. 1-6, Omega Publications, Medford, OR 97501

McKeever, James Dr., **The Future Revealed**, pgs. 234-251, Omega Publications, Medford, OR 97501

Prince, Derek, **The Foundation Series**, Book 1, Book 2, Book 5, Book 6, Book 7, Fort Lauderdale, FL 33302

Rosenthal, Marvin J., **Zion's Fire**, September-October 2010 issue, pg 14, P.O. Box 121048, Clermont, FL 34712 - 1048

Sandford, John & Paula, Elijah House, 17397 W. Laura Lane, Post Falls, Idaho 83854-4616

Shreve, Mike, **Our Glorious Inheritance**, **Vols 3, 5**, Conversion, p. 128

Strong's Exhaustive Concordance of the Bible, 1974 Edition, Abington Press, Nashville, TN

Wiese, Bill, **23 Minutes in HELL**, Charisma House, Lake Mary, FL 32746

Wilkerson, David, article on "Death", **Times Square Church Pulpit Series** newsletter, February 1993, NY

Wuest, Kenneth S., **Wuest's Word Studies**, **Vol I**, Chapter on Romans, Wm. B. Eerdmans Publishing Company, Grand Rapids, MI 49502

Wuest, Kenneth S., **Wuest's Word Studies**, **Vol II**, pgs. 107-111, Wm. B. Eerdmans Publishing Company, Grand Rapids, MI 49502

To order additional copies of

Eternal Life Principles & Beyond

Madeline's work is a truth seeking and teaching ministry to prepare the hearts of the Believers for their faithful walk with God affecting their eternal hereafter life.

To order additional copies direct, visit www.lulu.com

Rights for publishing this book in other languages
the author may be contracted through

Madeline M. Vance

727-796-5755

Email: madeline@madelinevance.org

Website: www.MadelineVance.org

If you have found the information in this book worthy of continued publishing for the benefit of others in the Body of Christ, please purchase additional copies and give as gifts. Thank you.

Unauthorized reproduction is a violation of the law and of Christian ethics.

www.ingramcontent.com/pod-product-compliance
Lightning Source LLC
Chambersburg PA
CBHW080542230426
43663CB00015B/2676